The
Electric
Muse
Revisited

It is through the support of the folk music charity Square Roots Productions that this book has been published. For more information please visit www.folktracks.org

**SQUARE ROOTS
PRODUCTIONS**
**NEW & OLD ROUTES
TO FOLK MUSIC**

The
Electric
Muse
Revisited

The Story *of* Folk *into* Rock *and* Beyond

**Robert Shelton, Dave Laing,
Karl Dallas** *and* **Robin Denselow**

Updated with new chapters
by **Robin Denselow**

OMNIBUS PRESS
London / New York / Paris / Sydney / Copenhagen / Berlin / Madrid / Tokyo

Copyright © 2021 Omnibus Press
(A Division of the Wise Music Group)

Cover painting by Tristan Adams, jacket design by FreshLemon
Picture research by Susannah Jayes

ISBN: 978-1-913172-08-4

Printed in Malta

A catalogue record for this book is available from the British Library.

Lyric Permissions

'Chords of Fame'. Words & Music by Paul Ochs 1979 Barricade-Music Inc. Universal Music Publishing Ltd. All rights reserved. International copyright secured. Used by permission of Hal Leonard Europe Limited.
'Requiem'. Written by Harvey Andrews. Published by Onward Music Limited, Roundhouse, 212 Regents Park Road Entrance, London NW1 8AW.
'City of New Orleans'. Words & Music by Steve Goodman © 1970. Reproduced by permission of Sony/ATV Tunes LLC, London W1F 9LD.

Contents

INTRODUCTION

There have been many influences on the growth of rock music from its brash beginnings in the 1950s to its contemporary spectrum of styles and sounds. The most pervasive have been the many varieties of folk music. From the world of blues, ballads, rags and reels, rock has gained a new range of techniques, aims and ambitions. The importance of Bob Dylan in this respect is of course, well known. But even the music of so untraditional a performer as David Bowie would not have made such a tremendous impact if he too had not learned from folk music that songs can be entertaining and poetic at the same time.

The natural habitat of folk music is societies in which culture has not become industrialised, and people are not segregated into performers and listeners, the one active, the other passive. Yet one of the most marked features of British and North American culture in the last twenty years, as the mass media and the entertainment industries have expanded in scope, has been not merely the survival of folk music as a cultural force, but a major growth in its influence and in the numbers of people involved in it, whether as musicians or devotees. That fascinating paradox is one of the main themes running through this book, which traces the myriad forms taken by what has been loosely called the "folk revival" and examines its effects on the dominant popular music of the period, rock.

Strictly speaking, the folk revival is not so much an event as a continuous process stretching back over more than a century, and involving people as disparate as the Harvard professor, Francis James Child and the Glasgow-born Cockney traditional jazz banjoist, Lonnie Donegan. Each symbolises one of the two main aspects of the revival. Professor Child was the prototype preservationist, the compiler of a famous collection of traditional ballads which have since been used as source material by many singers. (Folk-song recordings often refer to songs by the opus number given to them by Child, as well as by the traditional title.) The preservationist attitude was based largely on the (generally accurate) belief that the oral transmission of folk music – the handing down of songs from generation to generation through their memorisation rather than through written records – had virtually broken down by the last part of the nineteenth century.

Such tender concern for the integrity of folk music has never been a feature of the activity of the popularisers of the songs, like Lonnie Donegan, whose recording of Leadbelly's "Rock Island Line" sparked off the skiffle movement of the late 1950s in Britain. Inspired by Donegan thousands of young people formed themselves into skiffle groups, and learned his eclectic repertoire of American folk songs from both black and white sources, plus a smattering of numbers deriving from pre-war jazz. What drew them to skiffle was its rhythmic intensity compared with the moribund popular music of the day, not its roots in folk traditions unsullied by commercialism. The point was proved when rock'n'roll appeared on the horizon with its even stronger rhythms, and the skifflers exchanged their acoustic guitars for electric ones. Nevertheless, through skiffle and rock'n'roll, elements of certain kinds of folk music entered the mainstream of commercialised entertainment and had a significant effect on it. A similar but more far-reaching process occurred in the early 1960s in America when the younger singers of the mushrooming folk-song movement merged their approach with that of the new British pop sound to produce what came to be known as "folk-rock", a music which at its best could fuse the pungency of folk poetry with the power of rock rhythms.

But for all its faults, the preservationist attitude has provided an essential underpinning for the flourishing folk music scene of today, and indeed for the maturity of an important segment of contemporary rock music. Without Francis Child, no Bob Dylan or Steeleye Span. And it is easy to underestimate the courage of the early song collectors. In the face of apathy or ridicule from their peers, city intellectuals travelled through alien territory – whether it was the countryside of Somerset or Mississippi – notebook or tape-recorder in hand, persuading the folk to sing and play for them. Even if they accompanied their findings with laments that the end of the tradition was at hand, when often it proved to be far more robust, the results of their work are the foundation stones upon which the whole edifice of later folk-song movements was built.

The work of the collectors had, however, certain important but unintended effects. For, while they felt themselves to be simply making an objective study of folk music, the collectors played a part in shaping the picture which emerged. This often happened in Britain because the researchers brought to the culture of a lower-class, peasant society the values of the educated middle class. Victorian prudery, for example, caused Cecil Sharp and other collectors to "tidy up" songs containing explicitly sexual imagery. The original manuscript versions of some folk songs that later became school-room standards were not published until 1958, when James Reeves presented them in his valuable study, *The Idiom of the People.*

There was, in addition, the problem of the transcription of the music itself. The British collectors, steeped in the art music of their period, were accustomed to thinking of music in written terms, conforming to the scales and tempi of the classical forms. But folk music of any kind is produced in a very different way. In an interview, Louis Armstrong once spoke of blues and jazz being made by the kind of man who "doesn't know anything about (formal) music – who is just plain ignorant, but has a great deal of feeling he's got to express in some way, and has got to find that way out of himself."

The arrival of machines capable of recording the sound of folk song meant that the distortions which inevitably followed from the translation of the music into classical notation could be avoided. It was now possible to capture those aspects of vocal tone and inflection for which notation had no symbols. Then, of course, these field recordings were also a kind of interference (if a less damaging one) with the operation of the tradition since they tended to enshrine one particular variant of a song for posterity, in contrast to the process of oral transmission which involved the re-moulding and modification of music as it was handed on from one singer to another.

Perhaps the most crucial modification of the tradition produced by the activities of the preservationists occurred when it came to the use of the collected material in performance. The songs were transplanted by the singers who learned them following their publication by collectors into contexts very different from those in which they originated. Some, though, were closer to the spirit of the original than others. While the British collectors from the beginning were imbued with the feeling of the drawing room and the music teacher, many of the pioneers discussed in Robert Shelton's chapter on the folk revival in the United States were of a more radical temper. Like the poet Walt Whitman, men such as Charles Seeger and Carl Sandburg felt that the cultural heart of their country lay with "the people".

From there it was a short step to the liaison of political radicalism with folk song, which has always been a far more important aspect of folk revivalism in America than in Britain, though, as Karl Dallas points out in his chapter, there was a political impetus behind certain aspects of the revival in England. On the other side of the Atlantic though, songs were created from within popular movements, and a clear line can be traced from the martyred union organiser Joe Hill through Woody Guthrie's "Dust Bowl Ballads" to contemporary performers like Pete Seeger and Joan Baez.

If folk music as such can only be produced outside the commercial structures of the entertainment industry – which is the argument of hard-core traditionalists – then one of the nearest ways a modern industrialised society can contain its own equivalent to the traditional folk situation is in the solidarity of a political movement or of work. There has, in fact, been a rich vein of work songs created since the Industrial Revolution, though the music itself has been most surely rooted in those industries where there is a certain continuity between the patterns and methods of working before and after that revolution. Mining and cattle-ranching are two very different, but important, examples. The University of Illinois Press recently published a book of songs from the repertoire of a cowboy folk singer, Glenn Ohrlin, collected for the most part during the last thirty years. The introduction to the collection (*The Hell-Bound Train*) includes a succinct statement of the role of work songs: "Work is a centripetal force, bonds individuals into folk-like societies, and work songs, broadly defined, encode the behaviour of members of such societies." A similar description can be made of some social and political movements in which songs have played an important part, notably the black civil rights campaigns of the early 1960s. Robert Shelton's chapter includes a study of the way that movement generated a new development of the gospel music tradition in response to the exigencies of the struggle.

These forms of survival of the traditional folk process are nevertheless exceptions to the general musical development of the twentieth century. The music most people listen to is one kind or another of popular music, and the devotees of folk have been forced to take up a stance towards this situation. At one end of the spectrum are those who insist that folk music can have nothing to do with pop or rock, since they are the product of an industry dedicated only to making money for its shareholders. As James Reeves puts it: "We can – not always, but often – *feel* the difference, even if we cannot define it, between something made for love, fun, or pleasure, and something made for money."

On the other side are the musicians and critics who make and champion the wide variety of music that is usually categorised under the vague title "folk-rock", people for whom the musical resources of popular music and the access it offers to a mass audience are of greater importance than its entanglement with commerce. It is impossible to chronicle the development of the folk revival over the last two decades without taking the almost ceaseless debate over the relationship between folk and rock into account, a debate which has been by turns shrill, dull, hilarious and sometimes illuminating.

Despite the transparent opportunism of many popularisers and commercialisers of folk music, when the smoke of the battle has cleared, the balance of the argument seems to lie with the folk-rock fraternity, not least because attempts to integrate folk and rock have produced some of the best music of the last dozen years.

The preservationist view, in any case, rests on two misconceptions about the character of popular music. It is first assumed that since pop is an industry, all its products are equally tainted by the commercial environment, Bob Dylan as much The Osmonds. Apart from the fact that this attitude is far too flattering about the ability of businessmen to dictate popular taste, a closer look at the way pop works suggests a more complex picture. As in the cinema, each work produced within popular music appears as a result of a mixture of tensions and pressures that come from artists and audience as well as record companies and managers. And in each case, the mixture is different, with one or other of the pressures dominating. The pre-history of

Barry McGuire's prototypical folk-rock "protest" song, "Eve Of Destruction", recounted in my own chapter, is a prime example of how art, commerce and politics intermingle in many pop records. The second flaw in the traditionalist approach is the belief that folk music can be insulated from popular music, even though both exist in the same society with its centralised media. There is, rather, an inevitable interaction between the two, as is evidenced by "traditional" singers who happily include in their repertoire music-hall songs alongside the ballads of the tradition, or a group like Cream making use of a folk-song melody as a bass line in one of their own songs.

The many forms of interaction between folk and rock in Britain and North America are the subject of the chapters by Robin Denselow and myself. Here it is only possible to make some general points about the significance of the resulting music. The first thing to be noted is the crucial difference in the cultural situation of musicians on either side of the Atlantic. For while rock music was pre-eminently a synthesis of various American folk or semi-folk musics from both sides of the colour line, British musicians who wanted to create songs related to their own environment had no equivalent source within the popular music mainstream. The various streams of folk-rock in Britain have been the product of this search within folk for themes, and of the dissatisfaction with the insularity of the traditionalist clubs felt by many younger musicians. The result is music for which rock provides the grammar and the various British traditional musics provide the vocabulary – either directly for a band like Steeleye Span who adapt traditional songs *in toto*, or indirectly for Fairport Convention or Richard Thompson, who compose new songs using the elements of the tradition.

In North America itself, the influence of the folk revival of the early 1960s has been both greater and more diffuse on the vast expansion in aim and scope which rock music has undergone since that time. Graduates of the folk scene, from Bob Dylan and Paul Simon to Joni Mitchell and Jackson Browne, have played a major part in rock's growth into a music capable of transcending the narrow confines of the Tin Pan Alley pop philosophy. The stance towards the conventional notions of the entertainer and the star they brought from folk music has, at times, called into question fundamental aspects of the music industry, in a more effective way than the broadsides of the traditionalists. In the process, both they and their British counterparts have also liberated folk music from the danger of ghettoisation and stagnation which might have been the fate of the revival. In the best folk-rock music the tradition is not simply revived but transformed: the revival has got away.

The story of the relationship between folk and rock, the successes and failures, is still unfolding. This book takes it up only to early 1975, and it has been able only to sketch in the broad outlines of a many-sided and controversial process. But if it can persuade some readers to listen to some of the music it describes with new ears, its job will have been done.

Introduction to the new edition

On September 30, 2019, there was an extraordinary concert at the Royal Albert Hall in London. Richard Thompson was celebrating his 70th birthday, and doing so as part of one of the most memorable folk, rock and folk-rock line-ups ever assembled on one stage. "I don't like being the centre of attention, strange as it may seem," he said before the show. "I just want to have a few friends over."

Those friends included David Gilmour, the Pink Floyd guitar hero, who revived his cover version of Thompson's song "Dimming Of The Day", and Hugh Cornwell, of Stranglers fame, who played with Richard in a school band in north London, when they were both 14. And then there were the folk-rockers. There were past and present members of Fairport Convention, the band with whom Richard made his name in the late sixties and early seventies, and who can be credited with inventing English folk-rock. They included the other co-founders of the Fairports, Ashley Hutchings and Simon Nicol, along with drummer Dave Mattacks, who had joined them and the late Sandy Denny in recording that legendary folk-rock album *Liege and Lief*, back in 1969.

Also on stage that night was Maddy Prior, still one of our finest folk singers and leader of Steeleye Span, that other great folk-rock band started by Ashley, and also still going strong. And there was Martin Carthy, that remarkable and maverick folk guitarist who once played with Steeleye.

All of these artists featured in the first edition of *The Electric Muse* when it was published in 1975, and their later musical adventures are chronicled here. So too are the stories of the later generations of experimental folk musicians, from Eliza Carthy to Olivia Chaney and Teddy and Kami Thompson, who also appeared at Richard Thompson's birthday bash.

They were all in impressive form that night, but then so too is folk-rock, and the fusion styles that have moved beyond matching traditional songs against electric guitars and drums. The old songs and stories have proved strong and memorable enough not just to survive such experimentation, but to prosper and take on new life. As Martin Carthy put it, as he sat backstage during the rehearsals for Richard Thompson's show, "what has happened, and continues to happen, is that you can't hurt this stuff by messing with it. I have done some duffers, and some pretty good stuff as well, and it didn't hurt the music at all."

The first *Electric Muse* charted the rise of folk experimentation up until the mid-seventies, when the English folk-rock boom was at the height of its popularity, with Steeleye Span notching up hit records, playing major stadiums and collaborating with David Bowie and Peter Sellers. Those original chapters, by Dave Laing, Karl Dallas, Robert Shelton and myself, are all re-printed here – along with new chapters bringing that colourful story up to date.

It's the story of how folk and folk-rock fell from fashion after the glory years of the seventies, but then returned in a new folk revival, with English traditional music now fused not just with electric guitar-based rock, but with punk, hip hop, reggae, electronica and other styles that have become part of the contemporary musical landscape. It's a story that of course includes the continuing careers of the great seventies veterans, and those who followed them. A story that includes that remarkable singer June Tabor and her excursions into folk-rock with Oysterband, and the constantly surprising blend of experimentation, exquisite acoustic work and new composition from Eliza Carthy – one of the key figures in keeping the music alive. Then there's the punk folk of Billy Bragg, the sometimes startling and constantly changing work of Jim Moray, and the musical adventures of Jon Boden, leader of that massively popular big band, Bellowhead – who followed on from Steeleye in proving that folk could prove popular with stadium and large festival audiences.

And it's also the story of the new guitar bands, False Lights and The Rails, and the newcomers who are determined to revive the scene and bring traditional songs to new audiences. Sam Lee and Stick in the Wheel would hate to be labelled folk-rock. They have moved beyond that. But in their love of the old songs and willingness to experiment they show how the original folk-rock spirit lives on.

It was, of course, impossible to include every artist who set out to re-work traditional songs in the years since *The Electric Muse* first appeared, but I have told the story with the help of many of the key players. Thanks for your time – and your music – to Jon Boden, Billy Bragg, Eliza and Martin Carthy, Olivia Chaney, Simon Emmerson, Ashley Hutchings, John Kirkpatrick, Sam Lee, Jim Moray, Simon Nicol, Maddy Prior, Stick in the Wheel (Nicola Kearey and Ian Carter), June Tabor, Ian Telfer, and Kami, Linda and Richard Thompson.

PART ONE

The Electric Muse
The Story of Folk into Rock

ONE

Something Happened in America

ROBERT SHELTON

The clock ticks away all the hours,
The pictures are ragged and brown,
Could that really be me, looking young, feeling free
And marching my hopes into town?

We played in the cold water fountain,
We danced with the blind and the lame,
And the lion of stone who believed the unknown
Just remarked that we all looked the same.

And where did the beautiful people
Put all their beautiful things,
The love that we carried on banners of smiles
And songs that we all used to sing?

The times they were only for changing,
The day of destruction was nigh,
The lonely one told us he'd love us and hold us
And gave us a sad lullaby...

From "Requiem"

Something was happening in 1958 in America, but unlike the mythic "Mr Jones" we knew what it was then, and, with the sharper vision of hindsight, we know even more now.

There was a massive search for a new set of values. The cities were clogged. Commercials on television were choking the spirit with goods, not needs. Packaged culture was everywhere, but the naked lunch at the end of the fork was not nourishing and scarcely edible. There was a craving for another kind of meal, and, to a large degree, that change in the cultural diet was provided by the folk revival.

3

There was clearly "something wrong" with American youth in the late 1950s, a malaise and a searching. Earnest debates were held on the question of national purpose by some of the American leaders who had not been able to articulate a national purpose in their long public careers. It was the backwash of the McCarthy era, when a wildly accusative demagogue senator from Wisconsin had nearly succeeded in silencing all dissent under the flag of anti-Communism.

They called those who went to colleges and universities in the 1950s "The Silent Generation", because they were so apolitical, so little interested in social action, so meek in their acceptance of the verities of the American way of life. How did "The Silent Generation" become "The Singing Generation"? It was largely through a search for a better set of values than they were offered in the classroom, or the boardroom of the advertising agency.

A new version of the romantic return to nature and to honest values was spawned first by the beatniks, the coterie that included the writers Jack Kerouac, Allen Ginsberg, Lawrence Ferlinghetti and Gregory Corso. They wrote of freedom, travel, sensation and transcendence. Their ethic was not, however, picked up in a mass form, for the Beats proposed solutions that were too vague, too chancy, too personal and too escapist to form a mass movement. Only the fringe went the Beat route, while the majority turned, from 1958 through 1963, down the folk route. The folk revival offered something that promised to be considerably more wholesome and constructive, more purposeful and social than what the Beats proposed. Kerouac went *On the Road*, while Woody Guthrie had travelled the same road, but with a more assured destination.

What the folk revivalists were saying, in effect, was: "There's another way out of the dilemma of modern urban society that can teach us all about who we are. There are beautiful, simple, relatively uncomplicated people living in the country, close to the soil, who have their own backgrounds. They know who they are, and they know what their culture is because they make it themselves; in their whittling, their embroidery, their painting, but mostly in their singing. Look to the country, confused, uprooted city boys and girls, and you will rediscover yourselves."

It was romanticism to a high degree. As romantic as Wordsworth's rejection of London for the Lake District, as romantic as Rousseau's

4

espousal of the "noble savage", as romantic as Gauguin's flight to the South Pacific. It was part of a grand tradition, in which the victim of over-civilisation finds himself rejecting the comforts and traps of that civilisation and turning instead to the simple truths, for the seemingly uncomplicated fusion of life, thought and action that the so-called "primitive" enjoys.

Oversimplification? Of course. And the generation that set out to identify with the folk ethic of the 1950s found, inevitably, that the "untouched" or uncorrupted simple man no longer existed, at least not in the Western World. Often, too, there was disillusionment at finding things were not all that simple, that rural poverty bred its own special despairs, that there was narrowness, fear and xenophobia out there in the country.

The folk revival that began in 1958 was a gathering storm, a fad, a social movement, a mania, a craze and a cultural epidemic. The able historians of the vital popular music of the 1950s, mostly British, have shown us what riches were there, but those riches were being hidden by the gloss of the music business, and by the decline of vitality in rock'n'roll, which had already had three enormous years of creativity.

Pop, rhythm'n'blues and rock'n'roll were city musics, talking about a certain type of life and a certain set of resolutions to the problems of that life. Straight from the country, folk music seemed a deeper alternative. Then there was the great wave of payola scandals of the late 1950s. It became evident that disc jockeys and recording companies and businessmen were manipulating public taste, offering and accepting commercial bribes, leading America's dancing youth down the primrose path. Folk music seemed the pure alternative. It seemed to be beyond business, beyond manipulation, to spring from fresh wells of untainted water. What could be more appealing?

The folk revival of 1958 offered a seemingly new alternative culture. But this was not new, either. Folk music is the oldest known genre of music, and it was constantly being rediscovered by sophisticates. Part of the very folk process itself has been its recurring waves of popularity. So, although the revival that began in America in 1958 was to be the largest in history, it was just another link in the chain of earlier revivals.

Because so much of what has happened in the history of folk song has been carried by word of mouth, we are forever trying to find out what happened before. Unlike the more well-established academic disciplines, folk music has not been so clearly charted or historically documented. But the sources do exist, on recording, in the Archive of American Folk Song of the Library of Congress, in regional and state folklore societies, in learned monographs and scholarly works.

Although the work of literary folklore and music scholars seems miles away from listening to a country blues in a 1958 coffee-shop, there is a connection. It was some of those scholars, collectors, field-recording men and interviewers who helped keep a viable native folk tradition alive. It was some of the great scholars and collectors, as avid a group of savants as one might encounter, who made it possible for one to hear an old song done by a pop-folk artist. Someone had to keep the lines of communication open for the great folk revival to plug into its loudspeaker.

The mention of just a few scholars and collectors can indicate how they kept the roots of the folk tree alive. One of the most important nineteenth-century scholars was a Harvard professor of English literature, Francis James Child. His landmark collection, *The English and Scottish Popular Ballads*, was to become a highlight of poetry and balladry. In league with other early folklore scholars, Child was primarily interested in literary content. He codified the 305 principal "classic" ballads of the English-speaking world in a canon that is still in use today to identify this or that ballad as variants of "Child 12" or "Child 205". His pioneering work has in recent years undergone its long-needed completion – with the addition of the music and its variants – by a zealous professor at the University of California at Berkeley, Bertrand Bronson.

John A. Lomax was a different sort of researcher. He did not work primarily in the library, but out in the field with native source singers. Beginning with his fascination with cowboy songs and the music of Texas blacks, Lomax in the early years of the century began a lifelong career of ballad-hunting among the poor and obscure. He and his son Alan, who carried on his work, were among the greatest collectors in the history of folk song. Long before the music business or even the audience had recognised the intrinsic worth of those simple tunes, the

Lomaxes had tried to light the fires of enthusiasm among the leaders of the intellectual community.

Still another famous pioneer collector was the Briton, Cecil Sharp, who carried his quest for old English songs to the Cumberland Mountains of Kentucky, where he was to find many English songs intact and in daily use by such singing families as the Ritchies.

Falling somewhere between the academics and the field collectors was the writer, Carl Sandburg. A poet in the grand tradition of Walt Whitman, Sandburg also "heard America singing", as Whitman had written. Sandburg, too, was fascinated by the poetic outpouring he encountered in the farmhouses and ranch houses of America. While Sandburg was touring colleges in the late 1920s to research his giant Lincoln biography, he supported himself by singing folk songs. Ultimately, he published one of the earliest and best folk-song collections, *The American Songbag*.

Charles Seeger, patriarch of the Seeger clan, was a musicologist at Harvard who early sensed the depth and substance of folk song. He went on to become one of the most highly regarded scientists who are known as "ethnomusicologists". This new breed of scholar studies the musics of folk and primitive peoples stylistically and relates the music to the total culture of its people.

The early scholars in folk song often worked for pittances. They included such people as Vance Randolph, Newman Ivey White, Dorothy Scarborough, Samuel Bayard and many others. In our own time, people whose work contributed greatly to the basis of the folk revival of 1958 are such scholars as Kenneth Goldstein, Richard Dorson, MacEdward Leach, John Greenway, Margaret Flanders, Archie Green, D.K. Wilgus, Fred Ramsey, Roger Abrahams, Ellen Stekert, Sam Charters, Harry Oster and Harry Smith.

RECORDING IN THE FIELD

Invaluable work in the early years of commercial recording was done by the field men who flourished in the early 1920s. Such men as Ralph Peer, Eli Oberstein, Frank Walker and Art Satherley recorded the earliest folk blues and country traditional material. (In just one historic week in 1927, Ralph Peer made the first recordings of both the Original Carter Family and Jimmie Rodgers, two of the great names in folk and country music.) In a later era, it was the devotional zeal of Moses Asch which led to recordings of some of the best of the world's folk music on such labels as Stinson, Asch, Disc and Folkways.

But the heartbeat of folk music, its continuance and periodic revival, lies with the performers themselves. One could cite the famous union organiser, Joe Hill, who used folk song to build and strengthen the first militant labour movement of the Wobblies (Industrial Workers of the World). In the 1930s, others who used folk song as a tool in labour organising and struggles were such battlers for social justice as Aunt Molly Jackson, Jim Garland and the Dixon Brothers. The urban East, however, got wind of folk music through professional performers who were to become "stars". Burl Ives, the Kentucky giant, was one of the first to break through to a mass audience, in the 1930s and 1940s.

Ives made an appealing interpreter, with his fine light voice, his relaxed country manner and his strong repertoire of songs. That he later left the field to become a straight pop singer and actor does not detract from the early contribution he made. Another strong personality in the revival of the late 1930s and early 1940s was Josh White, the preacher's son from Greenville, South Carolina. Josh was steeped in the black song tradition, but he was also a first-rate populariser who could add elements of sexuality and theatricality to heighten his interpretations. With the heavy interest in black life and culture that flowered during the era of Roosevelt, Josh White also became a spokesman and interpreter for blues and religious song. In the same period, the Chicago folk world was illuminated by the work of Big Bill Broonzy, a sophisticated blues performer who could juggle tradition and popularisation with skill.

It is not surprising that there was a major early revival of folk song during the 1940s, a period of national testing, with World War II, and of re-affirmation of democratic principles in the post-war period. Then the "popular" heritage of America as both a political democracy and also, at least in theory, an economic democracy, brought forward some of the material that lay in folk song. The "common man" was fighting and winning the war, and it was natural that folk song, the music of the "common man", should enjoy great popularity.

During the 1940s, folk song was an entertainment medium in city concert halls and cabarets. A long and distinguished roster of performers emerged: Richard Dyer-Bennet, John Jacob Niles, Cynthia Gooding, Oscar Brand, Joe and Tom Glazer, Marais and Miranda, John Langstaff, Sonny Terry and Brownie McGhee, Hermes Nye, Susan Reed, Paul Robeson, Earl Robinson, Harry and Jeanie West and Hally Wood, to name a few.

It is a sad commentary on the erosion of time that many of these names from the 1940s are barely known today. However, as the line from Gil Turner's song says, "They carried it on." They kept the music alive, kept it from becoming just notes in a scholar's library. A few of these older stalwarts continued to work right through the folk "arrival" of the 1940s into the "revival" of the 1960s. In several cases, however, changing audience taste, the quest for new and younger performers, and the vagaries of luck led to the cruel discarding of some of the pioneers.

Two names from the 1940s would have to be inscribed in any "Folk Music Hall of Fame". Leadbelly and Woody Guthrie were romantic archetypes of what folk music, black and white, was all about. Both were rural singers who moved into the city performing scenes to make overwhelming impressions that were to last for decades. Leadbelly, or Huddie Ledbetter, was a dynamic fount of work songs, story-songs, blues and ballads. The Lomaxes discovered him as a prisoner at Louisiana State Prison at Angola in 1938 and they helped him sing his way to freedom (much as Harry Oster was to return to the same prison and help bluesman Robert Pete Williams gain his freedom).

Leadbelly's enormous drive and energy is hinted at on recordings on Folkways and the Library of Congress label (reissued commercially on Elektra). He was a John Henry-esque titan, a dynamic man in all respects. Such songs as "Midnight Special" and "Goodnight, Irene" are still ringing down the years with the vigour and depth of Leadbelly.

Woody Guthrie was to cause even more imitators in lifestyle and music-style than Leadbelly. Guthrie wasted away for nearly a dozen years before he died in the autumn of 1967. He was suffering from Huntington's Chorea, an incurable degenerative nerve disease. Such was his incredible output of songs and writing, so strong was his

9

romantic, rootless searching for the heart of America, that there are still boys setting out along Woody's "dusty highways". Guthrie was the pivotal figure, who rambled, with his famous sidekick Cisco Houston, a long time before it was fashionable to swallow up the American landscape. He heard a certain magic in American country music, from the Carter Family and others, and he freely borrowed the melodies as bases for his own songs with new lyrics. It would be difficult to find many "original" melodies among the 1,000 or so songs of Guthrie, yet his own poetic folk process made them into something else again.

Woody was a true-life figure out of John Steinbeck's classic novel, *The Grapes of Wrath*, a little guy hemmed in by his environment and ultimately finding his own way of liberating himself from that environment. To know Woody is to know and understand a great deal about the early Bob Dylan, who was so enraptured by Woody's lifestyle that he set out to relive it. (Ramblin' Jack Elliott, another city boy who had travelled with Woody, was once described by Guthrie: "Jack Elliott sounds more like me than I do.")

The Guthrie songbag is studded with bright lights. "So Long, It's Been Good To Know You" was a classic of leave-taking. "Car, Car" is a children's song that comes to life with each new generation, and Guthrie's Whitmanesque love of the best of American life was reflected in such songs of patriotism as "Pastures of Plenty" and "This Land Is Your Land". Woody blew out of the Oklahoma Dust Bowl and then, in California, Washington State and later New York, he fell in with such early folk-community leaders as Will Geer, Millard Lampell, Alan Lomax and Pete Seeger. Guthrie became strongly identified with the urban folk movement and with radical politics. Yet, as Dylan himself later learned, the artist is ultimately beyond politics. It is not just his radical humanism, but his artistic poetry that makes Woody live on. His recordings and writing should be studied by all who would understand what the American folk movement is about. For the reader, of especial interest is his early autobiography, *Bound for Glory*, and a later collection of his writings, *Born to Win*, which I was privileged to edit.

THE SEEGER CALLED PETE

The stature of Leadbelly and Woody Guthrie in the American folk-song firmament is impregnable. A younger man, who had been linked to both in his youth, and who more rightly deserves to be considered the "father of the American folk revival" was the lanky, lean son of Charles Seeger: the human banjo, "America's tuning fork", Pete Seeger. No music-maker of any genre occupies quite the position that Seeger does. The bearded stringbean in the old work shirt and denims, bent over his long-necked five-string banjo, has, in thirty years of performing, done as much as anyone to shape popular taste in folk, topical and protest music. Seeger is the eternal teacher, but is rarely the pedant. He has always believed that there is a power in music to inform, to stir, to rally, to direct and to cause social and personal interaction. His career has been a study in reverence for the creative spark that courses through the world's peoples. He hears melodies everywhere, and he relates them to the causes he most venerates: peace, equality, decency in a troubled world.

Pete's career falls roughly into three periods: the young folknik rambling with Guthrie, visiting folk singers on his own in the country; the period with The Almanac Singers and The Weavers; and his solo career since leaving The Weavers. Whether on his own or with groups, Seeger was a quietly commanding figure. His enormous range of songs, his ability to learn material quickly, his ingratiating personality all pushed him to the fore. It was Seeger who formed a bridge between the revival of the 1940s and the late 1950s, and it was he who helped keep the flame of folk, topical and protest song alive during the days of political repression of the early 1950s.

Seeger was a guiding light of the folk magazine *Sing Out!* and he helped Sis and Gordon Friesen to found the eminent little bulletin of topical songs, *Broadside*. (The number of songwriters, including Bob Dylan, who got stimulus and encouragement from *Broadside* was enormous.) Then there was Pete Seeger as songwriter. Because of his own ingrained modesty, he would often sing one of his songs without even telling an audience who had written it. But, certainly, "Where Have All The Flowers Gone?", "Guantanamera", "Waist Deep In The Big Muddy" and "If I Had A Hammer", whether written solely by Seeger or in collaboration with others, were classics.

11

An understanding of the revival that began in 1958 must take into account the two earlier groups that set a style for pop-folk performance. The Almanac Singers were organised in the early 1940s by Seeger, Millard Lampell, Woody Guthrie and Butch Hawes. They named the group after their residence, Almanac House, on 10th Street in Greenwich Village. It was long before there was any discussion about performing style or popularisation versus tradition, but the Almanacs had a zest, a tang and a naturalness that was not quite to be heard again until the 1960s.

The Weavers came together in 1948, the year of the famous third-party candidacy of Henry Wallace. It was the last bountiful year for American radical political expression until 1960 signalled the end of the McCarthy era. The Weavers – Seeger, Ronnie Gilbert, Lee Hays and Fred Hellerman – were born of the idea that the driving songs of Leadbelly were so powerful that it would take at least four ordinary mortals to do justice to them. After their first professional job at the Village Vanguard, The Weavers embarked on two years of national popularity which included two hit records, "Kisses Sweeter Than Wine" and "Goodnight, Irene". It wasn't long, however, before the ominous stench of the political blacklist was spreading. It harassed and limited the work of The Weavers and ultimately led to the group's disbandment. However, Harold Leventhal, who had been Woody's agent and an important figure behind The Weavers, was determined to see the group reorganise. In 1956, they assembled for a historic reunion concert at Carnegie Hall and continued mainly as a recording group until 1964. In between, each of The Weavers pursued individual careers, and Seeger was replaced, in succession, by Frank Hamilton, Erik Darling and Bernie Krause.

A very different sort of folk star of the 1950s was Harry Belafonte, whose approach was more stylised, personal and polished than the folk community had known before. It later became quite a frequent game of the folkniks to bait and berate Belafonte, yet his early contribution should not be slighted. Belafonte had an unerring ear and sense of taste for the songs that were to become classics of the folk canon. He was also the focal point for a boom of another style of folk song, calypso, in the mid-1950s. This Caribbean-born, highly rhythmic sort of topical song had its own vogue in the middle of the

1950s, and it laterally led to the emergence of The Kingston Trio and the rampaging folk revival that followed. So, while many have discounted Belafonte as being overly commercial and arch, one has to admit, in retrospect, that he was a most important unifier of two periods in the emergence of popular folk music.

THE TWO-HEADED REVIVAL

From the beginning of the latest revival, there was a split in the theory and practice of folk-song performance. The "ethniks" felt that traditional style was everything; anything less than the rough-voiced approximations of native singers, whether white or black, was a disservice to the origins of the music and its rural practitioners. The other camp, the popularisers, felt that original sources were fine, and to be respected, but that for the modern, sophisticated city audience something had to be added: polish, musical suavity, nicety of phrasing, harmonies, instrumental filling out and augmentation. As in Britain, the sparring between these two camps still continues. There is no one "true way" to do a folk song, despite debates and arguments to the contrary. Of course, the song can be done in the traditional way that has evolved over the years in a given community among a generation or more of singers. But once a song has left its native seed-bed and becomes a vehicle for public performance, nearly anything goes. Only the limits of aesthetic taste and proportion determine how it should be performed.

Tastes, of course, differ, but it is the straitjacketing of style that led to so very many foolish clashes within the folk and pop world in the last fifteen years. When Bob Dylan said: "It's all music, no more, no less," he was discarding the eternal debate about performing styles. For a long time, jazz was divided about traditional versus swing versus newer schools such as bop or cool. Somehow it all looked quite silly in the jazz world, but the purist versus catholic debate raged on through folk circles. Still, we can learn from the clash over styles, and it does help us organise the turbulent flood of the post-1958 folk revival by looking at the polarities of traditional versus commercial styles of performance. (Even that polarity is difficult to defend because in many instances traditional styles became commercial and some commercial approaches were strongly traditional.)

For the pivotal start of the most recent folk revival, we must look to The Kingston Trio and their big hit of 1958, "Tom Dooley". Nick Reynolds, Dave Guard and Bob Shane were three well-scrubbed collegiate-looking West Coast musicians who had an affinity for Caribbean and other sorts of folk and contemporary pop music. They used conga drums and guitars, were definitely "acoustic" in approach, and made much of movement and energy in their performances. Despite the apparent calypso identification in the name of the trio and their percussion, most of their material was deep in the American folk vein. "Tom Dooley" was a Southern mountain ballad that Frank Warner had collected from the singing of Frank Proffitt, an old Carolina farmer who had known the song for years. Indeed, if any single song were to symbolise the breakout of the folk revival, it would be "Tom Dooley". The Kingston Trio were not scholars, not aficionados of tradition. They just regarded themselves as a pop group working in a new idiom. They helped ignite a cultural explosion on college campuses, on the juke-box, on the radio (still retreating defensively from charges of payola manipulation) and in live performance.

Not everyone was pleased with the Kingstons' style. Nothing so clearly indicated the strong lines of contrast and dissent as two performances given at the first Newport Folk Festival in July 1959. The Kingston Trio was the extrovert box-office attraction, billed as the stars for the total of 13,000 paid admissions to the festival. But to underline the difference, a few hundred persons at Newport, at least, were just as keen to hear the delicate, introverted traditional songs of Jean Ritchie. She was the woman who, to use singer Ed McCurdy's phrase, "had left the mountains although the mountains had never left her". For many, the thin and delicate melodies and the beguiling lightness of the dulcimer of Jean Ritchie were a language apart, not easy to understand, somewhat old-fashioned and quite tame for tastes honed only on the exuberant dynamism of The Kingston Trio. As the debates ranged over the years, the show-business stylists and the traditionalists were able to prosper together. Each could teach the other and could influence the other. Soon, traditional performers were becoming "ethnic stars" and pop stars were studying ethnic song. It was a curious and often confounding inter-relationship.

With the commercial success of The Kingston Trio, it was not long before there were imitators. Although each was different in style and approach, The Limeliters, The Brothers Four and The Chad Mitchell Trio can be regarded as offshoots of The Kingston Trio. So, too, were The Tarriers, The Rooftop Singers and The Highwaymen, and dozens more either too short-lived or too inconsequential to be listed. The most successful offshoot of the Kingston Trio format was to be Peter, Paul and Mary. Albert B. Grossman, then the Chicago-based manager of Odetta, and later the manager of Bob Dylan, took an analytical look at the Kingstons and methodically set about building another folk trio. His plan was to centre the new trio on a girl singer, and his search for the component parts was long and arduous. At one point, he scrutinised the work of a group that Logan English was pulling together in Greenwich Village, with Molly Scott as the girl singer. Grossman continued to look. He found his people: Peter Yarrow, with a light tenor voice and a great deal of knowledge about folk song; Mary Travers, a tall blonde with sex appeal and a past steeped in the left-wing folk-song scene; and Noel Stookey, a singer and comedian who had worked the Village clubs. To build the group a musical director, Milt Okun, was chosen. He had worked with Belafonte, The Brothers Four and The Chad Mitchell Trio. When the name of the new group was decided upon, Noel became Paul. "If I created Peter, Paul and Mary, you know who I am," Grossman once told me with a bearish grin.

Despite the seemingly mechanical origins of Peter, Paul and Mary, this was to become a group second only to The Weavers in its popularity, its intelligence in material and arrangements, and a light-hearted stage personality. Peter, Paul and Mary were style-setters. Their frequent hits, their homages to singers like Pete Seeger, their touting of the young Dylan, all this cast them into a leadership role. They took to the political hustings, were evident at all the major civil rights functions, and made a strong identification between their music and their social philosophy.

In the late 1950s there was a "changing of the guard" among the ranks of folk singers. Old veterans were being replaced or eclipsed by newly emerging talent. Odetta, the powerful black woman who seemed a female cross between Leadbelly and Paul Robeson, soon eclipsed the area where Cynthia Gooding had reigned. Briefly, the very adept Bob Gibson came to the fore. Another disciple of Seeger, with a highly fluent banjo and guitar style, and the smoothest of voices, Gibson would have been a major figure, but personal problems and bad luck prevented it. Nevertheless, Gibson had been such a major influence on other musicians that he truly earned the title of "a musician's musician".

Other second-rank performers began to emerge. Billy Faier, who knew so much about the potential of the five-string banjo, was astounding people with the artistic horizons of such a lowly folk instrument. Dave Van Ronk, the rough and gruff Village denizen, who specialised in creative re-shapings of black song material, left a strong mark on the folk scene. Jack Elliott, who had rambled with Woody Guthrie, and who knew Guthrie's style and manner inside out, was the closest to an available replica of Woody. Although the son of a doctor from Brooklyn, Elliott had so immersed himself and his music in the rambling Guthrie mould that his origins were forgotten.

THE HOOTENANNY SHOW

What started in 1958 became, by the fall of 1962, such a deep part of American popular music that one of the three major US television networks, the American Broadcasting Company, launched a weekly television show that was called *Hootenanny*, after the slang name for a folk-song conclave. The show stretched the borders of popular interests in all sorts of folk music, but it also started a major conflict on aesthetics and politics. Because of the articulateness and the prominence of many city folk performers who got into the fray, *Hootenanny* may very well have been the most controversial American TV show of its time.

The hootenanny craze spawned by the show was a study in the mechanics of American merchandising, fad-chasing and cashing in on what is topically popular. For a year there was a surfeit of folk recordings and performers. One shoe manufacturer even brought out hootenanny boots. Two get-rich-quick-or-perish magazines, carrying the hootenanny emblem, were produced by the ever-present American publisher looking to cash in on a craze. (One, lamentably, was edited by this writer in a less-than-happy season of trying to turn opportunity towards a useful professional goal.)

The show, the fad and its extremes were all anathema to the old-guard folk fan who had always felt that folk music was, by its very nature, a bastion against commercialism. This discontent chose to focus on the fact that Pete Seeger, the obvious father of the hootenanny wave, was blacklisted for political reasons from appearing on the TV show. Even though Seeger was acquitted of a Contempt of Congress citation for resisting the political witch-hunts, his long espousal of left and radical causes left him under a cloud, at least as far as television was concerned. (Later, on Public Broadcasting, he had his own series.)

A boycott against the *Hootenanny* TV show was started by a group of singers, led initially by Judy Collins and Carolyn Hester. The ensuing ruckus nearly tore the folk community in half. Some performers felt the TV show would become even worse aesthetically if the boycott robbed it of people who knew most about folk song. Some performers adamantly refused to appear when invited, taking the position: "no Pete Seeger, no me". But in other cases, the opposition to the show was a vortex of irony. Some performers who had never been asked on the show were its most rigorous opponents, while in other cases, top acts like Peter, Paul and Mary disdained the show on political grounds, even though they would never have appeared because it was bad business practice for them to be competing with their own highly successful college concerts.

What can be said in estimation of the effect of the hootenanny fad of 1962–63? The answer must be pro and con. The TV show was among the weakest aesthetic adventures in the history of either TV or the music world. There was a basic disbelief and lack of understanding of the musical materials offered. The very performers who might have enriched the show were so ticked-off at the Seeger blacklist that their absence tended to relegate the show to mediocrity. (Imagine an *Old Grey Whistle Test* in which more than half of the best talents were boycotting it? What would remain?)

As to the larger hootenanny fad, it almost became a study in excesses, where clapping along to shaky or non-professional performers became the order of the day. The integrity of folk song was assailed by the fad, but it was not an altogether negative phenomenon. There were a few quality country performers, like Mother Maybelle Carter and Doc Watson, who would never have enjoyed such a wide audience without TV. Probably the clearest estimation of the two-year hootenanny craze is that it did as much good in broadening the appreciation of folk song as it did harm. We survived it. Folk music survived. Publishing and TV survived, and so we relegate it to the history of Curious American Phenomena.

The history of the folk revival of 1958 onwards is strangely pock-marked with philosophical disputes and internecine wrangling. It would scarcely enrich this survey to document the fights over style, money, personal ethics, and individual conduct that raged. The majority of reasons for the endless disputes can probably be found in two factors: (1) it is essentially a youth movement, and young people are battling their way towards their own standards and rules and fighting the inexplicable traditions of the past; (2) idealistically impelled movements are constantly running into contradictions in a society that has all but forgotten its idealism. The impact of commercialism and the attendant need and desire to make money have caused problems every step of the folk road. Had the elder members of the folk community, myself included, offered more guidance on this score, perhaps there would have been less professional jealousy, less carping, less competition and manoeuvring for coveted places.

But this frank discussion of the conflicts and confusions of an ever-spiralling popularity for folk song should not outweigh both the pleasure and the value that the revival brought to so many millions. In a sense, the dissemination of knowledge and recorded or live performances of folk and folk-derived musical expression has been one of the marvels of our time. It has opened countless doors on experience and enhanced understanding of those who had been the overlooked little creative people of our world. That, in itself, was an enormous achievement of the folk revival. That is why the folk-music revival has to be regarded as a recurring one, a cyclical movement that says that folk music, the oldest style of all musics, is here to stay.

THE GRASS ROOTS OF TRADITION: THE BLUES

No single popular musical form is more important in this century than the blues. From the blues stem dozens of types of folk music, skiffle, jazz, gospel, soul, rhythm'n'blues and rock'n'roll. This book surveys the permutations of folk music into rock; the glue that holds it all together is the blues. The way to find out how rock developed is to go back to the primitive blues, and all the elements that it would later take great masses of electronic equipment to express are there in those old one-man bands. Just a singer and his guitar. The blues form the foundation stones on which the castles of rock are built. Nearly all the leading stars and stylists of rock learned the alphabet of the blues before they started to spell their own words. At its heart, the old country blues is a lonely music. It was forged out of a man or woman and their own spirit, lamenting, protesting, commenting, soothing, and in some instances, expressing self-pity about the sort of life the blues singer had to lead. So the blues grew to be a description of a state of mind, a mood or a condition, not just the name of a song-style. As it spread, the blues came to wear many faces – the face of trouble, the face of love, the face of joy and escape.

Nearly every major star of our era has, at one time or another, paid his homage to early bluesmen and what they learned from them. Elvis Presley lets you know that it was the work of Arthur "Big Boy" Crudup that led him into rock. Bob Dylan has paid his tribute to Bukka White in "Fixin' To Die" and so venerated Big Joe Williams and John Lee Hooker that he helped bring them forward. The Beatles were deeply impressed with the work of Chuck Berry, who stood midway between the basic blues and rock, a giant transitional figure. And The Rolling Stones' influence from Muddy Waters was so great that it even led them to take their name from a blues by Muddy.

African American blues grew up and developed in the period following the emancipation of the slaves, in the last third of the nineteenth century. The basic ingredient of the blues was the field holler, a plaintive sort of West African-derived chant, used while picking cotton or working on a levee. The field holler, also called the arhoolie, was a haunting personal cry among Southern blacks that softened the pains of work, and that did battle with the enervating, lonesome existence of a field hand.

19

Then the field holler, with its modal, minor haunting trail, met up with more Europeanised folk forms, such as ballads. From that marriage came the basic country blues style. At least three distinct types of country blues can be listed: (1) Mississippi Delta blues, as recorded by the late, great Robert Johnson, contemporary John Lee Hooker and early Muddy Waters, to name a few; (2) Texas-style country blues, as performed by Blind Lemon Jefferson, Leadbelly and, contemporaneously, Sam "Lightnin'" Hopkins; (3) Eastern Seaboard blues, notably from Leroy Carr and Sonny Terry and Brownie McGhee.

Above and beyond these major types, there was the "holy blues", the mixture of sacred words with blues music. A whole spate of kerbside preachers, often blind, used to make the outdoors their tabernacle. Two of the greatest of the "holy bluesmen" were Blind Willie Johnson and the late Reverend Gary Davis.

Not only is the blues an infinitely flexible and varied song form, but it speaks volumes about the society it grew from. A portrait of black life in America could be drawn through the lyrics of country and folk blues. Such a portrait, which admittedly dwelled upon the poverty-stalked side of life, has been drawn masterfully by the British blues scholar, Paul Oliver, in *Blues Fell This Morning: The Meaning of the Blues*. Oliver's study is both a source of wonderment and shame, a document of suffering drawn in bold strokes, a musical-sociological masterpiece. (There was little surprise that it was the work of an Englishman. The outsider often sees things more clearly. The average man-in-the-British-street knows more about the blues than his counterpart in America.) Oliver used the canvas of blues lyrics on which to draw a realistic, compassionate portrait of an oppressed people.

In one sense, country blues can almost be found to be a form of topical song. Although the social conditions that gave rise to the blues may be changing dramatically, they still fester in the Deep South and in the black ghettoes of the North. Behind the beat and the cry of the blues is a message about social disorganisation and suffering. Because the white majority began to tune in to the message of the blacks in the civil rights movement of the 1960s, the blues began to have an even greater urgency and immediacy than they ever did. Whatever impact the many able white city interpreters of the blues have had in the folk revival, it is still the Southern black blues performer who must be regarded as the keeper of the grand tradition. So many fine old blues men have been "unearthed", "rediscovered" or "discovered" since the late 1950s that one must be wary of the cliché that "such and such is the *last* of the great country blues performers".

With the inroads of mass communication and the shift in cultural values of rural blacks, there is much evidence to indicate that the old country-blues tradition is ebbing. Still, one recalls the laments of the English folk-song collectors at the end of the last century who said that the rural tradition had died with the industrial revolution. The alarms of the conservatives in folk song, and there are many, even if they fly the banners of radicalism, are probably without foundation. The existence of a folk-arts revival in the midst of a period of unparalleled American prosperity promises as much for the continuance of a country-blues tradition as for the continuance of the Spanish *cante jondo*, the Rumanian *doina* and the Portuguese *fado*. The blues will probably never die as long as there is personal unhappiness. Folk arts may often be embattled, but they have nothing if not durability.

Even within the seemingly limited form of country blues, so many stylists were brought forward in the folk revival as to stagger the listener. There was the late Mississippi John Hurt, the sweet-voiced and wryly witty bluesman and songster. There was Skip James, with his high and keening voice carving his initials on your memory. There was bold and blustery Big Joe Williams, driving out with energy, as would a turbulent talent like Bukka White. Son House, who, with Robert Johnson, shares the title of "king of the country blues", was rediscovered even later than many others. Son House's own life-cycle, from early work, to obscurity, to rediscovery, was emblematic of how the folk revival not only revived old songs, but old singers at the same time.

The parade of folk bluesmen marches on. There's Blind Snooks Eaglin, rasping out his street-corner shouts. Roosevelt Sykes, who calls himself "The Honey Dripper", is at his piano keyboard, making the blues laugh and chortle. There's Howlin' Wolf, out of Chicago, hoarse and intense. There's long, tall, cool Memphis Slim with short and fat Willie Dixon; they are city men now, smart and sassy, but the beat of the old blues is deep within them. There are Sonny Terry and

Brownie McGhee, veterans of folk audiences everywhere, doing what they've done for years, and loving every minute of it. Sleepy John Estes is there, singing about the rats in his kitchen, sad and desperate blues. And Furry Lewis and Mance Lipscomb, Memphis Willie B. and Tampa Red. And among the legion of great blues instrumentalists, there is Fred McDowell, making his guitar into an orchestra with a bottleneck on his little finger. There was old Sonny Boy Williamson II, playing his mouth-harp as if it were a golden trumpet. And there was Josh White, a sophisticated and suave interpreter, who knew all about blues from the country. The blues, in the hands of these and many others, was a universal language with a thousand dialects.

The folk audience became highly knowledgeable about country blues. There was ample opportunity, on stage and recording, to study one of the very best "rediscoveries", Sam "Lightnin'" Hopkins, whose sets were studies in the many faces of trouble. His highly personal songs told of love unfulfilled and devotion unappreciated. He transformed such blunt complaints as "Have you ever been mistreated?" into artistic statements with voice and guitar. He posed such poetic questions as: "Have you ever seen a one-eyed woman cry?" And his guitar was like another voice, echoing his own, completing phrases, conversing in a voice-and-string dialogue.

There are two black singers it is worth focusing on, for their stories symbolise those of so many others. Two of the most revered figures in the folk revival were Mississippi John Hurt and Muddy Waters. Their careers tell a long tale about the blues and black music.

Mississippi John, who died in 1966 in his seventies, had lived long enough to have been brought from total obscurity to become an "ethnic star" of the folk revival. His story typifies the revolution in personal lives caused by the revival. Until his rediscovery in March 1961, he was presumed dead by collectors of his 1928 recordings. Found in his home hamlet of Avalon, Mississippi, John Hurt was moved with awesome speed to a national prominence that baffled him as much as it delighted him. Far from being the "primitive" music-maker one might have expected to find in the hills at the edge of the Mississippi Delta, Hurt was a weaver of subtle, complex sounds. His performances had the introspective quality of chamber music.

Hurt's first impact was visual. He was a short, stoop-shouldered former railroad-gang worker, cattle herdsman and farmer. His face was a study in corrugated bronze. Deep furrows between his eyes pointed down a large nose to a strong projecting jaw, where two crescent-shaped creases seemed to place the singer's mouth between parentheses. Pulled down to his ears was his trademark, a stained brown round-brimmed felt hat, which Mississippi John had purchased years earlier from a mail-order catalogue.

John tuned his instrument as carefully as a classical guitarist. The instrument he played after 1961 was a gift of the Newport Folk Foundation, in appreciation of his appearance at the Newport Festival. To him, the guitar was less an instrument than it was an equal partner in a two-member group. Phrases passed from his mouth to the strings and back again, in lively colloquy. The strings alternated a set of bass and treble figures, moving often with a jogging syncopated ragtime flavour, or becoming a gently philosophical extension of a voice used in similar fashion.

In a dark, lustrous, dulcetly projected voice that persuaded attention rather than commanded it, Mr Hurt sang sacred songs, blues or wry little erotic confections such as "Salty Dog" or "Candy Man". His repertoire wasn't large, but it bore up well on repetition. His style was not that of his area. While most of the Delta blues singers were shouters of rough, tortured, intense plaints, John was almost the meditative musical philosopher, with no forbidding regional dialect to make his lyrics difficult to follow.

After Hurt recorded for Okeh Records in 1928, he virtually dropped from sight, playing only for occasional country dances and neighbouring school and church functions. In March 1961, Tom Hoskins, a Washington disc collector, traced Mr Hurt to his Mississippi home. Tom Hoskins's only clue was a line from a disc referring to Avalon as his home town. When Hoskins caught up with Hurt, he told him he was taking him to Washington to record him. Hurt was convinced that Hoskins was "an FBI man. I knew I hadn't done anything sinful, but I went along to Washington anyways. Now I'm sorry that FBI man didn't come looking for me years ago." So were we all. At John's death, many felt it was like losing a kindly uncle or grandfather. As symbol, man and musician, John Hurt represented the country performer whose music formed a bridge to a more sophisticated culture. The folk fan went on from collecting records to collecting people. That was the greatest moment of humanity, wholesomeness and selflessness during the folk revival. It was the shining hour of American folk song.

The story of Muddy Waters is fascinating in its contrast to that of Mississippi John Hurt. In 1940, Alan Lomax was hunting songs for the Archive of American Folk Song of the Library of Congress. He was on the trail, in the central Mississippi Delta country, of Robert Johnson, who had actually died years earlier. Instead, Lomax found and recorded McKinley Morganfield, a young field hand who used to augment his meagre earnings by playing and singing the blues at Saturday night fish-fries.

Morganfield, encouraged that a collector liked his music enough to record him, made the break for personal freedom to Chicago, where he changed his name back to Muddy Waters, his childhood nickname. Muddy fell in with the lively Chicago blues scene, playing at rent parties and finally being recorded on the Chess label. Muddy's musical style changed as his life changed. Instead of the moody, dark and angry music he had sung down in Mississippi, he got into a much more projective and extrovert style. His guitar was amplified, to be audible in noisy South Side clubs. He added a bass and a drummer and such masterly mouth-harp stylists as Little Walter Jacobs. Muddy became a strutting, powerful blues man and his recordings were selling well around Chicago and elsewhere. One of the songs he recorded after the war in Chicago was "Rolling Stone", which was to give the name to one of the most celebrated rock bands on the planet, a leading American rock paper and a Bob Dylan song. So the path of Muddy Waters went from Delta country blues to hard-edged Chicago rhythm'n'blues, parent of rock'n'roll. In one man's career, from farmhand to star, is thus embodied a totally different route from that of John Hurt. What would have happened if Hurt had gone to Chicago in 1928 and made a life in music? That remains a tantalising cause for speculation.

THE BLUEGRASS GROWS ALL AROUND

The other major tributary of American folk song is, of course, the white European tradition, which came over with settlers from

England, Scotland, Ireland and Wales. Because America is such a polyglot culture, there are also active traditions of Indian, Scandinavian, German, Central European and Slavic folk musics. But we are talking about the mainstreams that contributed to a national folk music.

As has been noted, there were remote areas of America where some old English and Scottish songs were more alive among traditional singers than they were in their native regions. It's as if a set of songs and ballads got themselves lodged in a corner of the Cumberlands or the Clinch Mountains, in the Great Smokies or the Appalachians and stayed there, while "progress" in Britain was wiping out folk traditions.

The first people to put city listeners in touch with the great white country tradition were the collectors, and then the recording men who went out into the field, to tape old-timers with rare repertoires of musical relics. As the folk boom gathered in intensity, more and more labels, whether general or specialised, began to issue the sort of recordings that only the Library of Congress, Folkways or Stinson had issued earlier. The field recordings began to appear on Riverside, Prestige, Vanguard, Folk-Lyric, Elektra and Folk-Legacy. Soon the major labels were onto the game, and if not issuing field recordings, it became de rigueur to have a solid folk catalogue as part of the label's backlist.

There still was no better way to make contact with rural folk-ways and its people in their setting than by attending various conventions and festivals in the South. There was nothing comparable in the black culture, for the blues men tended to be loners, not given to festivals any larger than a Saturday night party. So, we began to take off on rambles out of the Northern cities to meet the white folk music world on its home ground. We tried the Old Time Fiddler's Convention in Virginia, but were discouraged, in our purist zeal, by the large proportion of electrified country and rock'n'roll being played there. We were looking for purer country air. Other citybillies went to Galax, Virginia, a mountain furniture-making town with a folk festival that banned all electric instruments. Others ventured where Pete Seeger had gone in the mid-1930s, the Asheville Folk Festival in North Carolina, run by the late Bascom Lamar Lunsford, the "minstrel of the Appalachians".

One rural folk festival that seemed to embody the very best of country folk song and instrumentation was in Union Grove, North Carolina. "This ain't exactly a town, it's just sort of a wide place in the road," the clever country folk told us when we arrived. The Old Time Fiddlers' Convention there, now nearing its fiftieth year of continuous performances, carries a sound of grass-roots America we must strive to keep alive. The annual meeting is one of the finest examples of a living folk-art tradition in the US. As the computers, the machines and the mass media maraud their way into an unknown and impersonal modernity, it is the scrape of the fiddle, the ring of the banjo and the cry of the human voice – such as can be heard at Union Grove – that will remind us of the America we came from. It will, hopefully, also remind us of some aspects of the America to which we might one day return.

Even though the numbers of city kids who went out to the country grew, it was necessary to bring the performers to the city before contact with the mass city audience could develop. At first, it was as if each active city performer "adopted" a country performer to escort, tout and make popular. "Adoption", however, did not connote any patronising, for the city performer was getting valuable lessons in the style of his country master. Thus, Mike Seeger was sponsor of The Stanley Brothers, and many another fine bluegrass band; Ralph Rinzler squired about Bill Monroe and Doc Watson; and John Cohen became Roscoe Holcomb's "discoverer" and good friend. The list grew, and this true collecting of country musician by city musician ran counter to the more detached world of earlier folklorists who, in their pressured haste, tended, as one country singer put it, to "milk the cow dry and throw the empty hide away".

This "importing" of native folk talent was evidenced principally at folk festivals, which will be discussed in detail below. But one group that began in New York and spread its work around the whole country was The Friends of Old-Time Music. In a series of concerts, the Friends were able to transplant from the South-east to Greenwich Village in one season such ethnic stars as Doc Watson, Tom Ashley, Mother Maybelle Carter, Horton Barker, Almeda Riddle and others. (Samuel Charters tried the more difficult task of bringing his blues rediscoveries, such as Gus Cannon, Furry Lewis and Memphis Willie Borum to a New York University concert.)

In discussing the broad spectrum of American white folk music genres, it may be useful to work backward in time, rather than forward. The primary question is: where does folk music end and commercial country music begin? In the extremes, it seems easy to answer; in the subtle centre, it is a very vexing question. The whole body of American folk and pop music is such a thickly woven mesh that certain styles are continually crossing and re-crossing other styles. Nowhere is this interweave more evident than in the music generally associated with Nashville, the music called country and western. A good many performers in the fifty-year history of country and western began as folk performers. Some never left the precincts of folk music at all, while others are continually walking both sides of the musical street, changing their performing style for a given song or instrumental.

Because much of contemporary country and western music has become so sophisticated, it is difficult to recall that nearly all of it was born in folk-orientated style. There has been an unfortunate tug-of-war between those folk fans who regard country and western music as an area for their study and enjoyment and those who make minute distinctions between what is pure folk and what is "corrupted" or commercial. It is this sort of elitist approach towards folk and its peripheral musical expressions that has retarded the folk movement's ability to stay in touch with mass taste. Ethnic snobs and traditional determinists think, with much persuasive argumentation on their side, that "their" music is superior. At the same time, they are denying themselves the vast excitements and stimulations of kindred and tangential musics, which, while not "pure", have much to commend themselves.

The country and western music world that works out of Nashville (and Bakersfield, Shreveport and Dallas) is an exceedingly complex and lively one. Country and western is America's "other popular music", rich in folk origins, folk traditions and variations of folk music. Country music, if put on a soundtrack, would be the clang of an electric guitar; the subtle fretting of Merle Travis's unamplified guitar; the piercing, stirring "Gloryland March" of Wilma Lee and Stoney Cooper; the yodelling of Kenny Roberts; the devilish banjo tricks of Don Reno; Pappy McMichen's bow sliding across his 1723 Italian violin, which he had to call a fiddle; Johnny Cash pointing his guitar at an audience as if he were going to hold them up; a screaming "Howdy" from beneath cousin Minnie Pearl's straw hat; Jimmy Wakely singing to his horse; Zeke Clements explaining how to skin a cat to make a banjo; Archie Campbell telling a racy story one minute and singing a gospel song the next; Ralph Peer telling rustic auditioners to relax and sing out in a Southern hotel room; Ernest Tubb speaking like a benign Lincoln in a ten-gallon hat; Hank Williams crying his lonesome words into a microphone; Jimmie Rodgers hearing a train whistle in the night. It is a rare and exciting sound.

It would be intolerance towards those folk traditionalists who dislike country and western not to admit the validity of some of their complaints. They find too little quality and too much ordure in country and western, a complaint that I would agree with in saying that the top 20 per cent of quality country music is superb, and the rest makes it difficult to persuade people to listen to the best. It's the same with pop music, soul music and even folk song. One can agree that there is a great deal of sentimentality, piety and platitude in country music. It can become carnival and hokum, nonsense and frivolity, but the quality will out. Listen to the hard-driving "honky-tonk"-style singing of a Buck Owens or a George Jones; listen to the involvement of a Bill Anderson singing about poor folks or about suicide; listen to the surging emotion of Tammy Wynette; place Roger Miller's "King of the Road" in a continuum that makes a direct line of descent from the hobo songs of Cliff Carlisle. See how Hank Snow and Johnny Cash are latter-day twigs off the sturdy branch that produced Jimmie Rodgers, "the Singing Brakeman" and "the father of country music", way back in the mid-1920s. It is all there.

One area where the folk fan and lover of tradition seemed most closely in touch with country music is that large overlapping zone called bluegrass. Thanks to the popularising of such city stalwarts as Mike Seeger and Ralph Rinzler, bluegrass is widely known to nearly every folk fan. Here is a style of rural ensemble music-making that is almost an equivalent to the rural string-band jazz, on one hand, a link to jig and reel bands of Scotland and Ireland, and a compelling cousin of the varied instrumental bands of European and Latin-American villages.

Bluegrass evolved from the string bands that flourished after the turn of the century. These string bands, such as Gid Tanner and The Skillet Lickers, and others with similar self-burlesquing names, had evolved from earlier banjo–fiddle combinations of the nineteenth century. That instrumentation was, in turn, an American variation of Irish and Scottish pipe and flute ensembles. This genealogical root-structure led, in the late 1940s, to the emergence of bluegrass music. Although the history of string bands is convoluted and largely undocumented, bluegrass is known to have begun among a series of seminal bands led by the great Kentucky singer and mandolin player, Bill Monroe. (Kentucky is called the "bluegrass" state, and Monroe's band was called The Bluegrass Boys.)

Monroe's various bands were the seedbed of bluegrass. Through its various formations passed nearly every major bluegrass stylist of our time. The leading offshoots of Monroe's Bluegrass Boys were Lester Flatt and Earl Scruggs, whose band, The Foggy Mountain Boys, became the nation's "glamour" bluegrass band. Scruggs's virtuosity on the five-string banjo is legendary. He gave the instrument a fluidity and a lyricism almost unknown among country pickers before.

When a listener to bluegrass, country or city style, hears the bright strains of "Flint Hill Special" or "Molly And Tenbrooks", a mental picture of one of these fascinating bands emerges. Usually, there are five or six colourfully jacketed musicians with string bow ties and broad-rimmed Stetson hats. One member of the band, often the bassist, is in a tramp's costume, with baggy trousers, galluses (braces) and a clown's hat. The bluegrass band clusters in a semi-circle, then almost breaks into a dance as the players bob and weave to get close to the mike. The faces are placid, unemotional. But the music is not. The banjo crackles with showers of notes, flying about like metal confetti in a windstorm. The fiddler whips his bow across the strings, doing daring slides and audacious double-stops. The bass is slapped gustily. The dobro, a steel guitar fretted with a metal bar in the Hawaiian fashion, makes a purring sound. The mandolin, suggesting a brittle, nervous cat walking a telephone wire, scampers at dangerous speed. Above it all, riding high and penetrating, is a tenor voice, or several voices in two- or three-part close harmony.

From Monroe's "school" of bluegrass have come, besides Flatt and Scruggs, such graduates as Mac Wiseman, Jimmy Martin, Carter

Stanley, Gordon Terry, Sonny Osborne, Clyde Moody and Chubby Wise. (It was Wise, a fiddler from Florida, whose smooth bowing and flashy effects gave much of the stylistic outlines to later bluegrass fiddling.) Of the songs best identified with Bill Monroe, whose own high-tenor singing is a marvel unto itself, are "Mule-Skinner Blues" and "Kentucky Waltz". His "Wayfaring Stranger" burns with religious fervour. Ironically, the first single recorded by Elvis Presley included Monroe's own composition, "Blue Moon Of Kentucky".

Flatt and Scruggs worked with Monroe during the pivotal period, 1945 to 1948, when the bluegrass style crystallised. Largely through the great interest in folk music shown by Earl Scruggs, this band was taken especially close to the hearts of the folk audience. It took a very small change in their standard country repertoire to make Flatt and Scruggs just as successful with folk audiences as they were on their flour-advertising TV and radio shows.

While Monroe and Flatt and Scruggs (who have since gone individual ways) are at the summit of bluegrass, the mountainside has been peopled by other able ensembles. The Dillards, from the Ozarks, salted their work with rich humour. The Stanley Brothers and The Clinch Mountain Boys had an unpressured mellowness in their folk-rooted old part-singing. The Lilly Brothers and Don Stover were country boys who emigrated to Boston and showed New England what bluegrass was all about. Around Los Angeles, The Kentucky Colonels grew out of The Country Gentlemen. The band featured the brilliant guitar-playing of Clarence White. (White later joined The Byrds and was killed in his twenties in 1973 in a car accident.)

Almost inevitably, certain young city folk musicians were attracted to the instrumental virtuosity attainable in bluegrass. There was a bluegrass band at Yale, The Gray Sky Boys; another at Harvard, The Charles River Valley Boys. Roger Sprung brought Scruggs-picking up to the Sunday free-for-alls at Washington Square Park in New York. Eric Weissberg, a New York banjoist who had studied at the Juilliard School of Music, became such a wizard at playing Scruggs-style banjo that even Scruggs sang his praises. After working in a variety of bands, it was Weissberg who brought banjo theatrics to the sound-track of the film *Deliverance* and his band by that name has been hitting the pop charts since 1973.

Perhaps the all-round best city-centred bluegrass band of the 1960s was The Greenbriar Boys. Ralph Rinzler, the scholar and disciple of Monroe, played mandolin and guitar. Bob Yellin was a florid banjoist, and John Herald had that wild and yelping high tenor voice that ranged through a hall like the clarinet of an old traditional jazz band. Of perhaps even greater importance was the musical-revival trio, The New Lost City Ramblers, who, while loving bluegrass, were specialists in the pre-bluegrass string-band music of the 1920s and 1930s. The Ramblers, led by Mike Seeger and John Cohen, in salty performances were paying great tribute to the old musicians from whom they had learned songs and styles. They tirelessly brought forward country origins. Ironically, at one point, this proselytising work of The New Lost City Ramblers helped the rural musicians to come to the fore, while the city trio slid to the back of the stage. This selfless form of activity is one of the little-known aspects of the folk revival that, in its strange irony, gave the whole interchange between city and country a glow of beauty, ethics and honour.

COFFEEHOUSES AND FESTIVALS

One of the strange aspects of the folk revival is that it grew alongside two new mediums for the performance of folk song, in coffeehouses and in folk festivals. An economic determinist explanation of the folk revival, which I find hard to accept, is that one reason for the folk boom was that it created a new musical labour force of cheap entertainment. This theory has it that the emerging coffeehouse scene demanded soloists who needed no band, no piano, no backing group – a self-contained musical entity that might also, in patter, supply a bit of comedy. The folk musician, city or country, was ideal for this. And the hushed, relaxed and intimate setting of a coffeehouse provided the ideal framework for listening to a folk singer/guitarist.

Americans have always been startled, upon visiting Britain, to discover how many folk clubs operate with regularity, most of them once a week in a room above a pub. Yet, if one were to survey the active folk coffeehouses around America from 1958 through the 1960s, the number would probably compare favourably to the number of folk clubs in Britain. Admittedly, there was a greater core of scholarship, knowledge, purpose and direction in the British folk

31

club rarely achieved in an American coffeehouse. In the latter, mood, ambience and atmosphere were the chief concerns.

American coffeehouses began in the Greenwich Village district of New York and the North Beach district of San Francisco, probably because these were both heavily Italian communities. The Continental tradition of the coffeehouse goes back to the origins of coffee, a date which slips my mind, if it was ever in my mind. So it was in places like The Figaro and The Rienzi that coffeehouse "hanging out" began. Soon, a new breed of place developed, like The Gaslight on Macdougal Street, where entertainment, beat poetry, comics and folk singers held sway. Then came the slicker places, like The Bitter End, where it wasn't the spontaneous Village spirit that was innate, but a heightened form providing a typical Village scene for the kids who came in from the comfortable suburban districts of Brooklyn, Queens and New Jersey.

University settings were ideal for the folk and coffee diet, whether The Ten O'Clock Scholar in Minneapolis, The Cafe Lena in Saratoga, The Club 47 in Cambridge, The Troubadour in Berkeley, The Buddha in the Midwest, and so on. By the height of the folk revival in 1963, there was a well-defined coffeehouse circuit throughout America. If you wanted to catch a local scene, that's where you headed. If you were a professional folk singer, that's where you worked.

Some of the more formal nightclubs and brand-new cabarets took the folk boom a step further. The Village Gate, The Purple Onion, the hungry i, Gerdes' Folk City, The Gate of Horn and dozens of lesser-known cabarets began to feature folk singers and instrumentalists. It seemed as though someone had tapped a well and the gushes of talent sprang out in profusion. The audiences listened to Casey Anderson, Hoyt Axton, Fiddler Beers, Leon Bibb, Theo Bikel, Sandy Bull, Judy Collins, Bonnie Dobson, Logan English, Carolyn Hester, Ian and Sylvia, Jim and Jean, Phil Ochs, Lisa Kindred... on and on, through the alphabet and the night.

Perhaps the way to best understand the coffeehouse scene and what a central place it played in the folk revival is to realise that both Bob Dylan and Joan Baez got their earliest performing experience in the coffeehouses of Minneapolis and Boston, respectively, before moving on. It was in the coffeehouses that they learned how to perform, how to please and handle an audience, how to shape material for the attention of an audience, and even how the material they did sounded bouncing off the eyes and ears of their listeners. Although the number of viable and interesting coffeehouses around the cities and campuses of America has diminished sharply, they made their contributions as an arena for what was then "the new music".

The festivals were the next outgrowth. The biggest and best-known of these was the annual one held at Newport, Rhode Island. It began as an offshoot of the parent jazz festival there, but in a short time it was to become a much bigger box-office attraction than the jazz festival. The first Newport Festival, in 1959, was co-produced by George Wein (of the jazz festival board) and Albert B. Grossman, who would later be best known for managing Bob Dylan. It started modestly with only about 13,000 tickets sold. The folk festival of 1960 was an appreciable improvement, aesthetically and commercially. But a spontaneous riot a few weeks later at the Newport Jazz Festival seemed destined to halt all music festivals in the Rhode Island resort city. However, in two years, after a series of meetings between Wein, Pete Seeger and Theo Bikel, it was decided to reconstitute the festival, put it on as a performer-run operation, and to build a companion Newport Folk Foundation that would plough money back into the roots of folk music.

Some of the greatest moments in the history of the folk revival occurred at the large concerts or the smaller workshops of the Newport Folk Festival, which has run since 1962 each year. The 1963 festival saw the upsurge of both the hootenanny craze and the implacable identification of the folk movement with the civil rights struggle. By 1964 a wonderful balance was being struck at Newport, between the show-business stars of folk song and the obscure but talented folk performers who were being brought up out of the remote hinterland. Several years of the folk festivals were recorded by Vanguard, lasting memorials of the power and scope of this great national event.

Yet size, prestige and publicity, such as were achieved at Newport, were not the only factors that made for highly pleasing festivals. Yale University undergraduates held a series of fine festivals at an old country hotel at Indian Neck, near Branford, Connecticut. The students at the Universities of California and Chicago mounted very skilful and ambitious student festivals. Scholars and collectors and other authorities were brought in to keep the academic tone just as high as the entertainment level.

The folk festivals around America during the early 1960s became more than just music programmes. With collegians and other young people hitch-hiking, coming in brightly painted cars and buses, and generally turning the events into pilgrimages, the festivals signalled a lifestyle. Few moments were greater than to be able to see city youngsters sitting beside old-timers from the rural South, learning a guitar phrase, a bit of lyric from an old ballad or blues, a bit of folklore in a story. There was the vortex, the heart of the whole matter passing along an art from mouth to ear, from old to young. It was something to be festive about.

SONGS OF PRAISE AND FREEDOM

African American folk music became "functional" when it was used to accompany work, or at funerals, or when it went to church. Curiously enough, the music also went modern, using elements of blues and jazz as well as the old hymns, spirituals and traditional gospel forms. The glory and the sanctity of the traditional African American spiritual has undergone so much change in contemporary life that city folk fans had to search to find the spiritual in its "pure" form. For anyone interested in rapid movement, change, flux and adaptation of tradition, black music in its modern gospel application and its subsequent use in the civil rights movement is one of the most exciting aspects of the entire folk revival.

African American gospel music has spread far from the churches in which it was born. During the late 1950s and 1960s, the fervour and vibrancy of black religious music had invaded the theatre, the music festival and even, for a brief time, the night club. Musical elements of gospel spawned a new school of jazz, played a role as "freedom" songs in the civil rights movement, made a deep impression on popular music in "soul", and became a solidly entrenched sub-division of American folk music. This impact of a religious music on popular art and entertainment may well be without precedent in the history of the church, although the development of the folk mass, the jazz mass, and even the rock'n'roll mass of the mid-1960s was clearly following a pattern long since established by black gospel. It was partially out of a need to make the music of the church vital to the congregants that modern gospel music developed. It began to take its present form after World War II, but its roots can be traced back to slavery.

Gospel music may be composed of traditional music of varying moods and tempos, using either biblical or colloquial language. Its lyrics may be simple in sentiment, but are always sacred, inspirational and devotional in content. Perhaps the most exciting and curious aspect of gospel song is that these sacred, devotional words are generally wedded to music and instruments that are so secular as to be indistinguishable from jazz, blues, or even rock'n'roll. Modern gospel is a strongly improvisational music, in which the voices play freely as if they were instruments in a jazz ensemble. (Churches of the Sanctified and Holiness sects use jazz instruments along with voices.)

What seems most overwhelming to new listeners of gospel song is the total abandon and fervour of the performances. Well-springs of energy seem to open up, as the singers get themselves more deeply involved in the surging rhythms, exultant crescendos and the enveloping descants. There was a time, not long ago, when many African American church leaders looked with disfavour on the secular, jazzy sound of gospel. Many churches with large black congregations continue to use the standard formal music of the hymnal. But the majority of black congregations have made the transition to the new blues-based gospel song. It has been estimated that there are some five hundred amateur groups in the country and more than fifty professional groups.

Gospel, too, has its stars. The late Mahalia Jackson was to become one of the most revered singers of any type of music, the glory and majesty of her voice and bearing leaving indelible recollections. Marion Williams and The Stars of Faith, working in the gospel pageant *Black Nativity*, with a script by the distinguished writer Langston Hughes, brought one form of gospel to thousands who may never have heard it inside the precincts of a church.

Many other names of distinctive gospel stylists should be mentioned: The Staple Singers, a family quartet from Mississippi, by way of Chicago, not only made history within gospel circles but also won the *Down Beat* award for the best vocal group of 1962. When the Staples went into gospel-rock, they became hit recording artists. Other names, other styles: James Cleveland, The Caravans, The Clara Ward Singers, The Soul-Stirrers, The Highway Q. C.'s, Ernestine Washington, The Five Blind Boys, The Stevens Singers, The Abyssinian Baptist Chorus, The Drinkard Singers, Maceo Woods, Carrie Smith, The Roberta Martin Singers, Alex Bradford, The Gospel Pearls, The Swan Silvertones, Tabernacle Singers, The Grandison Singers... a long and distinguished list, by no means complete.

Although there was a cresting of interest in gospel from 1962 to 1965, when many major record companies signed gospel performers, the majority recorded for specialised labels, such as Savoy, Tabernacle, Battle, Peacock and the like. Many pop listeners were drawn to gospel indirectly. When they realised that a lot of the "soul" and easy fluidity of the singing of Ray Charles was called "churchy" among the initiated, they tried to track the music back to its origins. Similar graduates of gospel were themselves pop singers, people like Della Reese, Aretha Franklin, Sammy Price and Dionne Warwick. Then, around 1955, the jazz world began to absorb the impact of gospel energy. The "soul jazz" movement borrowed heavily from the cadences, tempos and spirit, if not the letter, of congregational singing. Among those whose jazz improvisation began to reflect church sounds were Cannonball Adderley, Bobby Timmons, Horace Silver and the fine organist, Jimmy Smith.

Because gospel music, like its parent churches, is a missionary vehicle, there has always been an attempt to win converts. Few developments in this out-of-church work held more interest than its sorties into American night life. In the late 1940s, a few singers tried gospel music in the cabarets, but often at the expense of outraging the devout. Sister Rosetta Tharpe, Brother John Sellers and The Grandison Singers were the bold pioneers of this cabaret gospel, and they were often ostracised in the African American community for doing it. At one point, Clara Ward had one group bearing her name working in Birdland, the Manhattan jazz club, while another with her name worked the big casinos of Las Vegas.

But the move into the entertainment medium of the cabarets went much too far for the religionists with the launching of a pop-gospel movement and the opening of The Sweet Chariot, a somewhat tawdry mid-town Manhattan club built around gospel song. Leaders of gospel, from Mahalia Jackson down, saw the apparent distortion of the basic devotional content of the music, and soon the bandwagon gospel-cabaret fad went the way of all fads: down the drain.

Despite these forays, gospel continues to flourish in its native environments from impoverished storefront congregations to more affluent tabernacles. Radio evangelists, such as the Elder Solomon Lightfoot Michaux, Elder Beck and the Rev. C.L. Franklin (father of Aretha), have done much to spread gospel music into many homes since the heyday of radio in the 1930s. There is scarcely a major urban centre that does not have its Sunday gospel programmes on radio today. The history of gospel song is complex. Several kindred traditions have been tributaries to the mainstream of gospel music: the traditions of the spiritual, the jubilee, the hymn and the anthem. C. Albert Tindley, who is regarded by some as the father of modern gospel, was writing religious songs around the turn of the century, drawing upon the styles of spirituals and other traditional religious forms. Two important names in the composition of modern gospel are Thomas A. "Georgia Tom" Dorsey and Lucie Campbell. Dorsey, an itinerant blues piano-player, began to fuse the music of the blues with the message of the church as early as the middle 1920s. Lucie Campbell wrote many of the classics of gospel to be sung by Mahalia Jackson and others.

Some of the best milieux for hearing gospel music remain deep in the African American community, in churches, whether they be well-endowed large churches or close-to-the-people storefront tabernacles. At another extreme, one can hear quality gospel sessions at Harlem's leading cinema house, the Apollo Theatre. There, the involvement and rapport between the "preaching" singers is often so great that women in the congregation are known to faint with transcendence. Nurses are usually on hand.

But the most fascinating contemporary development in gospel lay far afield: gospel and its variations became a weapon in the civil rights movement that gathered force in the 1960s. Here, however, it was not a heavenly salvation of which the blacks and their allies sang, but of the urgent need for a better life on earth. Although the "freedom-song movement" was to burst with full fervour during the heart of the civil rights sit-in action, which began in 1960, there was already a long, involved tradition of African American "protest" song. African American folk music, which had been singing of a promised land since the days of slavery, became a vital force in the attempts to achieve that promised land in the 1960s.

In the course of a major survey for the *New York Times* in August 1962, I found that the integration leaders were all in agreement that music set the tempo of their movement. During visits to Albany, Georgia, Durham, North Carolina, and other tension points throughout the South, I found ample evidence that spirituals, hymns and gospel songs were helping to bolster the morale of integrationists and to disarm the segregationists of their hostility.

In the early 1960s, a new tributary of "freedom" songs, bold words set to old melodies, was making the deep river of black protest in song run swifter. The songs, old and new, were used at mass meetings, demonstrations, prayer vigils, on Freedom Rides, in jails and at sit-ins. The music rang with the bombast of election songs, the sanctity of marching tunes for a holy crusade and the spirit-building of fraternal anthems.

"The freedom songs are playing a strong and vital role in our struggle," the late Rev. Dr Martin Luther King Jr. told me in Albany. "These songs give the people new courage and a sense of unity. I think they keep alive a faith, a radiant hope in the future, particularly in our most trying hours." (This was six years before his assassination.)

The Albany Movement was a coalition of civil rights groups that struggled through 1962 to break down racial segregation in the south-western Georgia city. More than 1,100 arrests were made there of those demonstrating for an end to segregation. A young black leader in Albany, Charles Jones, said emphatically: "There could have been no Albany movement without music." The field secretary for the Student Non-Violent Coordinating Committee went on: "We could not have communicated with the masses of the people without music. They could not have communicated with us without music. They are not articulate. But through songs, they expressed years of suppressed hope, suffering, even joy and love."

In Albany, one could hear the majestic old spiritual:

Go down, Moses,
Way down in Egypt's land,
Tell old Pharaoh,
To let my people go.

Minutes later, one could hear a young black man, who talked of "the newtime religion", singing to the same melody:

Go down, Kennedy,
Way down in Georgia land.
Tell old Pritchett
To let my people go.

("Old Pritchett" was Chief of Police Laurie Pritchett of Albany.)

This conversion shows how the "freedom song" changed the lyrics to suit the immediate situation. Songs of this sort swept the South for at least four years, by word of mouth, through mimeographed song-sheets, and other speedy methods of improvised dissemination.

Freedom songs of the early 1960s, and their counterpart in the Northern topical-protest song movement, represented perhaps the greatest mass topical song-writing sweep to have affected America since the days of the organising drives for the labour movement in the 1930s. The songs were to be as controversial as those of the earlier labour crusades.

It was not only the new and more militant lyrics that were playing a strong catalytic role in the civil rights struggle. A Georgia official of the National Association for the Advancement of Coloured People, Vernon E. Jordan Jr., recalled the power of traditional religious music at an organising meeting: "The people were cold with fear. Music did what prayer and speeches could not do in breaking the ice."

Although there were many recordings of freedom songs, and although they were transplanted to concert and festival stages, those "performances" paled beside the real thing – hearing and watching the music being used in a "functional" situation. Gloster B. Current, national director of branches of the NAACP, summed this up: "They cannot hold a mass meeting in the South without music. You should really go there and hear it on the spot. The music sounds much different under the gun." Recordings and Northern concerts have long tended to make freedom songs sound like stale tub-thumping and sloganeering. Instead, try to visualise a group of fifty young black men on the stairs of a Southern church after a mass meeting. History put these "average" black teenagers in front of a microphone, and they are aware that, to use the Dylan line that was later used at the Democratic National Convention riots in Chicago in 1968, "the whole wide world is watching". A young woman on the steps of a Southern church chants:

> Over my head I see freedom in the air,
> There must be a God somewhere.

As Bernice Johnson sings, one can see, over her shoulder, a prowl (police patrol) car passing three times within fifteen minutes.

For an inkling of the emotional impact of freedom songs in action, imagine a crowded, sweaty meeting in Albany's Mount Zion Baptist Church. The heat broils mercilessly, despite six electric fans and dozens of hand-held paper fans. Dr King and his aide, the Rev. Ralph D. Abernathy, have spoken to their followers. The meeting closes with the traditional singing of "We Shall Overcome", which has been called the "Marseillaise" of the civil rights revolution.

Tired, dejected civil rights activists have found as much solace and strength in the music of the integration movement as have worshippers through gospel songs. The two uses of a kindred music are deeply rooted in black tradition. A white singer-guitarist, Guy Carawan, played a catalytic role in spreading the freedom song through the South, much as Pete Seeger had been the sower of folk and topical songs in the North. Carawan, of course, did not invent this use of protest song, for it goes back to pre-Civil War days. But as a musical organiser, he helped those in the early student sit-in movements to use music with greater effectiveness. After a while, students quite unaware of Guy Carawan, or their implicit debt to him, were singing songs he had helped popularise. His strong role cannot be emphasised enough, yet it was still a black phenomenon structured on the special traditions and needs of the black populace.

Not only the black people responded to the infectious songs. Police Chief Pritchett, although saying that "their singing is a method to incite them", added, "These people got a lot of feeling and rhythm. I enjoy hearing them sing. The songs are catchy." With a strange detachment, Chief Pritchett described the episode of December

1961: after more than 260 persons were booked in a mass arrest, his jail guards were singing and humming songs along with the prisoners!

Similarly, in a Charlotte, North Carolina, sit-in meeting of the Committee On Racial Equality (CORE), a policeman was observed singing along, before "he caught himself". Guards in the Mississippi State Prison in Parchman were observed doing the same. A jailer in Americus, Georgia, was said to have requested a song from a black prisoner. A white piano-player in Albany changed the lyrics of "When The Saints Go Marching In" to "When The King [Dr Martin Luther King] Comes Marching In". There are, of course, stories to the contrary: in Dawson, Georgia, singing was forbidden in jail. In Camille, Georgia, a prisoner was allegedly slapped for singing. In Rock Hill, South Carolina, a group was put in solitary confinement until they stopped their protests in music.

Two of the young activists intensely linked with the freedom-song movement, who were later to become well-known in the folk movement, were Bernice Johnson and Cordell Reagon. Bernice had a deep, booming, soaringly intense voice that reminded many of us of Odetta's, while Cordell was the tireless battler whose energy and purpose made many of the Northern folk liberals look a bit weak. Cordell and Bernice organised a group called the Freedom Singers, which gave many concerts and raised thousands of dollars for the Student Non-Violent Coordinating Committee.

"Songs are easy," Cordell explained, "a lot we make up as we go, mostly in jail. We were sitting around a drugstore today and I made up a song in rock'n'roll style. But the movement is constantly on people's minds. First they sing rock'n'roll, and then they go into these freedom songs." Encountering such dedicated young activists, who used music as their medium and their message, was a fabulous experience. It formed a great contrast with the middle-class youth of the Northern folk-music movement, who were, of course, trying to "say something" through their music, also.

The topical song upsurge in the North grew in intensity as did the civil rights struggle, but it went on to touch on other areas such as peace, women's rights, academic freedom and a host of other topical concerns of the 1960s. Out of the *Broadside* magazine group in New York came such people as Dylan, Phil Ochs, Tom Paxton, Gil Turner, Janis Ian and scores more. When Peter, Paul and Mary recorded a hit,

"If I Had A Hammer", written years earlier by Pete Seeger and Lee Hays, they were doing a Northern freedom song. When Dylan sang "Blowin' In The Wind", it, too, was a freedom song, and like the songs in the South, it was melodically related to an old spiritual, "No More Auction Block For Me". (When he got through with it, melodically and lyrically, it was his own composition.)

We have no gauges or thermometers to compare and contrast either the Southern black civil rights struggle and its songs or the Northern allied white middle-class civil rights campaign and the songs it took from the topical-song movement. Topical songs, throughout history, whether they were broadside ballads or commercial music-hall ditties, have, by and large, been of interest only so long as the heat of immediacy was still within them. But many went on to become classics. When Dylan wrote "It's Alright Ma (I'm Only Bleeding)", he probably wrote the most large-scale, sweeping and artistic topical-protest song of all time. How fascinating to see, in his concert tour of America of 1974, that reporters noted the greatest impact on his audience was the line about the President of the United States having to stand naked.

Artful songs of topical protest can become universal. The whole body of slave songs from the 1950s onwards remained in active tradition because the same need was there, and the songs filled the musical need. It is not a reflection on Phil Ochs's song-writing to find that his song about the sinking of a Navy submarine was quickly dated, while his poignant "There But For Fortune" survives as a perennial. Other topical songs were short-lived, but served their purpose nobly. When John Lennon and Yoko Ono came up with the simple chant, "Give Peace A Chance", they wrote an immortal line to an immortal melody. Until there are no wars, the song will have meaning, and then, it will retain its meaning in history.

THE RECURRING REVIVAL

If there is anything constant about the wildly erratic swings of change in popular-music taste, that constant is change itself. Because of the vigour of musical ideas, because of the clamour of the marketplace for new "product", because of the desire of critics and standard-setters for some degree of novelty, because of the skittishness of the passions of young listeners, change is always with us.

Compared to popular music, folk music moves very slowly indeed, and I'm not talking about tempo. By its very nature, folk music evolves over many years, passes through generations, survives even centuries and goes on, an anchor to the security of a popular culture. Yet when the slow-moving, glacier-like flow of folk music entered the folk revival of the 1960s, the heat generated by the interaction made folk music move faster than in any comparable period. There were more folk-like songs composed, more people about to perform and record, and the advent of the singer-songwriter, or singer-composer, meant that instead of a few isolated bards or troubadours, there were dozens in any given city across the American landscape.

The revival gained force, month by month, year by year until the end of 1964, and then it began to subside. A lot of factors can be advanced in explanation for the slowing down of the folk boom. The assassination of President John F. Kennedy in late 1963 was a factor. Those who had found their social ideals embodied in Kennedy's "New Frontier" suddenly had ample reason for feeling defeated by life in the death of the President. The most idealistic had found their music in the folk revival. With the jadedness of ideals came the need for another sort of music. So, too, with the idealism of the civil rights movement. For the first few years of the 1960s, it seemed that sheer enthusiasm and songs and marches were going to create a new society. Then the civil rights movement hit a stone wall of prejudice and the "white backlash". It was going to be a lot bigger job to end racism in American life than a lot of the kids had reckoned. Things slowed down, and the freedom songs didn't ring with quite the roll of triumph they once had.

And there were new sounds around. Not really new, because rock'n'roll flourished before the folk revival. But new people were doing new music. Dylan tried to get four tracks of electrically backed rhythm numbers onto his second album, *Freewheelin'*. He was only reflecting his own early, and continuing, interest in rock, rhythm'n'blues and other popular forms, even while still fascinated with folk forms. Tim Hardin was another who early on had wanted his folk-like ballads backed with electricity and rhythm. And into the East came a Chicago musician, Paul Butterfield, who learned about rhythm'n'blues "from the horse's mouth", right in the R&B clubs of Chicago's black ghetto.

The biggest current of interest in rock, however, came from England. A whole school of young Liverpool musicians, notably The Beatles, were fascinated by the rhythm'n'blues recordings of such masters as Little Richard and Muddy Waters and by the rockabilly songs of The Everly Brothers. From such influences British rock germinated in the early 1960s. The race was on, and scores of groups, such as The Rolling Stones and The Animals, began to perform rhythm'n'blues with an English accent. In many instances, the Britons seemed to understand what American blues were all about better than American whites. In not very much time, the so-called "British Invasion" brought it all back home. The English music seemed so alive, compared to the rather vapid stuff that could be heard on the *Hootenanny* TV show. There was a changing of the guard.

Largely unaware of their own great blues tradition, the American mass audience took to rhythm'n'blues, English style, as they had never quite taken to American performers. The discotheque began to consume as much interest as had the coffee-shop "hoot". For a time, the folk vigilantes were concerned lest this all added up to culture-theft. But the fears again were groundless. The British rock explosion only helped to stimulate tremendous interest throughout the world in American blues, from down-home Mississippi Delta, to Chicago, to Detroit. Again, travelling American bluesmen were finding, as had Josh White and Big Bill Broonzy in the 1940s, that their music cast a spell in Europe. Once prophets without honour in their own land, American bluesmen could, for the first time in their lives, make a decent living by touring Europe.

So by the end of 1964, the stage was set for a new rage in music. Dylan was to presage it with his tracks on *Freewheelin'* and The Byrds were to fully establish it with "Tambourine Man", done with electric guitars, drums, the works. Then came Dylan's two electric albums, and "folk-rock" was here, mixing the elements of folk with those of rock, holding on to meaning but making things dance.

The first few months of folk-rock were strange, indeed. Critics were caught off guard. Tangential performers like Barry McGuire and P.F. Sloan were being lionised for being copycats. Sonny and Cher aped Dylan's nasality and sold a million records. It was a confused, and confusing, period of transition. The audiences booed Dylan for part of a year; they almost booed him out of show business for eight years. But while some were booing him, the musicians were busy imitating him, and by the late summer of 1965, folk-rock was all about us. The path was clear for The Lovin' Spoonful, Janis Ian, Simon and Garfunkel. The singer-songwriters were plugging in.

After the first rigorous round of confusion, however, we could see that there was room for all sorts of music. Some of the ethnic purists began to hear what the new sounds were all about. The heavily political folk people began to see that folk-rock didn't mean an end to protest, but that protest was just to get a few thousand more watts with which to pump out its message. What had looked like a "sell-out" and "opportunism" turned out not to be malignant at all.

So the folk revival goes on. Less furious, less compulsive, less a mass phenomenon, but it's all there. And 6,000,000 people applied for tickets to hear Dylan do rock but also do folk and country-style material in 1974. "It's all music, no more, no less," he said in 1965, and it still has validity.

SOURCES

No list of twenty recordings could possibly cover all the rich and varied world of traditional American folk song or its urban revival counterpart. The recordings I've listed below should, however, certainly provide a solid introduction to the hydra-headed body of American folk song. The emphasis here is on the white and black mainstream of traditional material. Necessarily this tends to slight the myriad regional and ethnic sub-cultures, from Indian to Cajun, and so on, which proliferate in the United States. Wherever possible, I have listed multi-disc anthologies, which, while more expensive, do survey wider areas.

Anthology of American Folk Music (Folkways). Six LPs in three volumes make up a vintage collection drawn from 78s going back to the 1920s. A basic anthology that surveys rich pastures.

The Folk Box (Elektra). Unabashedly, I commend this because the choice of material and the annotations were mine. The four LPs attempt to cull the best from the Folkways and Elektra labels, arranged in survey form.

American Folk Singers and Balladeers (Classics Record Library). A vaguely similar collection, drawn from Vanguard's extensive archive. Prepared originally for the Book-of-the-Month Club, these four LPs lean mainly towards the urban performer and polished stylist.

Southern Folk Heritage Series (Atlantic). Seven LPs that take a fresh look at folk sources in the field by veteran collector, Alan Lomax. Especially noteworthy are the discs on black and religious music.

Pete Seeger's Greatest Hits (Columbia). The title seems odd for a singer who opposed commercial trappings all his career. But the contents bear out the title, portraying the career of the "father" of the folk revival.

Blind Gary Davis: *Harlem Street Singer* (Prestige). The marvellously rough and penetrating voice of a man who carried on Blind Willie Johnson's tradition of "the holy blues". Heartfelt blues vocal and guitar language, dressed up in religious togs by a kerbside preacher.

The Staple Singers: *Swing Low* (Veejay). Black gospel at its best; funky, voracious, genuinely involved. Daughter Mavis's voice shines through with power and clarity.

Muddy Waters: *The Real Folk Blues* (Chess). Muddy, that walking museum of the blues who travelled from Mississippi to Chicago and back, in style and in person, is in rare good form here.

Jim Kweskin and The Jug Band: *The Jug Band* (Vanguard). The music is black, the interpreters white, the fun incomparable as old junkyard instrumentation is brought out to display the pungency and wit of American "skiffle".

Johnny Cash at Folsom Prison (Columbia). The big man from the country with his special brand of white rural soul freeing a delighted audience of prisoners.

Robert Johnson: *King of the Delta Blues Singers* (Columbia). The dark and brooding country blues masterpieces of the vastly influential, late giant of the Delta style. Haunting and compelling.

Peter, Paul and Mary: *10 Years Together* (Warner Brothers). Because they were in the forefront of the popularisation of 1960s folk material, P. P. & M.'s retrospective is historically interesting and pleasant to boot.

Folk Festival at Newport (Vanguard). For several years, Vanguard conscientiously taped the mammoth Newport festivals. Any one of a score of the albums released makes a fine aural souvenir.

Joan Baez: *The First Ten Years* (Vanguard). That limpid voice, that social dedication and the always tasteful material make this Baez collection a must.

Bob Dylan: *The Times, They Are A-Changin'* (Columbia). Which early Dylan album epitomises his topical-folk period better than this?

Woody Guthrie: *Library of Congress Recordings* (Elektra). A service no less than public, this triple-LP set, drawn from old interviews with Alan Lomax, catches Woody in his prime, singing and talking about the roots of his folk art, an art that shaped two generations of singing and lifestyles.

Jean Ritchie: *Singing Family of the Cumberlands* (Riverside). The dulcet-voiced mountain woman in a musical companion to her book about a Kentucky folk community and its ambience in a remote hill pocket. Gentle, nostalgic, evocative and easy listening.

Leadbelly's Last Sessions (Folkways). Two double-LP albums of the late, great Texas titan, belting out his songs and blues with waning vigour, but still surpassing strength and grit.

Ed McCurdy: *A Treasure Chest of American Folk Songs* (Elektra). Two LPs that survey a mass of beautiful material. McCurdy's strong baritone is eminently listenable, his choice of songs intelligent. A "sleeper" album that irradiates any folk library.

The Weavers Reunion at Carnegie Hall – 1963 (Vanguard). The group that once starred Pete Seeger got together for a memorable, sentimental reunion with Pete and his successors. A classic bit of nostalgia.

TWO

Troubadours and Stars

DAVE LAING

During 1965, the folk revival described in the previous chapter gave way to "folk-rock" as a major market trend in American pop. The music business paper *Billboard* summed it up in a banner headline: "Folk + Rock − Profits". That trend lasted about a year as far as the record business was concerned. During that time Bob Dylan had his first big hit, Barry McGuire had his one and only hit, Sonny and Cher launched themselves on the road to cabaret and Glen Campbell recorded Buffy Sainte-Marie's "Universal Soldier".

But the effects of the folk revival on rock music lasted longer and went deeper than that particular bandwagon. Most of the seminal figures in rock in America over the last decade served their musical apprenticeships in the coffeehouses and on the campuses of the folk revival: Bob Dylan, Stephen Stills, John Sebastian, Neil Young, Roger McGuinn, David Crosby, Joni Mitchell, John Phillips, Jackson Browne − the list could go on and on. What these performers and others brought into rock was not just different sounds and musical styles, but a set of habits and attitudes which proved to be crucial in the expansion of rock's horizons in the late sixties.

To some extent, this was a familiar pattern in the history of popular music. Throughout the twentieth century, pop has periodically renewed itself by absorbing and transforming music that had previously existed outside the orbit of the mass media. Ragtime, jazz and the various forms of rhythm'n'blues that went to make up rock'n'roll all received this treatment. In the process, the original "folk" styles were usually diluted as they were uprooted from their cultural contexts outside the pop mainstream.

Where the folk revival differed from earlier styles that had been co-opted by Tin Pan Alley was in its "cultural context". Unlike the predominantly black forms which provided the basis for the earlier upheavals in pop, the revival was not rooted in a particular ethnic or social group. Its strength and growth in the early sixties was based on its relevance to the set of social changes which were slowly beginning to work themselves out in America, and also on the peculiarly parlous state of pop music at that time. In a sense, the power of the revival was the result of the unlikely coincidence of Martin Luther King and Frankie Avalon.

FOLK AND THE AVALON FACTOR

I think Philadelphia rock was the biggest kick in the ass folk music ever had. We all dropped that schlock and went folk around the same time.

John Sebastian

By 1959 – the year of the emergence of The Kingston Trio – the raw power of classic rock'n'roll had become dissipated. It was partly the result of the removal from the scene of a number of key figures: Buddy Holly was dead, Chuck Berry was in jail, Jerry Lee Lewis was in disgrace following the revelation of his wife's age on a British tour, Little Richard had given up the devil's music for the church, Elvis Presley was in the army and the clutches of Colonel Tom Parker.

But it also seemed that once that short joyous shout of revolt was over, rock'n'roll could not develop as a musical form except by regressing to a more conventional type of teenage music. Philadelphia rock may have retained the emphasis on the beat characteristic of rock'n'roll, but ultimately it owed most to the ballad styles that had ruled pop before 1955. The old guard of Tin Pan Alley breathed an audible sigh of relief when it appeared on the horizon. Although they hadn't baulked at making money out of Elvis and the rest, there had always been the danger of rock'n'roll blowing up in their faces – riots, "obscene" stage acts, etc.

The newer singers, however, had made rock safe. The music trade paper *Cashbox* editorialised about the "softer version (of rock) with emphasis on melody and lyric" and enthused over the fact that the kids were now "definitely listening to the story that goes with the song". In place of the mysterious and unintelligible lyrics about "Blue

Suede Shoes" and "Tutti Frutti" were comfortable boy-meets-girl songs of the kind that Tin Pan Alley had always produced.

Recent critical attempts to rehabilitate this phase of pop history have distinguished between different varieties of "soda-pop" music. There were the Elvis imitators from Philadelphia like Frankie Avalon and Fabian (bad), the instrumental groups like The Ventures and Surfaris (bad) and the Brill Building school of songwriters including Carole King and Neil Sedaka (good). But the performers of soda-pop themselves all shared one thing. In Charlie Gillett's phrase, they were "little more than puppets, dutifully doing as their producers instructed".

The centre of creativity in the music had therefore shifted from the singers and musicians themselves to the backroom boys and girls – the composers, engineers, producers and arrangers. In the best rock'n'roll records, the sound had been first and foremost the product of the particular features of a particular performer's style: Buddy Holly's "hiccuping", Chuck Berry's stinging guitar lines. In soda-pop and high-school music, the personal style was more often that of a songwriter or a producer.

All this, of course, made no difference to the mass of the pop audience. But to a small, significant section, it was all-important. These were the aspiring musicians in high schools and colleges around the country, many of whom had first been inspired to pick up a guitar by the rock'n'roll classics. They now found little of interest in "Poetry In Motion" or "Rubber Ball".

The point is fully discussed in Langdon Winner's essay "The Strange Death of Rock and Roll". Winner points out that "rock musicians take their training not in the Juilliard or Paris conservatories, but rather in the garage of the neighbour down the block. By this I mean simply that in the early stages of his career a rock enthusiast learns everything he knows from listening to records and other young musicians. Usually working together in small groups, the bandsmen copy and learn by rote the scales, chords and chord changes, and dozens of popular songs. In much the same way that a budding jazz musician must learn the solos of Charlie Parker by heart, the rock musician will absorb the current pop stylings into his 'bag'. Upon this basic foundation of 'listening' all of his subsequent playing rests."

Winner goes on to suggest that a "serious disruption of this process of education occurred in the early 1960s. 'Listening' as a means of learning rock and roll no longer proved fruitful... The very few interesting songs of the period were not enough to sustain the generation of neighbourhood garage student musicians. Faced with the wasteland which rock and roll had become, the most sensitive of the bandsmen turned their listening to other fields. In my case and that of my colleagues the refuge was almost invariably the world of jazz."

A very similar process was occurring at precisely the same time on the other side of the Atlantic. In Britain, too, the musical banality of pop in the late fifties and early sixties forced young musicians in many cities outside London to look further afield for records to learn from – to Chicago blues, rockabilly and the emerging vocal group sound of Tamla-Motown. And it was, of course, the impact of those groups from Liverpool, Birmingham, Newcastle and elsewhere which provided the catalyst for the emergence of folk-rock in America. Indeed, the first record to provide a rock version of a song which had first appeared in a folk form was British: The Animals' "House Of The Rising Sun". The group had learned the song from an early Bob Dylan album, and then came up with a rock version a full year before either Dylan or The Byrds did anything similar.

FOLK AS A WAY OF LIFE

> Peter, Paul and Mary sing folk music. In your hands you hold their first album. But to be more accurate, you hold a bouquet of song as fresh as the earth, and strong with the perfume of sincerity.
>
> Album sleeve-note, 1962

Langdon Winner and his friends were very much in a minority when they turned away from pop to jazz at the turn of the sixties. The majority of young musicians chose folk music as the alternative. As well as its musical challenge, folk offered something else – a sense of commitment, political or otherwise, and a whole way of life apparently diametrically opposed to the world of *American Bandstand*, the leading pop television show of the era.

The folk revival had established its own identity as a cultural force. It even had its own physical space in the major cities. Greenwich Village in New York or Yorktown in Toronto were the quarters containing the coffeehouses, the bars and the cheap tenement blocks. Folk had its own customs and rituals – the hootenanny and "come all ye", where anyone could get up and sing, and the collection taken up for a singer after his set. There were the folk magazines and specialist record companies as well. *Sing Out!* was for a while the centre of the revival and in its pages the doctrinal disputes raged fiercely over what was or wasn't real folk music. *Broadside* was a magazine devoted to publishing the songs of the younger contemporary writers.

Of the record companies, both Vanguard and Elektra began as one-room cottage industry operations. In the early fifties Jac Holzman, proprietor of Elektra, had borrowed a tape-recorder to record the Appalachian singer Jean Ritchie in her front room. He later made a breakthrough by taking on Theodore Bikel, a singer who had been blacklisted in the McCarthy era. Elektra continued to grow as the revival became a boom, signing up people like Judy Collins, Spider John Koerner and The Paul Butterfield Blues Band. In the mid-sixties Holzman extended his activities to the West Coast by recording Tim Buckley and his first rock bands Love and The Doors.

That brief description of Elektra's history suggests the complexity of the relationship between the folk revival and the entertainment industry in general, a point to which I'll return. There was an equivalent complexity within the revival itself, in the variety of musical approaches and styles that were described and seen as "folk" in the early sixties. The artistic stances involved can be roughly divided into four types.

The older generation of founding fathers included the people who had kept the music alive during the lean years of the fifties following the post-war success of groups like The Weavers. The central figure was of course Pete Seeger, but alongside him were folklorists and writers as well as other singers. The blend of old-style radical politics and unbending aesthetic conservatism about folk song that characterised much of the editorial comment in *Sing Out!* (though not Seeger's own work) set the tone for the series of Old v. New debates which rocked the revival from time to time.

The founding fathers were in favour of new songs being written, but they were usually expected to conform to the pattern of topical songs laid down by Woody Guthrie and others in the previous great age of radicalism, the New Deal era. The younger singers of the revival whose work tended to fit the formula, together with others who stuck to traditional material from Appalachia, Scotland or the South, made up a second group of performers, the disciples. The "protest" writers included Bob Dylan, Tom Paxton, Phil Ochs, Patrick Sky and Peter La Farge. There was an urban school of musicians dedicated to re-creating the country blues: Dave Van Ronk, Spider John Koerner, Tony Glover. And there were the sweet-voiced girls with a repertoire of Child ballads and mountain songs: Joan Baez, Carolyn Hester, Judy Collins, Buffy Sainte-Marie.

Most of the work of those people and dozens of others made up what was the orthodox mainstream of the revival in the early sixties. With the notable exception of Bob Dylan, they were not embroiled in the folk-rock saga, although later in the sixties many transformed their style and repertoire away from the orthodox notion of the folk tradition. Judy Collins broke new ground in her work with the arranger Joshua Rifkin (now best known for his part in the Scott Joplin ragtime revival), and her range of material tilted towards a chansonnier idea of poetry and music, including songs by Brecht and Jacques Brel. Joan Baez and Buffy Sainte-Marie are now among the former folk singers who have turned their attention to the submerged side of the country music tradition, and now record consistently in Nashville.

If the "founding fathers" and their "disciples" represented attitudes which placed supreme value on the idea of a folk tradition to be extended, the other two groups of revival performers consisted predominantly of people who worked in the folk context because there was nowhere else to go. They were the "displaced poets" and the "players" – the former neighbourhood garage musicians described by Langdon Winner.

The third group, the displaced poets, brought into the folk revival energies and sensibilities that in other times would probably have found expression in different ways. But at this point in time, the folk revival seemed to be one focus of activity which transcended both the academicism of the mandarin high culture and the triteness of the mass arts. In this respect, it looked in many ways like earlier cultural movements such as modern jazz or the Beat coterie in literature. And like those movements, there was an obscure but strongly felt impulse of opposition to prevailing social norms in even the least politicised corners of the revival. It was against commercialism *and* elitism, and for honesty and integrity.

The most consistently successful of the musicians who came to folk music out of these kinds of concern has turned out to be Paul Simon. He was a middle-class Jewish boy from New York who had enjoyed a small amount of success as a rock'n'roll singer with his school chum Art Garfunkel. In 1957, they had a hit with "Hey Schoolgirl", under the names Tom and Jerry. Afterwards, they went back to school and then on to college. There, Simon met a girl called Carole Klein who also wrote songs which they used to try to compose together in their spare time. In 1959, Carole got the chance to drop out of college to go and work full-time at one of the "song factories" on Broadway where young writers sat at pianos knocking out tunes for the current crop of teen idols to record.

Paul Simon advised against it, to no avail. Carole Klein became Carole King and one of the most successful of that generation of composers of teenage ballads. Simon's view was that the kind of pop music King would have to turn out was nonsense, an attitude common to every kind of folkie. Tony Scaduto's biography of Bob Dylan reports an impromptu duet between Bob and Ramblin' Jack Elliott which parodied current hit parade songs: "I killed my parents/'cause they didn't understand..."

If this hostility towards pop music sometimes smacked of snobbery – any civil rights protest song was necessarily thought to be preferable to any adolescent protest – it also highlighted the extreme restrictions on subject matter that existed in early sixties pop. The songs assumed an audience of teenagers and didn't admit anyone over high school age into the fraternity. They also dealt almost entirely in romantic situations or parental restrictions upon them.

The limitations of pop gave the young singers of the folk revival an immediate audience: the college-age generation. And it was of course a generation as much in motion as the one below it in the high schools. For the protest singers in the Woody Guthrie mould, the motion was primarily political and social: for the chimes of freedom and against the masters of war. But the rebellion of the civil rights generation also involved a break of some kind with a whole way of life and structure of feeling they had been brought up to inherit – what later came to be called the Middle American lifestyle.

Some of the displaced poets reflected the results of that emotional leap in their songs. Richard Farina, like Bob Dylan, spun together long energetic lines containing images tumbling one on top of another, reflecting a kind of dazzling chaos in songs like "Hard Loving Loser". Paul Simon was quieter and more self-regarding. Some of his work, notably "The Sounds Of Silence", sounded too much like a textbook on "alienation" or "identity crisis" set to music. But elsewhere in his early songs, the authentic note of uncertainty is caught exactly and without self-pity.

Words like "authentic" and "honest" were sprayed around a lot in the vocabulary of partisans of the folk revival. That sleeve-note to the first Peter, Paul and Mary album gushed to its close by saying: "Maybe everything's going to be all right. Maybe mediocrity has had it. Maybe hysteria is on the way out. One thing is for sure in any case: Honesty is back. Tell your neighbor."

Yet the work of certain singers had a particularly autobiographical power which justified such descriptions. Tim Hardin was the most outstanding. His earliest recordings were of blues and folk standards, the staple diet of journeyman musicians in the revival. But he soon developed an intensely individual style, owing little to the canons of the folk tradition. From that context he took only the plain, unvarnished character of his lyrics, in pieces like "Reason To Believe", "Don't Make Promises", "If I Were A Carpenter" and "Red Balloon". His voice tempered the obvious blues influences with a certain reticence which set off the almost confessional nature of his songs.

Hardin was a pioneer in the use of the electric guitar in the clubs, but never quite achieved his due recognition. His first album didn't appear until September 1966, by which time "folk-rock" was yesterday's news, and one of his best songs, "If I Were A Carpenter", was appropriated by Bobby Darin, who even sang it like Hardin – and had a hit. But he also pursued his own course unswervingly, and the determination to follow through every emotional turn of his life in his work led him into some less successful formal experiments.

55

Notable among them was the *Suite for Susan Moore and Damion*, whose subject was his feelings for his wife and child.

The kind of songs made by Tim Hardin, Paul Simon, and by Bob Dylan as he moved away from the traditionalist fold, came under attack from the old guard of the revival. One of the ablest polemicists among the latter, Josh Dunson, saw the significant difference between the two styles in "the change in the personal pronoun from 'we' to 'I'. The young song writers, as Woody Guthrie used to do, give their reactions in the first person, but, unlike him, they seldom notice others to their left or right. They write their songs while riding in subway cars, while waiting out in the cold for one or two hours, while trying to bum a ride, while sitting in a bar drinking, while alone in a room thinking.

"The songs that came from the older songwriters in the 1930s and 1940s reflected the intense feelings of unity and power that rallies of thousands and organizations of millions can render... The songs came out of the unshakeable faith and immense feeling that the singer had discovered the truth, a plan that was going to make the world one of 'bread *and* roses'."

This gap between the intentions and ambitions of the old and new streams in the revival was distinct and real, even when songs of both kinds appeared in the repertoire of the same artist. The difference could be summed up by saying that while the Dunson attitude required songs as providers of answers, the newer writers produced songs of questioning.

The reasons were strong. To begin with, the kind of old-left political solutions offered by the traditionalists had been discredited for young radicals as the Soviet Union was seen more and more clearly as behaving like any other Great Power. Then, the key movement of the early sixties – civil rights – involved young white people only peripherally, for obvious reasons. This was reflected in the music thrown up by that movement – adaptations of gospel songs like "We Shall Overcome" and "We Shall Not Be Moved".

There was also a problem of audience for those committed to the Dunsonian perspective. Tom Paxton's early records contained many songs straight from the Guthrie mould – about unemployed workers ("Standing At The Edge Of Town"), unions ("High Sherriff Of

56

Hazard"), travelling around ("Bound For The Mountains And The Sea"), and yet he sang them in the main to middle-class college students.

At the time this issue didn't surface, but at times later on some of the more astute among the committed folk singers began to see some need to connect in some way singing about "the people" with singing to them and, most important, singing in their idiom. Which meant a turn towards rock and towards country music. Phil Ochs was characteristically provocative about the issue in an aside during his famous Carnegie Hall concert of 1970: "What America needs", he said "is for Elvis Presley to become Che Guevara."

Folk-rock itself, though, found its practitioners mostly from the fourth of the segments of the revival – the players. These were the musicians drawn to folk because of the space it allowed them, those extra chords and changes. They were young, ex-high school or college students who came to Greenwich Village, to Yorktown in Toronto or to the coffeehouses of Boston and Los Angeles. They were the refugees from the garage bands of the rock'n'roll era, driven out by the blandness of soda-pop.

Often these players provided the back-up for established artists: Roger McGuinn of The Byrds played with The Chad Mitchell Trio and then with Bobby Darin, Richie Furay and Stephen Stills who later formed Buffalo Springfield were in The Au Go-Go Singers, and Barry McGuire sang with The New Christie Minstrels. Others got work as session musicians or even producers: John Sebastian played harmonica on dozens of albums by folk revival performers, sometimes with Felix Pappalardi (later of Mountain, and Cream's producer) on second guitar.

TROUBADOURS ON TIN PAN ALLEY

The folk boom has come and gone like a plague. As the scene came to its inevitable shift, some resigned and officially became salesmen, others became ethnic defenders of Mother Earth tradition even though there were no attackers.

Many grew their hair down to their wallets and jumped on the Beatle bandwagon in true hands-across-the-sea spirit. Palms upward as usual. Practically everybody tried drugs.

Somehow this led to a musical revolution. The Village Voice was
virtually panting with hip discovery. Discotheques spread like fungus.
Many were moved to proclaim a new era of culture for the masses.
Myself I also planned to form a new group of former folkies. We
would expand our hair, be backed by an electronic symphony
orchestra, would play sitars and various other eastern instruments we
learned of by reading record jackets, and we would talk about
free-form ultra Zen music on television. The group would be called
the Pretensions.

Phil Ochs, sleeve-note to *Jim and Jean*, Verve/Folkways 1966

The very success of the revival made it inevitable that folk would go
"commercial". The movement had in any case always had its
entrepreneurs, the people responsible for getting the singers and the
audiences together. They were the coffeehouse proprietors, the
festival promoters and the owners of small record companies. In
outline, their activities were the same as those of their counterparts on
Broadway or in Philadelphia. They provided the facilities for artists to
perform, they took the money from the customers and took their cut
before paying the musicians.

For, unlike the creators of the tradition, the folk revivalists were
professional musicians – even if that meant only a couple of dollars a
night collected from an unmoved club audience. Nevertheless, while
the revival remained a world apart from the mainstream of the mass
media, it could generate its own norms of creativity, honesty and
sincerity. While folk remained the interest of a small minority,
middle-men involved with it could not expect to make a fortune
from it. To run a club or a festival implied a commitment to the
music as well.

But as the revival became a boom, it attracted the attention of
people involved in the mass-entertainment world. They could offer,
quite simply, a larger audience to folk singers, through concert halls,
nationally distributed records and networked broadcasts on radio and
television. For folk musicians to get involved, however, meant
coming to terms with the rather different norms of the mass media.
At one extreme this implied an acceptance of a degree of control over
their work which many found unacceptable: the case of Pete Seeger's
blacklisting by the *Hootenanny* television show was the most dramatic
example. But in the two main forms by which folk was absorbed into

the popular music mainstream – supper-club music and folk-rock – the situation was less clear. Did wearing a tuxedo or using an electric guitar mean a loss of integrity, or was it just a compromise necessary to get across to more people?

For some of the diehards, there was no difference between the two forms. They were equally damned. Yet the impact on popular music itself was different in each case. While the supper-club folk set were comfortably assimilated into a pre-existing pop category, folk-rock turned out to be a major contributor to large-scale changes in pop as a whole.

The supper-club business basically involved transforming folk into a kind of "adult" entertainment, alongside the nightclub type of singing which had dominated pop before the arrival of rock'n'roll. The "intimate" nature of the nightclub performance – the patter between songs to try to establish rapport with the audience – had a superficial similarity with folk which was enough for groups like The Limeliters, New Christy Minstrels and Au Go-Go Singers to slot into the format.

There were problems of course. The folk music imported into the supper clubs had to be "tasteful". No anger, no raw edges. The "sincerity" of the music had to be kept in, while gently squeezing any suggestion of protest out. The usual way for this to be done was for urbane singers with impeccable manners to take their listeners on whistle-stop tours of exotic places: "Now here's an Israeli folk song… a Mexican folk song…" Folk music as a melodic equivalent of a package tour.

The traditionalists had nothing but scorn for everyone from The Kingston Trio onwards who participated in the despised mass culture. Sleeve-notes were one of the main ways for the folk revival to express opinions, and the anonymous writer on the back of an album by the purist white blues players Koerner, Ray and Glover sternly reprimanded the "Television and showbiz folkniks" who "have grown rich debasing our folk music and cramming our genuine national culture into the trite-and-true Tin Pan Alley pattern".

Among those castigated were Peter, Paul and Mary, the first of the younger folk musicians to have significant success in the pop field. They had certainly been brought together in a studied way by Albert Grossman, a former Chicago club owner and folk singer, in an attempt to break the barrier between the folk and pop audiences. But

59

despite the somewhat antiseptic character of their singing, the group made no compromises in their choice of material. It was through their records that Bob Dylan's songs reached out beyond the campus aficionados, and Peter, Paul and Mary broke the taboo on hit-parade artists expressing ideas about anything apart from what kind of girls/boys they liked, or how much they wanted to please their fans. They were one of the forerunners of folk-rock.

Because that vexed term soon became the property of the image-makers of Tin Pan Alley, it quickly acquired any meaning any user wanted to give to it. In particular it was attached to any song with a hint of "protest" about it. To start with, though, it described music in which a folk or folk-inflected song was combined with the instrumentation and arrangements of rock music. "Rock", not "pop", since it was the sound of the English Invasion groups spearheaded by The Beatles which provided the inspiration for the first amplified bands in Greenwich Village and Hollywood.

The sound of Merseybeat and of British rhythm'n'blues was recognised among younger folkies as authentic in a way American pop and even some folk music couldn't match. One Gary Burbridge of Grand Rapids, Michigan, wrote to *Sing Out!*:

> Since there has been a recent upsurge in interest in city blues, I think that some serious consideration should be given to some of the groups which are coming out of England. Such groups as The Kinks, Rolling Stones and Zombies and much of the music to which the Jerk is done today seems to capture the feeling of poverty and emptiness which other folksingers have failed to find. I think that one of the most important reasons for this is that these rock-and-roll singers are closer to the feelings that the poor have. The Liverpool sound is coming closer to the mark whether that is the aim or not.

This feeling that English rock musicians were somehow closer to the roots of true people's music – poverty – than their American counterparts crops up elsewhere. When Cream was formed, one critic attempted to explain their affinity for the blues by painting a picture of British life that was Dickensian in its bleakness: "When they were babies, London was bombed... what they grew up on, their soul food, is beans and chips (greasy French fries), eggs, bacon, and sausages that are part bread."

The first groups to take the first steps towards folk-rock were The Mugwumps in New York and The Byrds in Los Angeles during the summer of 1964. The Mugwumps proved to be an apprentice band whose members went on to other groups: Cass Elliott and Denny Doherty to The Mamas and the Papas, Zal Yanovsky to The Lovin' Spoonful. The Byrds were more durable. The original members had worked in the folk scene, though most of them had little commitment to the traditionalist idea. Apart from Roger McGuinn, Gene Clark had been in The New Christy Minstrels, David Crosby had been a singer, Chris Hillman was leading a bluegrass group around Los Angeles.

The Byrds established folk-rock as a viable style in both the artistic and commercial sense. They were reacting against what McGuinn was later to call the "commercial and plastic packaged" aspects of folk music. On the other hand they were significantly influenced by the success of The Beatles – early publicity shots showed the group sporting a variant of the "mop-top" hair style. The key factor, though, was the song: Bob Dylan's "Mr Tambourine Man".

A pre-release tape of it reached The Byrds via their astute manager Jim Dickson, whose idea it was for them to rearrange and record the song. A first attempt didn't generate much interest among record companies, but eventually Columbia came through with a contract, and the group went into the studio again.

What The Byrds (or rather McGuinn, since he was the only one to take part in the actual recording) did with "Mr Tambourine Man" has been described by Andrew Weiner:

> McGuinn all but re-wrote the song. He axed three verses, leaving the most "contemporary" of the original four in between the choruses. He slowed it down by half, allowing himself a very deliberate and clearly articulated vocal very much in contrast with Dylan's breathless rush. Using the bass guitar as a lead counterpoint to his own jungle jangle electric twelve-string he could play both lead and rhythm phrases, mostly the latter, jet-driven magic carpet textures that rise and fall in perfect cycles. But the voice is quite as important as the guitar, at once puzzled and cynically wise, weary and elevated, punkish and dignified...

Soon afterwards, Bob Dylan himself embraced a full rock sound with his fifth album *Bringing It All Back Home*. It seems likely that the success of The Byrds precipitated his decision to cut himself adrift from the folk scene at this point. Dylan already enjoyed a massive reputation on the campuses where folk was seen as serious music, to listen and not dance to. When he appeared at the Newport Folk Festival later that year, he was booed by some of the audience. But he had already made the transition to a new audience for whom "folk-rock" as practised by Dylan and The Byrds was the American answer to the British Invasion.

As such, folk-rock installed itself at the very heart of the pop music industry. After "Mr Tambourine Man", it was a new trend, a marketing concept which would be doggedly followed through by Tin Pan Alley.

For the traditionalists this was the end. The spirit of Woody meets Madison Avenue. And loses. The treatment of folk-rock by the music trade press tended to support such a view. The perfunctory reviews of new records involved running a commercial slide-rule over folk-rock, just as they did with any other kind of pop: "Positively 4th Street. Bob Dylan. Bitter follow up to guy's 'Like A Rolling Stone' about how nobody knows you when you're down and out. Flips flips... Where Have All The Flowers Gone. Johnny Rivers. Added go go beat to this one makes it a different song but still an effective side likely to be a biggie."

Despite all that, the impact of folk-rock on pop music in general was considerable. Perhaps the most successful single record was Barry McGuire's "Eve of Destruction", which eventually sold over six million copies. The story of its production and of its impact illustrates the rich and contradictory pop process which occurs when a new musical form enters the field, when finance, fashion, art and politics are inextricably mixed together.

The key figure to the appearance of the record was a perceptive Los Angeles record man named Lou Adler. He had been in pop since 1957, writing songs with Herb Alpert (one of which was a hit for Sam Cooke) and then producing surfing records with Jan and Dean. Adler told Richard Williams of the *Melody Maker* how "Eve Of Destruction" came about:

I'd heard the first Dylan album with electrified instruments. This is strange, but it's really true: I gave Phil Sloan a pair of boots and a hat and a copy of the Dylan album, and a week later he came back with ten songs, including "Eve of Destruction". It was a natural feel for him – he's a great mimic.

Anyway I was afraid of the song, I didn't know if we could get it played (on the radio). But the next night I went to Ciro's, where the Byrds were playing. It was the beginning of the freak period... there was this subculture that no one in L.A. knew about, not even me, and it was growing. The Byrds were the leaders of the cult, and the place was jam-packed, spilling out on to the street.

In the middle of it was this guy in furs, with long hair, and dancing; I thought he looked like a leader of a movement. Terry Melcher told me that he was Barry McGuire, and that he'd sung with The New Christy Minstrels. A week later we cut the record and it sold six million.

I didn't think it was a copy of anything. It was the first rock'n'roll protest song and Sloan laid it down in very simple terms, not like the folk people were doing. If you listen to the song today, it holds up all the way – it's the same problems. It's certainly an honest feeling, from a 16 year old.

Through this series of chance meetings, and Adler's careful orchestration of them, the end product – the single of "Eve Of Destruction" – was the meeting and mingling point of several significant musical and social cross-currents in 1965. From the folk revival itself came the notion of the protest song, even though, ironically, the Bob Dylan album given to P.F. Sloan, the composer of "Eve", was one which contained no protest material. Nevertheless, the earlier connection of Dylan and denunciation of political evil no doubt lingered on in Sloan's mind.

Then there was the Los Angeles "freak" movement, embodied in Barry McGuire. This was soon to manifest itself in the music of various "punk–rock" groups like The Standells and The Seeds, and more self-consciously through Frank Zappa's Mothers Of Invention, whose first album *Freak Out!* (the first rock double-album) set out to establish the principles of a new lifestyle. In 1966, the city saw one of the beginnings of the youth movement of the sixties when police clashed with kids on Sunset Strip. Stephen Stills' song for Buffalo Springfield, "For What It's Worth", was inspired by those events.

Finally, "Eve Of Destruction" along with "Mr Tambourine Man" stood at the head of a wave of songs released on to the market by record companies eager to ride the folk-rock-protest bandwagon. Some merely dressed up Bob Dylan material. The Turtles, featuring Howard Kaylan and Mark Volman – later to work with Zappa – weighed in with "It Ain't Me Babe". And also from Los Angeles were the king and queen of teen rebellion, Sonny and Cher. Their big hit, "I Got You Babe", was clearly aimed to suggest the Dylanesque protest sound, though the lyrics were a reworking of the vapid themes of early sixties teenage music: even though those adults don't like my hair and my clothes, it doesn't matter because I got you, babe.

Sonny Bono, despite appearances, was an old hand at making pop records. And The Turtles were professional pop musicians. Next to their rather slick records, "Eve Of Destruction" had a kind of rough-hewn grandeur. Barry McGuire didn't so much sing the song as shout it hoarsely. There was no way a listener could avoid having to listen to the words. The crude power of the record impressed even a traditionalist like Josh Dunson. Even though he felt that "it might well win the poll for the worst written pop song of the year", Dunson recognised the importance of its impact: "'Eve Of Destruction' is the first protest song dealing in specifics to reach the non-college-educated sector of the population. It is awkward and full of holes, but the earnestness with which it was bought by hundreds of thousands and blocked by dozens of stations might indicate a large segment of the young population other than college students is dissatisfied with our war policy abroad and double standards at home."

The main reason for the popularity of "Eve Of Destruction" among the mass of young people outside colleges was the fact that its author was one of them. P.F. Sloan was sixteen and a genuine street poet. He lacked the polished satire and irony of folk singers like Tom Paxton and Phil Ochs. Instead he dealt in rushes of rhymes and images, adding up to a semi-articulate teenage shout of rage. One of his other songs, "Sins Of A Family", had a verse which capped anything in "Eve Of Destruction": "What a sad environment/A bug-ridden tenement/And when they couldn't pay the rent/Was because her father was out getting liquored."

Folk-rock had its softer, poetic side too. Paul Simon and Art Garfunkel became rock stars without knowing it when "The Sounds Of Silence" became a massive hit. Simon was on a tour of folk clubs in Britain when Dylan and The Byrds began to probe the "folk + beat – profits" formula. Someone at Columbia Records in New York remembered the folk tracks by him and Garfunkel that were gathering dust on the shelves in a vault somewhere. It was decided that one of them suitably pepped up could capitalise on the new trend. Accordingly, a young black staff producer who had worked with Dylan called Tom Wilson dubbed guitar, bass and drums on to the Simon song. The first the composer knew of its success was when he saw an American hit-parade listing in a magazine in Europe.

If P.F. Sloan's offerings were folk-rock for drop-outs, "The Sounds Of Silence" and Bob Lind's "Elusive Butterfly" were more upmarket. Bob Dylan was the key influence on both styles, but whereas it was the tone of voice which Sloan and McGuire took up, for Simon and Lind Dylan the poet was more important.

Bob Lind was fairly typical of most of the writers and singers in what came to be known as "soft rock". Like Bob Dylan, he wrote songs with long, unfolding lines full of images designed to capture the detail of a relationship or a perception. But unlike Dylan, he always seemed to be just off-target, so that his earnest philosophy collapsed too often into anti-climax. At times it was all too easy for an unsympathetic listener to find his profundities merely ludicrous: "When you're so far down, the gutter looks like up to you/I will still be kneeling at your feet"... "My humanness astounds you as you realize how real I am."

THE ROAD TO YASGUR'S FARM

Besides the punk-protest of Sloan and the poetics of Lind and Simon, there was a third strand of "folk-rock": the groups. For both the first two strands, the words they were writing and singing were far more important than the sound of their records. The "rock" part of the folk-rock alliance was the poor relation. But bands like The Byrds, Lovin' Spoonful and Buffalo Springfield, along with the San Francisco groups, began to develop new kinds of rock music, as a real American alternative to the sounds of the English Invasion.

Collectively, they were returning pop music to the roots it had rediscovered in the rock'n'roll era: the urban varieties of the blues and of country music. In the case of the Los Angeles groups, The Byrds and Buffalo Springfield, they reached back through the work of Bob Dylan and The Beatles, each of whom had produced their own synthesis of those root musics. The Lovin' Spoonful, from New York, took a different route. Their early albums found the band zigzagging from jug-band music to country to blues to rock in a cheerfully eclectic manner.

To a large extent the Spoonful's beginnings were a development of the "good-time" sound of jug bands like The Even Dozen, which had included Maria Muldaur (née D'Amato) and John Sebastian, the prime mover of The Lovin' Spoonful. Jug-band music was folk song plus rhythm, from washboards and massed guitars. Its importance as a transitional form lay in the fact that it was folk music you could dance to (much of Bob Dylan's delight on hearing The Byrds' "Mr Tambourine Man" was said to have been due to his realisation that his songs could become music for dancing).

Sebastian spelled out his musical policy in his songs. He soon showed himself to be the best writer of lyrics in praise of American music since Chuck Berry himself. The Spoonful's first record was "Do You Believe In Magic", which sounded like a joyous shout of liberation, from the strictures of both production pop and folk purism. "The magic's in the music and the music's in me" sang Sebastian, and went on to prove it in a series of witty and inventive songs.

"Nashville Cats" was a sort of musical autobiography, describing his early exposure to those "yellow Sun records from Nashville" and the guitar pickers who "play clean as country water". Behind Sebastian's singing, lead guitarist Zal Yanovsky, a Canadian, was doing just that.

The Spoonful did love songs as well, in which the lyricism was invariably combined with a wry quality, which didn't undercut the sentiment but seemed to place it more securely. "Did You Ever Have To Make Up Your Mind" is punctuated by the gruff voice of a father saying "you better go home, son, and make up your mind" while the yearning romanticism of "Younger Girl" is made a little lighter with the line "Said she'd never been in trouble – even in town".

With each record, Sebastian's range as a songwriter expanded. "Summer In The City" was a superb evocation of oppressive days when there's no shadow in the city, and the cool evenings are full of romantic promise: "Hot days/Summer in the city/Back of my neck/Getting dirty and gritty". And even when The Lovin' Spoonful began to fall apart and John Sebastian became one of the founding fathers of Woodstock Nation, grinning beatifically at the crowds at festivals, his insight and wit didn't desert him. "Money" and "Younger Generation" were two of his finest songs, dealing with topics far removed from the concerns of the majority of folk or rock musicians. The former was a simple recital of the puzzling circulation of notes and coins and the power they have to get other people to do things for you: "You give money to me/To tickle your whims or blow up your mind/I give money to you/And pay you back in kind." The other song turned Sebastian's generation's revolt against the received wisdom of their parents on its head. What do we do when we have kids? "Hey Dad, my girlfriend's only three/She's got her own videophone and she's taking LSD/And now she wants to give a bit to me/What's the matter Daddy/How come you're turning green?/Can it be that you can't live up to your dreams?"

None of Sebastian's songs, or those of Buffalo Springfield or The Byrds, were political, in the sense that the protest songs of folk and folk-rock were. Yet a number of their members graduated to become the figureheads of the swelling youth culture of the sixties which had its finest hour at Woodstock. Crosby, Stills, Nash and Young, made up of ex-Buffalo Springfields Neil Young and Stephen Stills plus ex-Byrd David Crosby and Englishman Graham Nash, were the central figures in this confused and amorphous movement. They certainly sold more records than any other musicians associated with the mood of the times.

The mood and the movement didn't begin with C. S. N. & Y., though. If it had traceable roots, they were to be found in the growth of the Haight-Ashbury hippy culture in San Francisco, and in the central role of music in that culture's definition of itself. A sense of that unique social, cultural and political mix in its earliest stages is given in Ralph J. Gleason's description of an anti-war demonstration held in 1965:

> Poets Lawrence Ferlinghetti, Robert Duncan and Michael McClure
> had read to the crowd before the march and Ken Kesey's Merry

Pranksters were on hand, along with the Hell's Angels who eventually broke through the Oakland police lines on the second march and fought the Berkeley police. The vanguard of the march sang Beatles songs and midway down the line, on a flatbed truck, was the Berkeley political music group, the Instant Action Jug Band, led by Joe MacDonald, the band which evolved in a few short months into Country Joe & The Fish, one of the biggest successes of all the bands from the San Francisco scene.

The immediate musical influences on the local groups like The Fish, The Grateful Dead and Jefferson Airplane were the familiar ones: the instrumental styles of folk music and early folk-rock, plus the songs and even the films of The Beatles. *A Hard Day's Night* was a revelation to Americans expecting an English equivalent to the endless series of boring Elvis Presley vehicles like *Blue Hawaii* and *It Happened at the World's Fair.*

But what came out the other end was very different from any of the varieties of folk-rock, East or West Coast. The critical element was in a sense very similar to the 1940s folk model in which the singers were supposed to have "reflected the intense feelings of unity and power" deriving from the movements they sang for and about. Like those committed folk singers, the San Francisco musicians worked from a sense that they were part of something rather more significant than an entertainment industry.

The differences between Woody Guthrie and Joe McDonald were, of course, considerable. In the traditionalist version, the movement was a clearly defined political organisation with definite goals (unionisation of labour, support for New Deal social policies) and the singer's role was to keep up morale or proclaim the message. In San Francisco, the musicians were part of an ideologically diffuse community rather than a movement. And music, far from being just a useful adjunct to the community, was one of the main ways in which that community discovered and re-created its sense of unity.

Thus, the most important events were not mass meetings or rallies, but dances. To begin with, the dances were established as benefits to raise money for community causes – the legal costs of The San Francisco Mime Troupe for instance. Gradually they became events in their own right, with the development of light shows and elaborate psychedelic posters. Gleason described the atmosphere of one of them:

Inside a most remarkable assemblage of humanity was leaping, jumping, dancing, frigging, fragging and frugging on the dance floor to the music of the half-dozen rock bands – the Mystery Trend, the Great Society, the Jefferson Airplane, the VIPs, the Gentlemen's Band, the Warlocks and others. The costumes were free-form, Goodwill-cum-Sherwood Forest. Slim young ladies with their faces painted a la "Harper's Bazaar" in cats-and-dogs lines, granny dresses topped with huge feathers, white levis with decals of mystic design; bell-bottom split up the side. The combinations were seemingly limitless.

At each end of the huge hall there was a three-foot-high sign saying "LOVE". Over the bar there was another saying "NO BOOZE", while the volunteer bartenders served soft drinks. Alongside the regular bar was a series of tables selling apples...

Gradually, the various San Francisco bands began to take on individual identities. The Warlocks evolved into The Grateful Dead and their music developed through long, mesmeric instrumental passages, an acting-out of the spontaneity that was supposed to be the heart of the psychedelically fuelled "new consciousness".

Lyrics and voices were more important in the work of the Jefferson Airplane and Country Joe and the Fish. While the Dead seemed to embody the hippy tenet that reflection and analysis of experience were part of the old world, these bands wrote about drug experiences and political situations. "White Rabbit", which featured Grace Slick's keening voice soaring over the hard-driving playing of the Airplane, remains one of the best "drug" songs because of the way it perfectly matches Lewis Carroll's strange fantasy world with the more mundane hallucinations chemically induced in Haight-Ashbury.

The Airplane also recognised the existence of another, harsher world outside the peace and love of the hippy ghetto, even if their response was too often simply a stoned invocation of abstract "Revolution". Country Joe's attitude was both more varied and more subtle. Of all the San Francisco musicians, he was the one who made most of the folk heritage. He learned from Woody Guthrie the value of satire and ridicule as polemical weapons. Recently released live recordings show how he tried to use the communal atmosphere of the dance situation to arouse his audience to an awareness of the nature of American politics, as well as celebrating the values of their own lifestyle. In this respect, the famous "Feel Like I'm Fixin' To

Die" was his greatest achievement. Using a jolly tune, it exposed the logic of the American war effort in Vietnam through a parody of militaristic propaganda: "Be the first one on your block/To have your boy come home in a box".

Joe McDonald is the only musician to have survived the eventual collapse of the San Francisco scene with anything more than a cult approach. His folk roots and the implied political dimension in his music have been all-important. "Political" here is not simply a question of protest music – songs to sing at rallies – but an understanding that the hippy enclave could not forever just exist alongside the larger society it had rejected. It could either take more positive steps to oppose the Johnson-Nixon set-up, or be destroyed or else absorbed by it.

The end of the first, purely localised, phase of San Francisco music came in 1967, with the Monterey Pop Festival. Organised by a group of musicians, led by John Phillips of The Mamas and the Papas, another band associated with the indefatigable Lou Adler, it was intended as a showcase for the new rock music of 1967. As well as international figures like The Who and Jimi Hendrix, a number of San Francisco groups performed at Monterey. Among the audience were representatives of major record companies, including Clive Davis, president of Columbia. He said later that he had seen "the new music and the whole new culture that went along with it". He also went ahead and bought a large chunk of the music, thereby beginning the separation of the San Francisco musicians from the culture which they had developed. Soon Columbia were running advertisements for records by new groups with the slogan "The Man Can't Bust Our Music". Which was a little confusing for anyone who had always thought of corporations like Columbia as part of The Man.

That point of view was taken by the more radical community activists in San Francisco, like the Digger Emmett Grogan, who describes in his book *Ringolevio* the stratification of the psychedelic ghetto into street people and merchants: the property-less and the propertied.

But among the semi-coherent system of hippy belief, there was a reply to this sort of political criticism, expressed best by The Beatles in "Revolution": "You say it's the institution, well, you know, you better free your mind instead". Courtesy of the record companies, that message was beginning to go out beyond the Bay Area. Down in Los Angeles, the heart of the West Coast music industry, Lou Adler and John Phillips found their 1967 version of Barry McGuire in Scott McKenzie, another former folk-singing buddy of Phillips. They concocted a song called "(If You're Going To) San Francisco", and the record – very conservative in its style – sold in millions. Whatever the commercial interests involved, this over-simplified (Peace, Love and Flowers) version of the Haight-Ashbury philosophy struck a chord with large numbers of young people. The stage was set for the emergence of Woodstock Nation and its most accomplished musical representatives – Crosby, Stills, Nash and Young.

The Monterey Pop Festival had been held on the site of a long-established jazz festival, and events like this and the various long-standing folk festivals were one of the models for the growing numbers of rock festivals from 1967 onwards. But whereas the earlier festivals had been devoted to "minority" musical forms more or less ignored by the mainstream of American pop, and had taken their particular tone and intensity from that fact, rock festivals found themselves trying to re-create the intimacy in the context of heavy commercial and marketing operations.

This schizophrenia at the heart of the rock festivals was increased when the other model for them is taken into account. This was the approach of Be-ins and Gatherings of the Tribes that had grown up in San Francisco in the wake of the successful dances. They were held in the open air, bands played free of charge and most people went not to hear the music but, well, just to be there.

Sometimes the two impulses behind the festivals came to blows: in the clashes between security guards and kids taking the Jefferson Airplane's advice to tear down the walls, or rock stars demanding cash upfront before going out to communicate with their generation. But mostly the contradiction was softened, or obscured: at Woodstock, hundreds of thousands got in free without any opposition from the minions of the organisers, because the film and recording rights had already guaranteed that it would be a commercial success. The folk/community impulse was allowed free play on condition that the business interests were satisfied first.

For their performance at Woodstock, Crosby, Stills, Nash and Young were paid 5,000 dollars, thirteenth in the hierarchy of musicians in financial terms. A year later, they had two best-selling albums behind them and were drawing greater audiences and earning more money than just about anyone else in rock. Their meteoric rise was due to the fact that, more than anyone else, they seemed to reflect the confusions and contradictions at the heart of a new culture caught between the political and show-business definitions of itself. Not that C. S. N. & Y offered answers. If they had a message it was in the song Stephen Stills had written for Buffalo Springfield about the Sunset Strip riots: "There's something happening here/What it is ain't exactly clear".

Even the differing personalities of the four musicians seemed to mirror the various aspects of the new culture. David Crosby and Graham Nash, with their high, clear harmonies and softer songs, represented the peace-and-love side of things. The two former Buffalo Springfield people were more aggressive, in their writing, singing and electric guitar playing. A *Fusion* reporter described their performance of Neil Young's anguished masterpiece "Down By The River", at a festival in Big Sur: "Finally they begin. Crosby is angry at the wait, and once into the song he tries to pull Young in by jamming on him but Young is still fiddling, tuning, and finally he turns his back on the whole thing, walks over to the amps, and begins re-stringing his guitar. Nash and Stills pull the song along, twisting it about until Young gets through and jumps in, licking and a-picking on his electric. The song goes on for 15 minutes, with the best electric music ever made before an audience, but the concept is nowhere, the refrain is ridiculous: 'I shot my baby – down by the river.'"

That kind of tension and conflict was a feature of live performance by Crosby, Stills, Nash and Young, notably in the rivalry between Stills and Young, which dated from their days as alternate lead guitarists with Buffalo Springfield. On record, the tension came out less in individual songs than through the overall range of moods. The second album, *Déjà Vu*, had moments of optimism, in Joni Mitchell's "Woodstock" and Nash's "Our House", balanced against the powerful sadness of Young's "Helpless" and the mixture of humour and paranoia in Crosby's "Almost Cut My Hair".

The group lasted little more than a year. The tensions between the members proved to be even stronger than commercial pressures on them to keep going. It was also the year in which declamations about the new culture died away. The dream, as John Lennon said, was over.

COMING DOWN WITH KINNEY

As the new decade begins, there is a tremendous surge in leisure time activities in response to a demand to entertain all age groups. This was brought about by a shortened working week, a growing affluence and a burgeoning of a new youth generation whose impact upon traditional culture has been described as 'Youthquake'... 'Woodstock' [the film] proved what most young people already knew and had tried to explain to their parents – that contemporary music is more than entertainment, it is a way of life and a way of looking at the world.

Your company is actively involved with music in all its forms. Our Warner Bros, Atlantic and Elektra record companies have participated in this rapidly growing and highly competitive field.

Kinney National Services Inc., *Annual Report 1970*

I found him by the stage last night, he was breathing his last breath
A bottle of gin and a cigarette was all that he had left
I can see you made the music 'cos you carry your guitar
God help the troubadour who tries to be a star.

Phil Ochs, "Chords of Fame"

It is very strange making a living out of being yourself.

James Taylor, Warner Bros recording artist

Despite the optimism generated by Woodstock (Eric Burdon's anthem was typical: "You wanna see the future now?/Don't put our festival down/This time next year man/Ten million may be comin' round"), it was an end, not a beginning. The year 1970 brought the tragic fiasco of The Rolling Stones' outdoor concert at Altamont, and a new breed of folk-tinged musicians, the singer-songwriters.

The keynote records of the genre were James Taylor's *Sweet Baby James*, Carole King's *Tapestry* and Joni Mitchell's *Blue*. The songs were introspective and thoughtful, owing less to San Francisco or folk-rock than to the displaced poets of the revival. Indeed, the new singers were linked to the revival indirectly through the activity of performers like Tom Rush and Judy Collins. Unlike some of their fellow folk singers, neither Rush nor Collins wrote many songs themselves. They were contemporary folk performers by virtue of their judicious construction of a repertoire from the best songs composed by their fellow singers. In particular, both had a reputation for choosing material by unknown writers. Tom Rush was the first to record songs by James Taylor and Jackson Browne, while Judy Collins brought Leonard Cohen's name to the fore with her version of "Suzanne". Both singers had already helped to establish Joni Mitchell's name, through songs like "The Circle Game", "Both Sides Now" and "Chelsea Morning".

Taylor's rise to fame was meteoric. After only two records (one an unsuccessful album recorded in London for Apple) he was on the cover of *Time* magazine, hailed as the symbol of the cooling of America and the withdrawal of young people from the apocalyptic postures of the sixties. *Rolling Stone*, the *Time* of a younger generation, saw him as part of "The First Family Of The New Rock", along with his musical brothers and sisters, Livingston, Kate and Alex.

This "New Rock" came under immediate attack from rock'n'roll traditionalists whose arguments bore more than a passing resemblance to those of the old-guard folk revivalists a few years earlier. The most articulate version of the case for the prosecution came from Greil Marcus, writing in *Creem* magazine: "The rock, when it matters, is a means towards isolation and identity, a delightful buffer against integration into the social and cultural mainstream of the society. But now rock and roll *is* mainstream music, and that mainstream assimilation has brought not power but dissipation. Our connection with the music is dissolving..."

On this view, rock had been (in the fifties and again in the era of Bob Dylan and The Beatles) the musical expression of a particular group of people with their own culture set apart from the "mainstream" culture of television, Tin Pan Alley and *Time*. Now, James Taylor and his cohorts, like the Philadelphian soda-popsters before them, were selling the pass. Rock was respectable: in 1971, *Evergreen Review* included Simon and Garfunkel among their tongue-in-cheek list of "things liberals approve of".

74

There were indeed many question marks against James Taylor's kind of music, or at least against the way in which it was presented by acolyte and PR man alike. His biography could be read as that of a traditional artist: a man creating songs from the dark places of his mind, using art to conquer the chaos of life. Taylor had been inside mental hospitals and been addicted to heroin. His best-known song, "Fire And Rain", had one verse about a friend's death, one about "kicking junk before I left England" and a third "about my going into a hospital up in Western Massachusetts. It's just a hard-time song, a blues without having a blues form."

James Taylor most certainly took that autobiographical truth-telling attitude towards song-writing that had previously been evident in Tim Hardin and the earlier Paul Simon. Yet, like them, in his best songs the pages from a private diary are transmuted. So, "Fire And Rain" comes across as a distillation of a deep sense of loss and loneliness when a pillar of certainty in the singer's world suddenly and inexplicably crumbles. The song, again, was peculiarly appropriate to that particular historical moment, when the "counter-culture" was falling apart. And, like C. S. N. & Y., it was a tone and a nuance that mattered with James Taylor, not explicit statements.

Another source of adverse criticism was James Taylor's voice, which was said to be one-dimensional and inexpressive. In "Fire And Rain", in fact, the subdued delivery effectively sets off the highly charged lyrics. Any more demonstrative singing would have tipped it over into melodrama. But successive albums, on which Taylor's thin vein of poetry sometimes seems to have run out, do leave an impression of blandness. It remains true that his best songs seem to fall into a kind of "lullaby" category, notably "Sweet Baby James" and "You Can Close Your Eyes", from the third record *Mud Slide Slim and the Blue Horizon*. The former is a peculiarly hypnotic collage of images, moving from the lone cowboy to the lonely "turnpike from Stockbridge to Boston".

Taylor's singing is probably the most "folky" thing about his work – although the first music he heard at home was Guthrie and Leadbelly, his early years as a player were in soul and rock bands, in particular The Flying Machine, a short-lived New York group he formed with guitarist Danny Kootch. The criticisms of his singing tend to be based on a notion that the rock voice has to follow the ways of black music, where the range of vocal intonation and embellishment is crucial to the formation of a musical identity. But in white rural singing, that kind of approach was never the norm. In his *Rolling Stone* review of *Mud Slide Slim and the Blue Horizon*, Ben Gerson compared James Taylor's voice to the "high, lonesome quality of Appalachian music... a flat undemonstrative style which, nevertheless, bespeaks great emotion."

James Taylor, like Bob Dylan before him, was an archetypal example of a troubadour who became a star without wanting to. The situation into which he was catapulted placed pressures on him to present himself in ways entirely at odds with the ethic of his music. Gerson: "The Rolling Stones in their flamboyance can excite mass appeal: when James does, something has gone askew. James' career is the lie to his art, for if he is by nature an introspective recluse, the effect of his career is the opposite. The discrepancy which makes James' enormous success grotesque to the outsider is exactly what makes it personally threatening to him."

Taylor's response to the pressures has been to retreat, not only in his life, but in his work. None of his recent albums has matched up to *Sweet Baby James*. On the other hand, Joni Mitchell has made the contradiction between career and art (what British blues pioneer Alexis Korner once called the necessary schizophrenia of the professional musician) part of the subject matter of her songs. "For The Roses" captures the essence of the situation: "In some office sits a poet/And he trembles as he sings/And he asks some guy/To circulate his soul around".

Joni Mitchell was a product of the Canadian folk scene, centred on the Yorktown section of Toronto. That scene seemed slower to develop its own distinctive voices and several of them – notably Gordon Lightfoot and Joni herself – migrated south. Perhaps as part of a growing awareness of the cultural domination of Canada by the United States, the last few years has seen the emergence of a group of Canadian singer-songwriters, led by Bruce Cockburn, Murray McLauchlan and David Wiffen.

Joni Mitchell went first to New York, where she met Elliott Roberts, a man destined to become one of the rock entrepreneurs of the seventies when he teamed up with David Geffen, architect of

Asylum Records. Through him she got a recording contract and a producer, David Crosby, about to form his new supergroup.

From the beginning, she was unique among the many women emerging from the folk-song coffeehouses because she wrote all her own songs. Songs had been written for women before, but Joni Mitchell was the first in rock music to consistently express a woman's point of view from inside. It was always done through minute but exact touches: "Marcie's faucet needs a plumber, Marcie's sorrow needs a man." She was also a mistress of the more conventional contemporary folk song. "The Circle Game" (which various sources claim was inspired by Neil Young, himself a graduate of the Toronto folk scene) links the growth of an individual with the traditional theme of the turning of the seasons. "Both Sides Now" also uses metaphors taken from nature but takes in multiple points of view, though in the end "It's love's illusions I recall, I really don't know love at all".

That restless impulse kept Joni Mitchell moving as a musician. She had moved to California in the Woodstock era – she wrote the best (and now most poignantly ironic) song about that event – but unlike some of her male contemporaries she never succumbed to the idea that sunshine and financial freedom solved all problems. It may not be necessary to add that the fact of her sex clearly played a crucial part in all this. Even a star can be treated "just like a woman", especially if she lives in a community of successful musicians: "Maybe it's paranoia/Maybe it's sensitivity/Your friends protect you/ Scrutinize me".

By 1970, and her third album *Ladies of the Canyon*, Joni Mitchell was feeling the same pressures of success that James Taylor had suffered under. Her solution was different. She took a while away from music, travelled in Europe and came back to record *Blue*, an album entirely free of the occasional folksiness of her earlier songs. She began to use the full range of her voice, swooping down an octave from her customary soprano. And the shapes of the songs followed the voice and the sense of the lyrics, in a way unequalled since Buddy Holly had deployed his remarkable range of vocal effects. The words themselves became sharper, shorn of the more florid metaphors.

The process continued on the next two records, *For the Roses* and *Court and Spark*, where the love songs are joined by others probing the contradictions of a musical form caught between self-expression and commercial exploitation. In the context of that new theme, even love songs can seem to be about the audience as well as a lover: "You think I'm like your mother/Or another lover or your sister/Or the queen of your dreams/Or just another silly girl/When love makes a fool of me."

The considerable achievements of Joni Mitchell and other singer-songwriters return us to the criticisms of the "new rock" by the traditionalists. On one level, their music does work more like certain aspects of "mainstream" culture than the kind of communal folk art rock'n'roll was claimed to be. It's clearly the product of an individual sensibility and is received by listeners as individuals rather than as a community. Yet, as the lyricist and critic Clive James has said, there are only two states of grace in the arts: total innocence and total awareness. After the collapse of the Woodstock Nation dream, innocence was only possible in good faith for anyone too young to have experienced it. Hence the rise of groups like Grand Funk Railroad, playing to strictly teenage audiences. This was, in a limited sense, a communal situation. Its limits were those of simple anti-parent music.

Grand Funk were one of the two groups put forward by Greil Marcus as a possible rock alternative to the neutralisation of the music by James Taylor et al. The other was The Band. The importance of *their* work lay in the chance that they might re-unify the new cultural forces of the sixties because of their concern with America, its history and mythologies. Although the argument explicitly rejected any notion that music could provide political insight or leadership as such, it nevertheless contained the unstated assumption that rock music could once again become the central unifying force of a movement whose aims were ultimately more than purely musical.

The crucial weakness of this view was pointed up by the strong element of self-consciousness in the "new rock": both James Taylor and Joni Mitchell realised that the limiting peculiarity of the rock'n'roll life was that to communicate you had to circulate your soul around. Only Mitchell, however, was able to make this awareness part of her music. And that kind of triumph was only available to her because she retained from her folk days a different notion of the aim of a singer to that projected by the entertainment industry.

FEEL LIKE GOING HOME

Good morning America, how are you?
Don't you know me – I'm your native son.

Steve Goodman, "City of New Orleans"

If it wasn't for her political connections she could probably be the top female country singer.

Nashville producer Norbert Putnam on Joan Baez

Following the decline and fall of Woodstock and all that, rock music began to fragment. There were two general kinds of response to the changed situation among musicians with folk music roots, influences or intentions. The first was that of the new breed of singer-songwriters – Taylor, Mitchell and the rest – using their own experiences as raw material for their songs. Elsewhere, a large number of people looked outwards and backwards, mining American history, tradition and geography.

The Woodstock philosophy had been an attempt to construct a new world, a future (or just a moment) radically cut off from America past and present. The new approaches – and they were many and disparate – shared a desire to locate a continuity, to re-make or discover roots and traditions through which past, present and future could be connected. Nearly all of them centred on "country" and one or more of the meanings of the word. "Country" as *the* country, a rural space, idyllic when set against the death-in-life of the cities, had been a resonant counter-cultural theme. And there were acoustic bards a-plenty to express that feeling in music. Beyond that was "country" as country music in its various phases and forms.

Here, as in so much else, Bob Dylan made the first move, when he recorded *Nashville Skyline*. Following him, various folk and rock singers and musicians went on to integrate different aspects of the music into their work. Some were after the sound and the skills of the Nashville session players, particularly the younger men who throughout the late sixties were steadily eroding the dominance of the stereotyped country and western sound that had made country so profitable and so despised by other musicians.

Others sought out the "essence" of country music, seeking in it a solidity lacking in contemporary rock, much as earlier musicians had turned to the blues. Finally, there were attempts to look anew at the whole American folk and popular music heritage from a contemporary perspective, notably in the work of Ry Cooder and Arlo Guthrie.

Although in the main their style isn't touched by country music, the acoustic bards relate to their audience in much the same way as a lot of mainstream country performers. Most of the listeners to the latter are city dwellers, the white working-class people who came in from the country a generation or two back. Their music gives them a picture of country life and values in a nostalgic fashion. Similarly, the people who listen to John Denver warbling about smoking round a campfire, or Seals and Crofts singing about flowers blooming in the desert don't actually live the rural communal life. What is presented is a generally idealised vision of something most of the audience won't ever experience. At its worst, it becomes a way of escapism from the problems of the city.

John Denver has been the most successful of these singers. He learned his folk-singing at college in Texas, and immediately found his place in the easy-listening side of the revival. After an engagement at a Los Angeles club, he took his place in a re-organised Chad Mitchell Trio. He wrote "Leaving On A Jet Plane", a hit for Peter, Paul and Mary, and he shared many of the characteristics of that group. Like them, he has always been on the borderline between the real innovators among writers and singers, and the performers who simply dilute new music to fit the preconceptions of the pop mainstream.

Most of his songs are too bland and romanticised to succeed, almost a reversal of the failings of the "art is pain" school of singer-songwriters. At best they can evoke a diffuse mood of well-being, rather than a precise feeling. The one major exception is "Rocky Mountain High", which holds the interest because it presents a moving picture instead of a still life, and a range and tension of feelings. It tells of a young man coming to the mountains and finding contentment there. But the song doesn't stop at that typically blissful point. It goes on to describe the threat to the rural life from the encroachment of the mining industry. And against that contrasting image of "scars upon the land", the glowing descriptions of forests, streams and mountains take on a substantial presence.

The urban counterpart to Denver was the late Jim Croce. Both favoured relaxed, melodic songs and performed in a style close to the clear, open singing of James Taylor and the white, rural tradition. While John Denver came on as a sort of cross between a nice hippy and Huck Finn, Croce looked like a mixture of a Marx Brother and a construction worker (which he had been for a while). Although he produced a large number of easy, flowing love songs, his most interesting work was usually the product of sardonic observation of cameos from city life: "You Don't Mess Around With Jim", "Working At The Carwash Blues". The immense popularity of both John Denver and Jim Croce in the early seventies can probably be traced to their studied casualness and the anti-show-business approach they took to their music: a "no-frills" policy which again entered the pop mainstream via the folk scene.

Croce came from Philadelphia and the local attenuated folk scene there. Chicago also had a similar set of clubs, and from them emerged two of the better songwriters of the past few years, Steve Goodman and John Prine. Goodman's classic song is "City Of New Orleans", a railroad song in which the precision of description gradually widens the perspective until the train becomes a metaphor for America itself. John Prine is better known, partly because of the superficial similarity of his voice to Dylan's. And even though some of the sources of his style are the same – the classic country songs of Hank Williams for instance – Prine's approach is different. Because he didn't come up through the folk revival and the cosmopolitan cross-currents of influences in which people like Dylan, Phil Ochs and Judy Collins swam, his songs seem to be grafted straight onto a far earlier and more genuinely folk tradition belonging to "thousands of anonymous people who sang country because they lived in it communally, and who sang about work because they worked for a living".

It's not coincidental that it was Kris Kristofferson who was instrumental in getting Prine his recording contract. Both men have an ambiguous relationship to Nashville country music, or, more accurately, their modes of writing illuminated country's double status as both a folk and a pop music. It wasn't until the 1950s that country and western music had become fully industrialised. Prior to that time it had retained a strong element of rural folk music – songs made by country people for their own communities. The basic cause of the change was demographic – the move from the land to the towns as agriculture became mechanised or economic and natural disaster hit the small farmer.

The key figure in that change was Hank Williams. His songs were perhaps the finest flowering of country music in its folk form, but their immense sales finally clinched its acceptance by the major institutions of show business. But that folk side of country didn't die. It lived on in the "old-timey" musicians who played bluegrass music, and in aspects of the work of some of the biggest figures in Nashville country and western, notably Johnny Cash. This isn't the place to go into the details of Cash's career and his music, but it's enough to say that he was a key figure in Bob Dylan's move towards country music. And Dylan, of course, set the pattern for large numbers of rock and folk performers to reconsider country music as a vital part of their heritage.

There were The Byrds (at this time headed by the ever-present Roger McGuinn and Gram Parsons), who cut their *Sweetheart of the Rodeo* album. There were the later groups who wanted to merge rock and contemporary country music: The Flying Burrito Brothers and Poco. And there were bands of young musicians starting from older versions of country and western, with fiddles and mandolins rather than guitars: The Dillards and The Nitty Gritty Dirt Band.

Dylan's own generation of folk-revival graduates also took notice, and pre-eminent among them was Joan Baez. From the earliest days of her career she had been typecast as the figurehead of what I called earlier the "second generation" of the folk revival. When *Time* magazine, in 1962, decided to feature the revival, it was Joan they put on the cover, casually picking a guitar and gazing out into the distance.

Although she was from the beginning serious about politics, her repertoire consisted entirely of traditional songs, both American and British. Bob Dylan was among those who noticed this apparent contradiction between her beliefs and her art. Richard Farina (a very talented songwriter who was married to Joan's sister Mimi, and who died in a motorcycle accident) described a conversation with Dylan: "'Take Joanie, man,' said Dylan, 'she's still singing about Mary Hamilton. I mean where's that at? She's walked around on picket lines, she's got all kinds of feelings, so why ain't she stepping out?'"

It was eventually Bob Dylan's own songs that changed Joan Baez's mind about contemporary material. She began to feature "With God On Our Side" in her concerts, and also toured with its composer – an important step for Dylan since at this time Baez was the most popular figure on the folk scene.

Despite that, she didn't follow Dylan and the rest into folk-rock. She preferred to remain a folk singer, playing on campuses and in concert halls, including more and more new songs in her performances. She spent more and more of her time and effort in political work, founding the Institute for the Study of Non-Violence and appearing at rallies and meetings.

Her music was marking time. Although she recorded songs by The Beatles, Tim Hardin and others, the depth of her work wasn't keeping pace with the deepening of her non-musical activity. The answer came from an unexpected quarter: Nashville. Again, Bob Dylan had been there first, and his interest in country music and musicians made Joan Baez aware of that submerged "folk" side of country: the side that included Woody Guthrie, Joe Hill and songs about hard times and prisons, rather than the conventional Nashville output of romantic sentimentality.

When they heard who was coming, the musicians at Quadrophonic Studios decided to stick "Wallace For President" slogans on their equipment. The stickers were peeled off as soon as they realised that Baez was as good a musician as she was an agitator. That was in 1968. Since then, six Joan Baez albums have been cut in collaboration with producer Norbert Putnam and the nucleus of "new Nashville" session players who made the Area Code 615 records.

In that time, her own style has consistently matured. Her political commitment is as strong as ever, but it has become totally indissoluble from her music. "Prison Trilogy", on *Come from the Shadows* (1972), is a narrative that fits easily into an established country tradition about hard times and jail, a tradition extended dramatically in Joan Baez's coda: "They might just as well have laid the old man down/And we're gonna raze, raze the prisons to the ground." The same album contains her song "To Bobby", which is both a criticism of Dylan's move away from commitment ("You left us marching on the road") and an attempt to understand his situation: "Perhaps the pictures in the *Times*/Could no longer be put in rhymes/When all the eyes of starving children were wide open."

That song showed how far Joan Baez had moved from the image of the self-satisfied "protest" singer preaching to audiences whose understandable reaction was annoyance. In her live shows, she sings John Lennon's "Imagine", but changes one crucial word. Instead of "Imagine no possessions, I wonder if you can", the line becomes "I wonder if *I* can". There is still unevenness in her work, though. The second side of *Where Are You Now, My Son?* (1973) is a long documentary ballad about Vietnam which falters because the medium of song isn't right for it. The best political songs are those which take the customary lyric topics and place them in an unexpected perspective. That's what Country Joe McDonald does on *Paris Sessions* (1973) and what Baez herself does in "Rider, Pass By" from her 1973 album. Using archetypal images that might have come from a traditional ballad (mysterious horsemen, "ancient waves"), the songs explore male–female relationships in a time when "Dancing on their broken chains/Ah, the ladies are no more".

The 1962 *Time* article about Joan Baez thought it significant that there was "no show business" about her. She has remained faithful to that tenet of the revival, and if it means that she's lost a chance to reach a wider audience via the publicity machinery of the record business, the gains are correspondingly great. She can, to a large degree, control the way in which her music is disseminated, and thus close the gap between the intention and the effect of her work more than the unwilling singer-songwriting stars.

Gordon Lightfoot is another singer working on the border between folk and rock who, though based in Toronto, has recorded often in Nashville and Los Angeles. The smoothness of his voice and the ease of his melodies make him seem deceptively like another of the Denver/Croce breed of acoustic songsters. Yet beneath the immaculate surface of his music, Lightfoot has developed a personal synthesis of all the things a travelling troubadour in North America should think about. There are highway and hitch-hiking songs which capture the mixture of despair and exhilaration of that condition: Lightfoot was actually the first to record perhaps the best highway song of recent years – Kristofferson's "Me And Bobby McGee". His best love songs can take situations of loss or unhappiness and keep the feeling this side of sentimentality: "If You Can Read My Mind" and "Talking In Your Sleep" are the most successful. And though there aren't many of them, Lightfoot's songs about his native Canada have probably contributed as much to the development of the Toronto music scene as the recent "Cancon" (Canadian content) edict which regulates the amount of foreign-produced music to be played on the radio.

The strength of Gordon Lightfoot's work lies in his use of his voice and in his mode of writing. The voice becomes another instrument much of the time – in a similar way to Joni Mitchell's style. The melodic flow of the songs seems tailored to the particular contours of Lightfoot's singing, as also are the lyrics. The best of these have a resonance and density which is reminiscent of songs which have evolved in a traditional manner. Lightfoot's hit album *Sundown* (1974) is rich in them. The title track combines an incantatory chorus with aphoristic statements like "Sometimes I think it's a sin/When I feel like I'm winning/When I'm losing again" in a masterly way.

Through Lightfoot and others, Toronto is beginning to assert itself as a centre of contemporary folk-based music. The same is true of Austin, Texas. The city is the state capital and university town, which has led to the concentration there of a number of "progressive country" singer-songwriters such as Jerry Jeff Walker and Michael Murphey. These "cosmic cowboys" and their co-thinkers – like Jimmy Buffet based in Florida – form part of the movement which is beginning to impregnate country music with what might be called a rock or post counter-cultural sensibility. In a sense, it's the second stage of a development that began when Dylan first went to Nashville and Johnny Cash cut an album of songs dedicated to the cause of the American Indian. This process is still in its early stages, and is still viewed with hostility by many of the entrenched Nashville interests, but it promises to be one of the most significant musical trends of the seventies since it involves the revitalising of a folk tradition that had all but been buried under mainstream pop.

Another side of that process is represented by other players who, rather than add to a tradition by writing their own songs, give that tradition a new significance by their choice of material from it: they re-draw the map of American folk music. This attitude is different to the purism of much of the folk revival of the sixties, or indeed the purism of such movements as the British rhythm'n'blues of John Mayall, The Rolling Stones and others between 1962 and 1964. They were attempts at total re-creation of a musical form that had grown up in a very different cultural and social environment.

Among the best of the new cartographers of American traditions are Taj Mahal, Arlo Guthrie and Ry Cooder. Taj Mahal and Cooder had been together in The Rising Sons, one of the first folk revival blues bands (along with Paul Butterfield's group in Chicago and The Blues Project in New York). In 1965 *Sing Out!* reported that The Rising Sons were delighting audiences at the Ash Grove in Los Angeles. Further down the same column, incidentally, is the news that the "Troubadour management was impressed by the audiences drawn by The Byrds, a folk-orientated rock-and-roll group whose hit single of Bob Dylan's 'Tambourine Man' reached the top of the local pop music charts..."

Since then, both Mahal and Cooder have made a series of albums, exploring the rural blues and the white rural music of the Jimmie Rodgers and Woody Guthrie eras respectively. In contrast to the general trend in rock over the last decade, they are minimal artists – never playing a note when none will do. This was proved negatively in the case of Ry Cooder during his various collaborations with the Stones, notably on the inconsequential Nicky Hopkins *Jamming with Edward* album. He was schooled on the Los Angeles session scene, and first shone out on Randy Newman's *12 Songs*, with his mandolin and bottleneck guitar playing.

Although Cooder remains very much a part of the Los Angeles recording world, his own albums have gone over much the same territory as a lot of the recent work of the current king of mainstream country, Merle Haggard. Both are again reaching back beyond Nashville countrypolitan to the time when Southern white music was a matter of working men singing to their peers about common situations: the age of Jimmie Rodgers, "the Singing Brakeman", and of Woody Guthrie, the itinerant worker and union man. That kind of approach might have seemed quaint and academic in the psychedelic era when the pastures of plenty beckoned beyond the hallucinations, but when the seventies are coming to seem as close to the thirties as the sixties, it becomes a question of learning from the experience of earlier generations.

All that is even more true of Arlo Guthrie, who has come a long and a generous way from *Alice's Restaurant* and his Woodstock appearance as the average hippy troubadour. At that point he seemed to be moving as far away as possible from the directions his father took. Which was understandable, particularly considering the fate of Hank Williams Jr. Then, a change came with *Hobo's Lullaby* (1972) and *Last of the Brooklyn Cowboys* (1973). The latter includes two traditional fiddle showcases for Irish virtuoso Kevin Burke, two songs by Woody, five by Arlo, Dylan's "Gates Of Eden" and three classic country songs from the thirties. That apparent ragbag in fact adds up to a very coherent attempt by Arlo Guthrie to recover his personal musical heritage: the fiddle playing connects with a family tradition via his own song "Uncle Jeff", about Woody's brother who was an old-time fiddler. And the title of the record suggests a perhaps over-pessimistic attitude to the future of the synthesis it achieves: an integration of the rural and the urban, conservative form and radical content. It's certainly an integration to be envied by any intelligent American radical who realises that the transformation of American society he or she hopes for cannot happen without the so-called "rednecks" rediscovering their own heritage as working people, the heritage out of which Arlo Guthrie's father created his music.

NEW MORNING?

This chapter has described the history of rock music in America over the last decade from one particular angle. Much has been left out: the influence of the English Invasion, of the new jazz, of city blues, the various currents of purely teenage or anti-parent music: bubblegum and heavy downer rock. But I hope enough evidence has been produced to suggest that the impact of the folk revival and its offshoots has been critical in the growth of rock into not only a multi-million-dollar industry but a major cultural form which affects the way millions of people in different generations and situations see themselves and the life around them.

At the very least that impact (or series of impacts) has been responsible for much of the acute instability and sense of crisis of identity the music has today. Before 1964, there were things to hold on to. Rock'n'roll had rocked the boat in the late fifties, but pop was back again as simple entertainment fitting neatly into the slot marked "consumer leisure-time activity". Then, along came "folk-rock".

On one level, it was a fad. A marketing concept, a bandwagon for opportunists to jump on, a craze over in a year. But it also introduced into the heart of mainstream popular music ideas which wouldn't go away. The idea that songs could concern themselves with topics far wider than the conventional love themes, that musicians could approach their work as self-expression, rather than "giving the people what they want".

This has led, of course, to a lot of very bad and self-indulgent music as well as some very fine records. It has also been partly responsible for the tragedies which have punctuated rock's history. In other times, to be a star might have been a burden, but the limits were known. One was an entertainer, part of show business. The audience went back to work next day, satisfied but unchanged. But as soon as a new dimension entered popular music – the singer as poet, as leader – tremors were set up. The late Lillian Roxon's moving piece on Janis Joplin summed up the role of the new rock star: "...I don't know if any of you have any idea how truly enslaved American women were by the whole shampoo, set, tint and spray routine. Janis set them free." Janis Joplin had been a folk singer in Texas and part of the doomed San Francisco experience. She and her audience knew, however blindly, that the music was more than entertainment. If the people "stoking the star-maker machinery/Behind the popular song" (Joni Mitchell) knew it, they didn't care. The attempt to compress her energies and those of her listeners into the habitual structures of the entertainment industry led to disaster.

Elsewhere the impact of folk ways on rock have been less cataclysmic, although substantial, setting up tremors rather than causing earthquakes. Folk "ways" because it hasn't been the actual music of the revival which has installed itself within rock, so much as a series of approaches to music-making which had taken root in the revival.

Ironically, the approaches which have had most effect on rock – for ill as well as good – have been those aspects of the revival which had least to do with the traditional mainstream. The notion of self-expression and autobiographical intensity owed most to literary sources, the idea of poet as truth-teller. One of the main exponents of this "school", Leonard Cohen, was already an established literary figure before he took to song-writing, while the origin of Robert Zimmerman's stage name in the Welsh poet Dylan Thomas is well known. More significantly, in the work of Cohen and Judy Collins (who has recorded songs by Brecht and Weill, Jacques Brel and material from the "Marat-Sade"), rock music has widened its scope to include the European chanson genres.

The opposite wing of the folk influence has been responsible for rock music becoming aware of a past to which it is heir in more meaningful ways than simple nostalgia for the golden oldies. In earlier phases of pop, the notion of the music as purely temporary and transitory, with no past or future, had achieved the status of an official ideology, which was very convenient for those involved in selling it. The most recent explorations of the past focusing on country music represent not simply musicological excursions, but a search for alternative purposes to those of the mainstream entertainment industry. The potential of this work is all the greater for its modesty: the lessons of the apocalyptic ideas of the Woodstock era have been learned.

Finally, what may come to be seen as the most significant effect of folk on rock has generally gone unremarked: the emergence of a number of women artists free of the conventional pop stereotypes. A list of some of them begins to suggest the importance of this development: Joni Mitchell, Joan Baez, Judy Collins, Bonnie Raitt, Mimi Farina, Carly Simon, Toni Browne and Terry Garthwaite, Maria Muldaur, Linda Ronstadt.

The general pop situation had been (and to a large extent remains) one in which female singers were forced into one or other of the three roles recently analysed by Michael Gray: those of the Virgin Mary, Eve and the Slave-Girl. The common denominator was that all the roles were passive and all were created from a male point of view. The only creative space allowed was in a performer's presentation of a song or an image.

This is not to say that the folk revival didn't have its female stereotype. But that sensitive ballad-singer role (early Joan Baez) was at least an active one. Baez and the others accompanied themselves, and they were able to develop artistically because the way wasn't blocked in folk music by the machismo style which dominated rock.

The existence of women singers and writers as major performers in the rock arena is an implicit challenge to that macho stance of the conventional rock band. And the implications of the current situation go further. If, as some of its defenders claim, the "masculinity" of rock is not optional but essential to the achievements of the music, then perhaps that kind of music may come to be seen as no more relevant to our time than the soda-pop of the early sixties. For not the least important aspect of the impact of the folk revival is the idea that music cannot be seen as separate from the rest of life. It cannot be confined to a sealed-off compartment marked "entertainment", and there may be occasions when it needs to be judged and found wanting by standards above and beyond those it provides for itself.

SOURCES

Written Sources

Sandy Darlington, "Cream At Winterland" in *Rock and Roll Will Stand*, ed. Greil Marcus (Beacon Press, 1969).

Josh Dunson, *Freedom in the Air* (International Publishers, 1965).

Josh Dunson, "Folk Rock: Thunder without Rain", in *The American Folk Scene*, ed. David A. DeTurk and A. Poulin Jr. (Dell Publishing, 1967).

Ben Gerson, in *Rolling Stone*.

Ralph J. Gleason, *The Jefferson Airplane and The San Francisco Sound* (Ballantine Books, 1969).

Michael Gray, "Sexist Songs", *Melody Maker*, June 1, 1974.

Michael Gray, in *Let It Rock*, June 1974.

Robert Greenfield, "Songs Of Innocence, Songs Of Restraint", *Fusion*, April 17, 1970.

Greil Marcus, "Rock-A-Hula Clarified", *Creem*, June 1971.

Melody Maker, February 5, 1972, p. 25.

Lillian Roxon, "A Moment Too Soon" in *No One Waved Goodbye*, ed. Robert Somma (Outerbridge & Dienstfrey, 1971).

Sing Out! September 1965.

Andrew Weiner, "Dylan, The Byrds and the First Hippy Hymn", *Creem*, April 1972.

Langdon Winner, "The Strange Death Of Rock and Roll", in *Rock and Roll Will Stand*, ed. Greil Marcus (Beacon Press, 1969).

Recordings

Children of the Revival

Tom Paxton: *Rambling Boy* (Elektra).

Peter, Paul and Mary: *Best of Peter, Paul and Mary* (Warner Bros).

Buffy Sainte-Marie: *Best of Buffy Sainte-Marie. Volume 1* (Vanguard double).

Paul Simon: *The Paul Simon Song Book* (CBS).

Tim Hardin: *I and II* (Verve double).

From Folk to Rock

The Byrds: *History of The Byrds* (CBS double).

Lovin' Spoonful: *Daydream and Hums of The Lovin' Spoonful* (Kama Sutra double).

The Mamas and the Papas: *20 Golden Hits* (ABC double).

Tom Rush: *Classic Rush* (Elektra).

Bob Lind: *Don't Be Concerned* (Fontana/World Pacific).

Singers and Songwriters

Judy Collins: *In My Life* (Elektra).

Crosby, Stills and Nash: *Crosby, Stills and Nash* (Atlantic).

James Taylor: *Sweet Baby James* (Warner Bros).

Joni Mitchell: *Blue* (Reprise).

Phil Ochs: *Live at Carnegie Hall* (A & M – Canada only at the time of writing).

Reworking a Tradition

Joan Baez: *Come from the Shadows* (A & M).
Arlo Guthrie: *Last of the Brooklyn Cowboys* (Warner Bros).
Ry Cooder: *Boomer's Story* (Warner Bros).
John Prine: *Diamonds in the Rough* (Warner Bros).

THREE

The Roots of Tradition

KARL DALLAS

REALITIES OF THE REVIVAL

Bob Dylan summed it up: "There's nobody that's going to kill traditional music. All these songs about roses growing out of people's brains and lovers who are really geese and swans that turn into angels – they're not going to die." He said it to Nat Hentoff in a *Playboy* interview in 1966, one year after he'd been booed at the Newport Folk Festival for playing electric "folk-rock", and one year after he'd been booed for playing the same sort of stuff at Forest Hills; the quote is revealing.

Later, when the Northumbrian traditionalist, Louis Killen, did a small concert at Woodstock at the height of Dylan's withdrawal from the music business, Dylan turned up disguised in dark glasses and revealed afterwards to Killen that one of the reasons he had hidden himself away had been not so much the trauma of folkdom's refusal to accept his electric experiments, as their later over-enthusiastic move from acoustic to electric music – at his bidding, as they mistakenly thought. But he had been pursuing a personal vision, not charting a recommended course of action for his peers, and when the rest of young middle-class America traded in their acoustic Martins for Gibson Les Pauls, the responsibility was more than he was willing to assume.

The music business, and especially the music press, likes to act as if the development of style were a matter of palace revolutions, of abrupt changes in fashion from one month to the next – a pose which has more to do with a desire for built-in obsolescence in marketing terms than with any cultural phenomenon. Musicians themselves, especially those who appreciate the music reporter's need for a headline story in every interview, often compound the confusion and will deliberately distort their reasons for any new change or experiment to make sure of getting space. So a new approach to music is presented as something which outmodes its predecessor, instead of as an outcome of organic growth or even, as in Dylan's case, instead of as something of entirely personal significance.

Dylan, of course, is notorious for his agility in refusing to play this press game – or for playing it according to his own, constantly revised rules, never revealed to his opponents in the media – and the more intelligent of his fellows do the same. I well remember Dave Swarbrick, at the time that Fairport Convention was going through the most unsettled period in its history, saying to me acidly of their latest personnel change: "And if you ask me if that's a logical development in our progression, I'll slosh you."

It is easy in this sort of atmosphere for the reporter to skim across the surface of the folk music revival and see the growth of electric folk – or folk-rock as the pop press prefers to call it, attempting thus in some way to link it with the music of The Byrds and similar American groups inspired by Dylan – as a radical break with the "purist" origins of the revival. It is tempting to see it as something which can be justified only by discarding some of the most cherished beliefs of the pioneer revivalists, as a form which can be explained only as something quite distinct from the folk club movement which it somehow invalidates and makes obsolete.

A large number of folk club revivalists share this opinion about electric folk, which is one of the reasons why they are opposed to it. Also, with their amplification and PA systems, increasing volume and expensive road crews, most electric-folk bands must of necessity take the music out of the intimacy of the club and into the wider impersonality of the concert hall or ballroom.

Nevertheless, electric folk can be understood only if it is seen in context as a kind of music which has grown organically out of the work of the early post-war revivalists and which successfully applies many of the principles which until recently had remained only a pious aim. In particular it tries to use traditional music as a means to revitalise and reinforce a truly national genre of popular music – or, as we would now put it, a British brand of rock.

Woody Guthrie, 1950s. *Gems/Redferns*

Lonnie Donegan, December 1957.
Mirrorpix

The Incredible String Band, late 1960s.
Gems/Redferns

The Byrds with Bob Dylan on harmonica, Ciro's nightclub, Los Angeles, 1965.
Michael Ochs Archives/Getty Images

Shirley and Dolly Collins, *The Sweet Primroses* rehearsals, 1966. *Brian Shuel/Redferns*

Fairport Convention, February 1969. *Gems/Redferns*

Steeleye Span (*Please to See the King* line-up), 1970. *Gems/Redferns*

Muddy Waters, The Country Club, London, December 1970. *Gijsbert Hankeroot/Redferns*

Ewan MacColl and Peggy Seeger, *A Kind of Exile* TV programme, 1971. *ITV/Shutterstock*

Linda Thompson and Richard Thompson, London, 1974. *Michael Putland/Getty Images*

Simon and Garfunkel, Madison Square
Garden, New York City, June 1972.
Hulton Archive/Getty Images

Bert Jansch, 1971.
Jans Persson/Redferns

Crosby, Stills, Nash and Young with Joni Mitchell, Wembley Stadium, London, September 1974.
David Warner Ellis/Redferns

Horslips, 1974. *Michael Putland/Getty Images*

The Albion Dance Band, 1977. *Gems/Redferns*

Billy Bragg, Labour Party rally, June 1987.
Mirrorpix

Shane MacGowan of The Pogues, March 1988.
Mirrorpix

Oysterband (the line-up that included John Jones, Chopper and Alan Prosser), 1990.
Martyn Goodacre/Getty Images

The work of the earliest post-war revivalists is full of evidence of their desire to become involved in the mainstream of popular music and to use all the facilities of the mass media to put their music across to the people. These musicians were for the most part of the left and worked in an international political climate where on the mainland of Europe the veterans of the Communist-led resistance seemed likely to have a big part to play in its future after the liberation: not an unreasonable idea, especially after Labour's landslide victory in the 1945 election. Later, with the disillusionment that followed the success of the Marshall Plan and the loss of popular support for Marxist ideas throughout Europe and especially in the newly socialist "people's democracies" of Eastern Europe where Soviet influence meant a stagnation of thought rather than the development that had been expected, the need for and possibility of such mass support seemed less obvious. And at the same time, the folk clubs had demonstrated how a musical movement could grow up almost entirely independently of the mass media, a true underground with heroes who never appeared on TV and rarely on radio, who only recorded, if at all, for small companies whose products were almost impossible to find in record shops deluged with the music of Bill Haley, Elvis Presley and their British imitators.

Such independence from the media did tend at times to make the folk clubs somewhat elitist in their approach, and the most hidebound of them became increasingly ingrown and cut off from any contact with the real "folk" who congregated in the public bars below the pub rooms they rented. And yet the existence of the folk clubs as a movement, a hydra-headed undirectable community which resisted all attempts to dragoon it into federations, ideologies or mutually warring factions, has an importance in the social history of Britain since the war, and a continuing function in the development of British popular culture which is seldom appreciable within the kilometres of space now devoted to folk music of one persuasion or another in the pop and popular media.

It was their initial willingness to use the mass media, and indeed the very existence of electronic media reaching into every home in the land, that distinguished the post-war revivalists, led by Ewan MacColl and A.L. Lloyd and the American, Alan Lomax, from all their worthy (and, in some cases, more worthy) predecessors who had relied on the printed word and the educational system for the diffusion of their discoveries. The very earliest collectors of folklore had been antiquarians. Later collectors had seen themselves as assembling "curiosities" or "last relics" of a dying culture into learned volumes intended for gentry similar to themselves. The great cataloguer of English and Scottish ballads, Francis James Child, was a professor at Harvard University, a scholar writing in 1898 for scholars. Even Cecil Sharp, Fabian socialist though he was, limited his appreciation of the popular potential of his researches in the early part of the twentieth century to campaigning to have them taught in the schools whose principal purpose was the production of efficient components for the factory machines, something which did no good turns to the national appreciation of our folkloric heritage at all.

Lloyd, Lomax and MacColl, on the other hand, burst upon our consciousness in 1951 in a series of radio programmes called *Ballads and Blues* in which the other prominent performer was the Eton-educated, ex-Guardsman cornettist, Humphrey Lyttelton. The suggestion that there was anything in common between jazz and folk music was a revolutionary one in England, though it had for a time been a truism of Marxist aesthetics in America (though not within the Soviet Union) that jazz was a people's music, and therefore politically OK.

There was also more than a hint of opportunism in this alliance with jazz musicians, for they were likely to be the only ones able to free folk accompaniments from the dreadfully stilted piano arrangements that had been foisted upon them during the twenties and thirties. It was some time before the charm of the English and Scottish folk song, sung completely unaccompanied and allowing free rein for vocal embellishments, struck the revivalists. When it did, there was another "revolution" and unaccompanied singing became the thing, though the lack of instrumental accompaniment in the traditions of these islands seems to me to have been over-emphasised, and is more likely a sign of decadence than of the purity of the tradition, as is sometimes maintained against all evidence to the contrary from parallel European traditions.

Although it is commonly believed that the blues-based folk of the contemporary singer-songwriter has its roots in the American-influenced skiffle explosion that followed the unexpected chart success of Lonnie Donegan's "Rock Island Line", actually the roots of Donegan's skiffle themselves lie in the *Ballads and Blues* period of the revival. When Ewan MacColl and Ken Colyer's Jazzmen and Jeannie Robertson, the great Scottish travelling singer later awarded a MBE for her services to folk music, shared the bill at a Royal Festival Hall fund-raising concert in the mid-fifties for the old *Daily Worker*, MacColl, with Colyer's band, sang the African American chain-gang song "Another Man Done Gone". Later, Bill Colyer came on to play what was described as "skiffle", the first time I had heard the term, though as a matter of historical fact this was actually after the session that produced "Rock Island Line" and Donegan had long left the Chris Barber band with which he had originally played banjo.

Even earlier, at a fund-raising concert MacColl and Lomax organised at the Theatre Royal, Stratford, in aid of Joan Littlewood's then unknown and struggling Theatre Workshop, MacColl's protegée Isla Cameron sang the Liverpool kids' song, "Johnny Todd" (later to become more well-known as the theme-tune to the *Z Cars* TV series) with jazz musician Bruce Turner playing a simple and effective clarinet obbligato between the verses.

This concept of jazz clarinet interpolations into a fairly straight-forward folk-song context – which is the direct ancestor of the electric guitar solos with electric folk bands like Fairport Convention and Steeleye Span – was further developed in 1956 by Lomax and MacColl in their "skiffle" group, The Ramblers. The remarkable Peggy Seeger, just arrived in Britain on her way back from a Moscow Youth Festival, also numbered among its personnel as did another of MacColl's protegées, Shirley Collins. This talented lady went on to become doubly influential in the development of electric folk, once in her collaboration with the eclectic "folk baroque" guitarist Davy Graham, and, later, on her *No Roses* album when her husband Ashley Hutchings, former bass player with Fairport and founder of Steeleye, put together an aggregation of electric and acoustic folk musicians as The Albion Country Band.

The Lomax-MacColl Ramblers were not a real skiffle group, either in the original, American rent-party sense of the word or in the somewhat bastardised folk-with-a-beat connotation given it by Donegan and his followers. It is interesting to recall that, like the *Ballads and Blues*, they also came out of the mass media, in this case a

Granada TV series which also presented, for the first time, some of the country's most distinguished traditional singers, men like Sam Larner and Harry Cox. Their repertoire was later to be ransacked by the younger traditionalists of the revival who felt, rightly, that they could not imbibe the true spirit of the tradition from the printed page, especially as "collated", "annotated" or otherwise "improved" by scholarly editors more concerned with analysis than revival.

This new generation of musicians was also becoming disenchanted with MacColl's popularising style of interpretation. Although MacColl later urged didactically that the techniques of tradition could and should be studied by the aspiring folk singer, in the early days of the revival he was much less sensitive to the sound of tradition. Though he came of a family of traditional singers, MacColl was having to find his own way back to his roots, just like the rest of us. There is a story, possibly apocryphal, that his first-ever public appearance was at a Salford cinema contest where he sang under a suitably grandiloquent alias in the style of Al Bowlly or one of the other contemporary crooner heroes of the Palais de Danse.

His mother, Betsy, is a fine traditional singer, and judging by the number of texts in MacColl's collections attributed to his father, the late William Miller of Stirling (MacColl's real name is James Miller), his father's repertoire must have been prodigious. Ewan, however, chose to proceed from talent-contest crooning to traditional-style performance by way of the expressionist theatre, performing before the war in a troupe whose name, the Red Megaphones, betrays its links with the street theatre of Brecht and the agitprop of Mayakovsky.

By the beginnings of the revival, MacColl's singing was still somewhat histrionic, and it was only much later that he became able to suppress his own ebullient personality and interpose instead a rather dry, analytical, impersonal relationship between himself and his material.

It was fortunate for the revivalists, looking at the same time for a more reliable model than MacColl and for source material that didn't hark back continually to transatlantic sources – as much of MacColl's still did – that the mass media came conveniently to their aid once again in the mid-fifties. The outlet was a Sunday morning radio show, *As I Roved Out*, which racked up remarkable audience figures at what was then a peak listening time. The programme was a strange hodge-podge, the result of a fairly academic field-recording collaboration between the BBC and the virtually defunct English Folk Dance and Song Society (EFDSS), at that time almost entirely given over to a combination of check-shirted American square dancing (popularised as a result of a visit by their Patron, the then Princess Elizabeth, to Canada) and a mincing emasculation of the once vigorous English country dance tradition.

Another programme, *Country Magazine*, had elicited an unsuspected interest in traditional songs as early as 1942. When the programme returned to the subject in 1953, hundreds of texts were sent in by listeners in the countryside who claimed to have learned them traditionally – and the EFDSS lent the BBC their director's son, Peter Kennedy, to tour the country with a tape recorder to check up on how living the tradition actually was. The results were remarkable, and invalidated once again the predictions of doom with which each previous collector had prefaced his collection of "final fragments" or "last leaves" for the preceding century or more. How remarkable can still be heard, for many of the recordings obtained in this period have been issued commercially as *The Folk Songs of Britain* (a misleading title, for these islands contain within them not one but several distinct traditions, but I suppose one should not carp at what is, for all its faults, the most comprehensive survey of living traditional music ever undertaken in this country).

Despite adherence to BBC rules which banned all bawdry (so a classic ballad like "Blow Away the Morning Dew" would be faded out at verse three) and forbade unaccompanied singing for more than a few stanzas, so that tapes were edited unmercifully (a practice which survives, without justification, in the gramophone recordings), the programme managed to remain fairly true to its subject while building up excellent listening figures. The programme was retired, brought back by public demand, retired again, brought back again, then finally retired for good.

It came at just the right time. Before it, the young revivalists were torn between the near-rock of Donegan's successors and the somewhat loaded political sloganising of MacColl and his entourage. After it, they had something of a repertoire and, just as important, the beginnings of a vocal style. They were still starved of a chance to hear much good traditional instrumental music – indeed, they still are – largely because Peter Kennedy came out of the dance section of the EFDSS and consequently had more wrong-headed preconceptions of what constituted good instrumental music than he had of song. For an example of his standards, one has only to listen to any of many execrable dance records he made for HMV at the time and wince at the heavy-footed insensitivity of them.

By 1956, the folk clubs were beginning to blossom. Though MacColl's own Ballads and Blues Club was one of the first in 1953, he had for a time written off most of the others as insignificant gatherings of dilettantes, as indeed some of them, like the Troubadour in Earls Court, tended to be. But a number of different types of club, in Bradford and Liverpool and various parts of London, were also springing up, rooted in their locality in terms of membership, if not in repertoire as yet. He began to recognise them as an important social force, which they have continued to be, to a greater or lesser extent, ever since.

Actually, John Foreman has pointed out that in providing musical entertainment close to premises licensed for the sale of alcoholic drink, the folk clubs are in direct line of succession to the old music halls which were killed off in the 1920s by the new kinema. Certainly, the loophole in the licensing laws which allows minors to attend functions held in rooms over pubs but not to drink in the bars, permitted the clubs to free themselves from the sort of proprietorial tyranny which made the American coffee-bar circuit so sensitive to commercial pressures, ultimately to the disadvantage and virtual demise of the American folk scene.

These days breweries and their managers are more aware of the increased bar takings which result from letting a room to a club which books "star" names – who do not need record or TV work to make quite a substantial living, such is the power of the club movement – and they are likely to withdraw lettings from a club which does not play consistently to packed houses. This has caused some artistic stagnation, though some of the more enlightened clubs in this position scrape through by booking big names three weeks out of four to subsidise the fourth week by an unknown talent or perhaps an "old boy" up from the country to play the role of a traditional singer.

Today, a club like the Young Tradition, which promoter Bruce Dunnet ran in the mid-sixties in the Scots Hoose just off Cambridge Circus (now a "disco pub" called The Spice of Life) would probably get short shrift from the licensee, and yet it is to the Scots Hoose that many of the tangled skeins of today's folk and electric folk lead if traced back. Dunnet's idea was to present the Celtic tradition, represented by the great Connemara singer Joe Heaney, then living in London, together with some of the best of the younger musicians who flocked to Soho. A somewhat Calvinistic Scottish Communist, Dunnet had little appreciation for the kids' lifestyle, their then novel experimentation with drugs, and their crashpads up in West Hampstead, but he had a good ear for talent. He had for a time run MacColl's Singers' Club for him, had been the first manager of Julie Felix, had almost managed The Rolling Stones (he turned them down only because he was aware he had no appreciation or understanding of the blues, especially sung by white kids) and when three of his singers banded together in unique and dissonant unaccompanied harmonies, he saw in them a potential new stream for the traditional music he loved.

The club staggered to an unceremonious close and most of its clientele and performers (the one hardly outnumbering the other) transferred their allegiance to the more successful Les Cousins (always called "the Cousins", never "Lay Cousangs" by its devotees) round the corner in Greek Street where, since it had no liquor licence, they could embrace each other, sleep all night, perhaps deal a little surreptitious dope while no one was looking. Dunnet gave the name of his late club, the Young Tradition, to the trio of Heather Wood, Royston Wood (no relation) and Peter Bellamy, who then became Cousins stalwarts, along with a whole collection of folk-blues guitarists seemingly sprung whole from the fertile fingers of Davy Graham; notable among these were Bert Jansch and John Renbourn, with singer-songwriters like Al Stewart, Roy Harper and the American Jackson C. Frank, as well as a promising young girl stalwart from the Scots Hoose, Sandy Denny.

This was at a time when, it would appear to an outsider reading the *Melody Maker*, the British folk scene was seemingly intent upon savaging itself to death. MacColl had formed his Singers' Club as a venue to be run by the singers themselves (as opposed to the old

Ballads and Blues, where in the last analysis policy decisions had been taken by the entrepreneur and British representative of the World Federation of Democratic Youth, Malcolm Nixon) and had ruled it by the dictum that all singers must perform repertoire only from their own culture and especially (unless they were American) not from America. His own hybrid character, a Salford-bred son of Scottish parents living with and accompanied by the American multi-instrumentalist Peggy Seeger, gave him plenty of leeway within the rules. However, for the first time barriers began to be erected in print between the hardline traditionalists headed by a new, less tolerant MacColl, who found their expression in my own magazine, *Folk Music*, and the folk-blues freaks who were strongly influenced by the singer-songwriters of America and expressed themselves through a more successful and more eclectic magazine, *Folk Scene*. A lot of the attitudes still being struck publicly in British folk music owe their origins to this period.

In actuality this was mainly a paper battle. The folk clubs were recognising much of the logic behind MacColl's nationalism, and the cowboys of every derivation from Stratford (East) to Strathclyde were becoming less and less influential. But at the same time the musical ferment that was to run through from Bob Dylan to the acid rock of the mid-sixties, and which, paradoxically, had its roots in the work of Peggy's half-brother, Pete Seeger, in Alan Lomax, MacColl's old collaborator, and in the radical songwriters of the pre-war era like the Oklahoma folk bard Woody Guthrie and the singing union organiser, Joseph Hillstrom ("Joe Hill"), whose anti-navy lampoon, "Stung Right" had inspired MacColl's own early anti-army song, "Browned Off", at the beginning of World War II, was also touching the folk clubs. An audience would turn quite happily one week from the semi-traditional stridency of a Young Tradition to the introspective self-regard of a Paul Simon the next, or to the complex guitar arabesques of a Bert Jansch, with no sense of inconsistency.

The tastes of the performers were equally hard to pigeonhole, especially since so many of them seemed to pass through the doors of a sort of commune in Somali Road, Hampstead, where at any one time one might expect to meet any or all of the following: The Young Tradition, Davy Graham, Louis Killen, Bert Jansch, John Renbourn, Donovan Leitch, Val Berry (a fine singer who never reached her full potential) or Anne Briggs. Anne had been discovered by Ewan MacColl in her native Nottingham, put into one of the first Centre 42 "taking culture back to the people" tours he had organised with Arnold Wesker, and had become the idol of the traditionalists for her jagged, intense singing. Though no one realised it at the time, least of all the music writers, the house in Somali Road was acting as a mixing pot, a forcing house for the hybrid that was later to find its flowering in electric folk. It was there that Annie Briggs taught Bert Jansch the appreciation of traditional song that was to burst upon us in his superbly surprising *Jack Orion* album, one of the most important precursors of Pentangle and hence of electric folk.

Meanwhile, the most important work MacColl was doing was not in the field of public polemic but, once again, in the mass media. Beginning in the late fifties and working in conjunction with the BBC producer Charles Parker, he evolved new techniques in radio production whose lessons have yet to be learned by the vast majority of radio people and which, paradoxically, inspired such envy among the higher echelons of BBC radio that, in due course, Parker was frozen out even from the Midlands backwater in which they obviously hoped his creative energies would be dammed up. This was at a time when BBC thinking assumed that all future development in broadcasting would take place in TV and that the only creative radio possible was on the elitist, middle-class-orientated Radio 3. Later the pirate radios were to blow a lot of these assumptions sky high.

Of course, the radio ballad – the form which MacColl and Parker devised – did not spring ready-made from their collaboration. MacColl's theatrical work in the days before he devoted himself almost fulltime to folk song was sufficiently noteworthy to cause the venerable Scottish poet, Hugh MacDiarmid, to lament his defection from drama to what he considered the inferior art of balladry. MacColl's play, *Uranium 235*, is still a neglected masterpiece of post-war avant-garde theatre. Then, too, following the *Ballads and Blues* series, MacColl had been involved in numerous attempts to present folk and folk-type material in ways that broke away from the recital concept, but which owed a lot to the ideas of American innovators such as Marc Blitzstein and Earl Robinson, composer of "Ballad for Americans". There was one remarkable Christmas Day programme he did with Lomax which preceded the Royal Speech with an affirmation of the traditional, neo-pagan elements of Yuletide that would have created a terrible scandal if it had not been so self-evidently brilliant. As it was, the powers that be resolved never to let such dangerous folk into such a sensitive time-slot again.

MacColl's very early song-writing collaborations with D.G. Bridson, such as "Johnny Miner", were remarkable enough to be well worth reviving now. Though their attitudes do tend to reflect the somewhat sentimental view of working-class life as seen from the standpoint of the middle-class liberal "Marxist", who was then trying to join in the equally unrealistic social-realist search for a working-class hero, or New Man, then going on in Stalinist Moscow, they did at least treat working-class people as worthy of respect in their own right, and not merely as caricature symbols.

In the radio ballads, MacColl and Parker replaced the didactic text between the songs with tape-recorded talk by real workers – an innovation which not only brought the programmes closer to reality, but also revealed the existence of a lively tradition of folk speech and behaviour which is clearly the soil from which folk balladry springs and has continued to spring throughout the industrial era. Exposure to this source material had a profound effect upon MacColl's own lyric writing, which became less sentimental and tougher in its realism. It was also less comfortable, which is possibly why, with the exception of "The Travelling People", a minor hit in Ireland for The Johnstons, none of the songs MacColl has produced since those days has evoked the same echoes as his earlier, more indulgent material, songs like the dreadful "Dirty Old Town", "Champion At Keeping 'Em Rollin'" and "First Time Ever I Saw Your Face".

Ironically, MacColl's increasingly intransigent attitude made such unpleasant demands upon his performers that the personnel of each radio ballad tended to be radically different from the one preceding, with the exception of a hard core of devoted followers. As a result, many of today's folk stalwarts can be heard, if only in the chorus, on the recordings later leased by the BBC to Argo for commercial release.

Of course, in economic terms, the radio ballads were incredibly self-indulgent, involving literally miles and miles of tape to produce perhaps only a few minutes which were usable, and it was ostensibly for financial reasons that the programmes were phased out. But it was undoubtedly their political stance, illuminating the way in which the development of the English motorway system was dependent upon the exploitation of immigrant Irish labour, for instance, in "Song Of A Road", or quoting one local councillor as advocating the physical extermination of gypsies in best Nazi fashion in "The Travellers", which made them discomforting to the BBC bureaucracy.

The real faults of the radio ballads lay in their unsatisfactory instrumental work – it is amazing, considering the imaginative experiments of their earlier days, the way MacColl and Lloyd's use of instrumental accompaniment degenerated so rapidly into formula – and, apart from the excellent use of Sam Larner's songs in "Singing the Fishing", the failure to integrate traditional songs with the original material which would have given the programmes more of a historical perspective. Also, as the least successful programme in the series, "On the Edge", demonstrated only too well, MacColl's own increasing alienation from the way young people's consciousness was evolving under the impact of electronic media was not merely causing him to ignore technical resources which would have expanded the breadth of his music, but was also diminishing his influence in a movement that was already developing independently of all attempts to control or direct it.

As significant as the numbers of today's revivalists who performed in the radio ballads are the numbers who did not. MacColl and his followers tended to take up an increasingly ideological stance towards the music, and his doctrines had less and less to do with reality as the young practitioners of the craft of folk song saw it, influenced as they were by the same factors that were creating modern rock'n'roll. This finally robbed the movement of a coherent attitude to what was pop and what the relationship should be between the two.

The effect of this was not entirely negative. The folk movement after the lessening of MacColl's influence became more and more pragmatic, less inclined to bend the available data to fit preconceived notions, and thus more able to evaluate realistically its own development than any previous revival. But pragmatism can become opportunism, the blind acceptance of the validity of anything and everything which found expression in the oft-quoted "they're all folk songs – I ain't never heard a horse sing" or the dictum of Douglas

Kennedy, former director of the English Folk Dance and Song Society, that "anything the folk does is folk".

At the beginnings of the revival, a little booklet written by A.L. Lloyd for the Workers' Music Association, *Singing Englishmen*, had provided some sort of necessary perspective without imposing any hidebound set of *a priori* principles upon it. But by the time of his later full-scale book, *Folk Song in England*, Lloyd seemed to have retreated into a sort of obscurantism which suggested that the term folk song was losing its meaning, "just as the thing itself fades and merges into a general stream of music, into that One Music that begins to embrace not only Western high art, popular and traditional musics, but also the musics of other continents and cultures, with Japanese koto players taking to the harpsichord, pop musicians experimenting with the bouzouki, a French composer writing Roman Catholic music in Indian style, and a Mongolian girl singing her horse-herding songs in conservatoire manner as if they were arias by Tchaikovsky".

However, though this may have some truth, for all the cultures of the world are indeed imploding under the impact of electronics, it lacks historical perspective. As the product of a class society, as we shall see in a moment, the concept of folk music may indeed lose its meaning with the end of class antagonisms, but I see no signs of that yet awhile.

In particular, I have never been able to understand the so-called difficulty, which Lloyd first expressed in an article, "What's Traditional?", in the first issue of my own magazine, *Folk Music*, of establishing usable criteria as to what is folk and what is not, so long as one realises that the subject under discussion is a process rather than a thing. Still more, I have always been surprised that Lloyd, who on the basis of his published work appears to be a Marxist, seems not to have fitted what he knows of the folk tradition (which is a great deal) into Marx's theory of historical materialism, in which human society progresses from classless primitive communism, through the class societies of slavery, feudalism, capitalism and socialism, ultimately completing the cycle with the re-establishment of a classless communist society at a higher level.

Though I am not a Marxist, I think Marx's analysis of the development of society is the only satisfactory explanation of the

106

origin of folk culture. The current flowering of interest in folk music under the impetus of electronic communications is but one symptom, to my mind, of the possibility as well as the urgent necessity of restructuring society along lines which break up the impersonal state and return it to a collection of true communities.

The distinctions between folk, popular and high art do indeed seem to be blurring, but this is a comparatively recent process. Throughout history, the three strains have been remarkably distinct.

Of course, folk and pop have been close bedfellows throughout at least the last 500 years of musical history. The earliest pop music of the unemployed minstrels thrown on to the dung heap of the developing townships of the medieval bourgeoisie was parasitical upon folk and classical forms to a remarkable degree. The broadside printers of Seven Dials in the nineteenth century, the direct predecessors of the sheet-music publishers of Denmark Street of pre-electronic (i.e. pre-1950s) pop, drew a great deal of their best-selling repertoire from the folk tradition – even if they tended to label the oldest and most venerable ballads they borrowed as "a new song". And it is tempting to see electric folk as but another step along this road, in which traditional material is performed with a rock beat, often utilising folk instruments like the fiddle and Appalachian mountain dulcimer and even the bagpipes, but in association with a rock rhythm section of electric guitar, bass guitar and drums.

But the electronic popular music of rock is so different in form and function from the old print-based pop of "moon and June", and so akin to the old pre-literate oral forms of folk music, that most of the assumptions made today about the relations between the two are misguided, based on theories devised at a time when the complete destruction of folk culture by the industrial state seemed only a matter of time. Now that the state itself is disintegrating around us, while folk culture goes on from strength to strength, they need to be re-stated.

THE THREE STRAINS

First was folk culture, out of which evolved the second strain, high art. The third strain, popular art, did not develop until spreading literacy and the growth of an urban middle class created the revolutionary concept of entertainment.

What do we mean by folk culture? Most academics try to define it as something static, or, if changing, only in the direction of decay: a certain type of song, with words of a certain character, using certain types of melody and scales. True, there are characteristics which one associates with folk song, but while they may help us in the task of recognition, they do not in themselves define it. They do not deal adequately with the common situation in which a song, fulfilling none of their criteria, will perform a folk function if none other is available to serve the purpose, nor the even more familiar process by which a song that is apparently "folk" is wrenched from its cultural environment and presented on the concert stage or on TV or in a printed collection and becomes something quite unfolk, either art song or pop song or the raw material of ethnomusicological research.

The problem is rather as if the theatre critic were to become confused between a play and its performance in the field of drama, with this difference: while it may be said that the works of Shakespeare can exist on the printed page, divorced from actors and the stage and audience, the folk song lives only at the moment when the singer emerges from the community of which he is a member to express its collective feelings through the medium of the song. He sings, in E.S. Carpenter's telling phrase, as "many-to-many, not as person-to-person", recreating a relationship between "singer" and "audience" which, in reality, makes nonsense of the two terms, and is as old as humanity itself.

The substratum of music and culture outside or below established high art and culture, which today we term "folk", did not emerge until class antagonisms produced the need for different modes of expression to express the divided nature of society. Until then, "folk" music was all there was.

The classical writers were all aware of its existence, though since many of them were spokesmen of the new ruling class, they were hostile to it. Plato in his *Republic* wished to banish all music except that of the stringed lyre and cithara from inside his perfect city, but allowed that "in the fields the shepherds would have a syrinx to pipe on". The syrinx, or pan pipe, is an ancestor of our modern mouth organ and is thus, indirectly, second cousin to the concertina. Henry

Mayhew interviewed a street musician who played the "pandean pipes" in the mid-nineteenth century and published the story in his *London Labour and the London Poor* in 1861.

A religious writer, St John Chrysostom, had noticed the special nature of folk song long before the term was coined by nineteenth-century antiquarians: "Farm workers treading the grapes, or training the vines, and doing any other work whatsoever, frequently sing. Sailors as well, when rowing do this. Women also while weaving, and when separating a tangled warp on the beam, sometimes individually, at other times all together, sing one particular melody."

In his essay, "The Part Played by Labour in the Transition from Ape to Man", Frederick Engels conjectured that the faculty of speech probably arose as a consequence of communal labour: "The development of labour necessarily helped to bring the members of society closer together by increasing cases of mutual support and joint activity, and by making clear the advantages of this joint activity to each individual. In short, men in the making arrived at the point where they had something to say to each other..."

At about the same time, a nineteenth-century sociologist, Bücher, expressed the view in his *Arbeit und Rhythmus* that speech originated in the act of labour itself, in the chorused grunting necessary to co-ordinate efforts which is the ancestor of the shanty. Thus, it could be said that this form of primitive song actually pre-dates speech, and is the very first form of art.

It was also the very first magic, for what one man could not do alone a group of men could achieve easily, and it would seem logical to ascribe the magical effects to the "song" chanted in unison rather than to the communal effort expended. Much early magic has this sort of rational basis.

The very earliest known representation of a human figure, a prehistoric painting in the cave of Les Trois Frères in the Dordogne, shows a magician wearing antlered headdress, playing on a musical instrument which might be a mouthbow, or it could be a double pipe like the aulos which Plato would ban from his *Republic* and which Aristotle described in his *Politics* as "not a moralising but rather an exciting influence".

Plato preferred the cithara, the stringed instrument which was played by Apollo in his victorious contest with the aulos-wielding

Marsyas, the old fertility god more widely known as Dionysus. According to Robert Graves, the myth of this musical battle dates from the period of Hellenic expansionism. It is from this period that we see the beginnings of a new stream of art music as the expression of the ruling class that emerged out of the old classless community, and the mythical contest is about the struggle between the old Dionysian strain and the new Apollonian music of class society. It is a struggle which has continued to the present day.

Myth says that the Dionysian aulos was first made from stag's bones by the goddess Athene and was believed to have curative properties. Theophrastus said that "persons subject to sciatica would always be free from its attacks if one played the aulos in the Phrygian harmony over the part affected". The Phrygian mode, later known as the Dorian (D to D on the white notes of the piano) under the somewhat confused nomenclature proposed by Glarean in 1547, was indigenous to the Celtic peoples of Galatea in Asia Minor who gave St Paul such trouble during the early days of Christianity. Next to the Ionian (major) mode, the Dorian is one of the most popular in English folk song.

A similar instrument to the aulos, the Arabic double-oboe, the rhaita, is still believed by its practitioners to have medicinal properties, extending even to the cure of bone-fractures. It has been suggested that this wild music, which can be heard in a recording made in North Africa by the late Rolling Stone Brian Jones, in 1968, acts in some way upon the alpha-wave patterns of the brain.

In the hands of the magicians, the aulos became the instrument of the aristocracy, formerly the elected leaders of the old communal clans, but with literacy and the invention of money this primitive class system was not enough. In the sixth century BC the old vestiges of the clans were decisively smashed by Kleisthenes' democratic revolution of the new trading classes.

The music of this revolution was played on the cithara (sometimes incorrectly called the lyre) and it was a music of the head rather than the heart. It was the product of a literate, hierarchical society whose social relations were based on money rather than the mutual help practised within the old tribal families. The old music, which was oral, arose from social relations based on communal ownership of wealth bound up in the earth and the tools with which to till it, and had its roots in even earlier social forms, which seemed disordered to the modern mind. The conflict between literate Apollonian "head" music and oral Dionysian "heart" music has continued throughout history, with Apollo representing the established order, always, even during the flowering of arty acid rock in the sixties.

As the feudalism which had supplanted slave society began itself to decay, a third strain of popular music evolved as the expression of the new class relations, and in many ways acted as a hybrid, parasitical upon the other two. For instance, popular music tended to originate in a written form, and indeed the period of its strongest development dates from the invention of printing, but much of its dissemination tended to be oral. Its forms were often those of art music reduced to cliché, but just as frequently it drew its content from folk culture.

The main distinction of popular music from both the other streams was that its only function was to entertain. We have already seen that folk music was functional, originally serving a magical purpose. The earliest art music was just as functional as folk culture, though the function was different, and has changed throughout history according to which class forces were in the ascendant.

With the growth of class society, the new aristocracy demanded that their bards celebrate their deeds and give their people a sense of history, a unique concept, for humanity had hitherto lived in what George Steiner has disparagingly called "the mindless present". As Tacitus said of the Celtic German bards: "These ancient songs are the only sort of history annals they possess."

Later, as class society became still more stratified, and man moved from slavery into feudalism, the bard had become a minstrel. The decentralised Celtic civilisation had been smashed by the legions everywhere but in Britain, where bardic culture survived until the Norman Conquest, despite the Roman occupation. By then, the Normans were singing metrical "cantilenae" rather than the chanted prose epics of the Celts and Norse aristocrats. When they conquered England their minstrels came with them, and so did their harps, originating from the Apollonian cithara, displacing the native crwth, the true Celtic "harp", which was as often bowed as plucked. Modern offspring of the crwth, like the Eastern European rebec, have a sharply Dionysian sound.

With the decay of feudalism, the minstrels were thrown on to the labour market, often finding employment as "waits", employees of the urban burgesses whose first role was as a sort of police force. But not all of them could aspire to this status, and they scraped a living in the taverns.

To musical historians, the watershed point in the destruction of the minstrel tradition was Simon de Montfort's crusade against the Albigensian heretics of Provence in 1209, the most cataclysmic disaster to strike an established feudalism, though throughout the thirteenth and fourteenth centuries the minstrels were leaving the banqueting rooms of the castles and applying their talents to the quite different needs of the city alehouse.

Since many of their customers would be former peasants driven by the decay of feudalism into the city, they would often cannibalise rural traditions, though usually what they presented was a townsman's view of country life, rather than the authentic article. For instance, the celebrated thirteenth-century *rota* or round, "Sumer Is Icumen In", probably the earliest English popular song we know, is a carefully contrived work, full of stylistic innovations like a six-part canon that were not to be adopted in Continental Europe until much later, and a repetitive drone-like bass burden which is possibly an imitation of the bagpipes. The words are lyrical. Nothing happens except to add a generally pastoral atmosphere: "Groweth seed and bloweth mead, and springeth the wood now... Ewe bleateth after lamb... Well singest thou Cuckoo, nor cease thou never now." (I have modernised the spelling.)

The setting is a familiar one in folk song, but only as a backdrop for the action: "Now the winter is over and summer is come, and the meadows they look so pleasant and gay. I spied a fair maid and sweetly sung she, and her cheeks wore the blossom." So much for the dramatis personae, but before the first verse of this folk song is over the man and the maid have begun conversing. By the end of verse three they are married.

Though this was collected as recently as 1906 in Dorset, the form was already well set by the time of the "Sumer" rota, as we can tell from another thirteenth-century manuscript which contains the oldest known folk ballad, "Judas". It is a pity we do not have a tune for it; the comparison would be interesting. But the text is remarkably different in style from "Sumer Is Icumen In". While the pop song merely records an impression of spring bursting into summer, "Judas" is packed with dramatic narrative. And even in my modernised version, the body rhythms of the original still come through (the early ballads were danced as well as sung: the word "ballad" is etymologically the same as "ballet"). Jesus sends Judas into the town with thirty pieces of silver to buy victuals for the Last Supper and says that on the way he will meet his kinsman. To a certain extent this is reminiscent of the gospel story (Matthew 26: 18) where the names of the disciples are not mentioned individually. But the kinsman he meets is not the owner of the house where they shall meet, as in the Scripture:

> He met with his sister, the sinful woman:
> Judas, then were worthy me to stoned you with stone.
> Judas, then were worthy me to stoned you with stone.
> For the false prophet that thou believest upon.
> *She entices him to sleep in her lap and while he is sleeping the thirty pieces are stolen − the ballad does not say by whom.*

> He tore the hair from his head, that it all flowed with blood:
> The Jews out of Jerusalem supposed that he was mad.

> Forth came the rich Jew that was called Pilatus:
> Wilt thou sell thy Lord, whom they call Jesus?
> I will not sell my Lord for riches of any kind,
> Unless it be for the thirty piece he gave me to mind.

> In Him came our Lord as His apostles sat at meat:
> Why sit ye, apostles, and will ye not eat?
> Why sit ye, apostles, and will ye not eat?
> I am bought and sold today, for to buy our meat.

> Up stood him Judas: Lord, am I that?
> I never heard a single soul speak of you with hate.

The ballad ends with the familiar prophecy that Peter will deny his Lord three times, which also occurs in a better-known religious ballad, "King Herod And The Cock".

That Judas would sell Jesus merely to get back the lost dinner money seems a little far-fetched until one goes into it and finds that we are dealing with one of those very ancient legends that are possibly older than the gospels in the Bible – which were, after all, also orally transmitted epics for many years before they were written down. For instance, the still widely current "Cherry Tree Carol" tells of an event described in the apocryphal gospel of Pseudo-Matthew but unknown to most clergymen.

Similarly, the great ballad scholar Francis James Child has traced the story of "Judas" to reports of a lost writing of the apostle Bartholomew in which the silver was originally coined by Abraham's father and had passed from hand to hand down the generations as "the price of him that was valued, whom they of the children of Israel did value", ending up as the tribute brought to the infant Jesus in Bethlehem by the wise king, Melchior.

This ancient ancestry and continuity over the centuries – in many cases right up to modern times – is in vivid contrast with the constant flux of popular song which has a living existence in people's mouths of about a century at most. Today, nobody sings songs like the "Sumer" rota outside the ranks of early music revivalists, but ballads whose form and attitude to their content is identical with that of "Judas" are still being sung in tradition now.

Indeed, so defined is the form of "Judas", and so like so many other ballads collected over the next five or six centuries, that we may presume it was far from being an isolated example of what was then being sung. Its sacred subject was no doubt what appealed to the friar who presumably noted it down. What of the songs he thought too trivial, or too profane, to preserve? We shall never know. The holy man's interest was probably the content of the ballad he noted rather than its form, and certainly not its music.

In its beginnings, of course, popular music was not such a distinct category as it was to become later, in the heyday of mass literate culture. Composers like Guillaume de Machaut (1300–1377) could produce solemn works like his *Mass for the Coronation of Charles V* as well as over 200 *chansons balladées*. And it is paradoxically true that while a proper recognition of the value of ballad texts was not to dawn upon learned gentlemen until the seventeenth and eighteenth centuries, the new popular culture based upon the printing press seized upon them with both hands.

Many of the earliest printed ballads were clearly from traditional sources, and it is interesting how many of them have magical aspects, often consisting of riddle stories, in which young maidens have to solve puzzles set them by mysterious, seemingly superhuman strangers, or lose their virginity. Four out of the first ten ballads in Child's famous collection of 305 classic archetypes were printed on broadsides. One of them was allegedly written by one Thomas Deloney, though if we compare it with other songs he is known to have composed then it becomes obvious that he must merely have noted it down. Deloney, described by a contemporary as "the balleting silk weaver of Norwich", was one of the new breed of songwriters who poured out songs and snatches to entertain the new middle class of London, satirised by Shakespeare in the character of Autolycus, the balladmonger of *A Winter's Tale*.

Henry Playford's 1707 collection of *Wit and Mirth, or, Pills to Purge Melancholy, being a collection of the best Merry Ballads and Songs, etc. (with airs)* was possibly the first collection of the new popular songs to give them a sort of respectability. Respectability, of course, is not really the right word; for "merry" read bawdy. After the censure of the Puritans, the young intellectual gents of Restoration England took a great joy in the supposed frankness of the songs of common folk. And if traditional songs were not saucy enough, why then, new ones could be written to make matters even more explicit.

These early ancestors of the modern rugby song were re-edited a few years later by Tom D'Urfey (1653–1723), himself a tavern poet and songwriter who was a worthy successor to Deloney. He wrote such popular songs as "The Roast Beef Of Old England" and a broadside parody of "The Froggy And The Mouse". When his critics complained that he wrote doggerel, he stammered out: "The Town may da-da-damn me for a Poet, but they si-si-sing my Songs for all that." His collection had no pretensions of folkloristic scholarship, though songs clearly from tradition could be found alongside what the nineteenth-century novelist, folklorist and critic, the Rev. Sabine Baring-Gould, called "filth of the most revolting description". But D'Urfey deserves some sort of place among the ranks of the early collectors, as does Deloney.

Not all the cheap ballads were folk in origin. Nor were all of them products of the lower classes, for until the growth of the newspaper the customers were mainly the new middle class, and only songs of interest to them, of whatever origin, were reprinted. This fact must colour what we know of traditional song in this period, which is entirely through the medium of the broadside and the ballad book.

The broadside ballad or broadsheet – so called, because it was printed on one side of a single sheet – went into something of a decline in the eighteenth century, though the influence of the street ballad persisted in the work of popular poets like John Gay and William Cowper. But the break-up of the rural communities which was plunging so many country people into the urban sinks of the newly growing industrial society gave the cheap printers a new market in these compulsory proletarians – and, incidentally, provided the publishers with a new source of repertoire.

A.L. Lloyd has described the nineteenth-century broadside as "the greatest influence of print on folksong" and many of the versions of folk songs collected in the past hundred years obviously owe their origin to broadsides. Though it may be true to argue, as he does, that all the versions of "Banks Of Claudy" or "The Dark-Eyed Sailor" that one finds are traceable back to a single, printed source, it may not necessarily follow that the only reason the songs are known is because of print. On the contrary, what probably happened is that, faced with the authority of print for a single version being sold in every market town for miles around, the local singers abandoned their more individual variants of the story. For print imposes conformity. As Gordon Hall Gerould says in *The Ballad of Tradition*: "The circulation of songs in printed texts necessarily dislocated the normal curve of things, since it spread them widely in a fixed form and indicated the melodies by which they should be accompanied. In place of the slow process of dissemination that had been customary, from singer to singer, from older folk to younger, there came in at a single stroke a totally alien process, swift in operation..."

The ballad printers found the old songs a great source of material – though they often labelled them "a new song". One of the most successful of the printers, James Catnach, who set up in 1814 in competition with the already established Johnny Pitts in Seven Dials, sent men round to collect ballads from the singers in the country inns. Perhaps he did this because Pitts warned his own writers of the dreadful consequences of writing for Catsnatch, as they nicknamed him.

As well as ballads, both Catnach and Pitts sold accounts, true and fictional, in prose or verse, of the events of the day, chiefly of murders and executions. These were pinched from the newspapers as often as not, because while the poor could not afford the sevenpence a newspaper cost in 1814 (including fourpence tax) they were willing to fork out a halfpenny for a quarto account of a murder. Catnach's first big success was Weare's murder in 1823, of which he sold the 250,000 sheets he printed in his own shop, and also countless other sheets sub-contracted out to other printers – who were not above printing off a few more and selling them for themselves. For James Bloomfield Rush's murder, the wretched verse-maker only got a paltry shilling (twelve pence), though Catnach's street salesmen are alleged to have sold 2,500,000 at a penny a time.

Strangely, though Rush's story was the all-time broadside best-seller, it did not strike roots down into the tradition like Catnach's "Confession and Execution of William Corder The Murderer of Maria Marten" which sold a mere 1,166,000 copies in 1828. As is so often the case in the folk process, in which stories are refined down to their basic essentials, not all the sixteen couplets of Catnach's sheet, allegedly written by Corder himself, have survived in tradition. When Joseph Taylor went to the studio of the Gramophone Company in 1908 to sing the song – with twelve other songs from his repertoire – he had only three verses, which compress the narrative to the murder and omit the "take warning by me" moralising which was customary in such broadsheets:

If you'll meet me at the Red Barn
As sure as I have life
I will take you to Ipswich town
And there make you my wife.

This lad went home and fetched his gun,
His pickaxe and his spade,
He went unto the Red Barn
And there he dug her grave.

With her heart so light she thought no harm
To meet her love did go.
He murdered her all in the barn
And he laid her body low.

The theme of the pregnant girl who is murdered and buried by her lover is far older than Maria's tragic fate; the American ballads,

"Pretty Polly" and "Omie Wise", are remarkably similar to Catnach's ballad in economy and horror. Possibly it is this similarity to one of the great elemental themes of classic balladry which commended it to the folk, or perhaps the fact that it sang so well to one of the most popular tunes in the English tradition, known variously in its different versions as "Come All Ye Faithful Christians" or "Dives And Lazarus" or "Star Of The County Down". The tune was also used by Taylor for another of his songs, "Briggs Fair", which so took the fancy of Frederick Delius that he used it as the basis for his "English Rhapsody", *Brigg Fair*.

The abolition of the Stamp Tax on newspapers removed the main attraction of the old broadsides, which in any case were being revealed in all their inaccuracy and untopicality by the new immediacy given to newspapers by their improved news-gathering resources, especially after the invention of the electric telegraph. As a consequence, the role of the ballad as song, rather than the fallible narrative of an allegedly true event, shifted from Seven Dials just up the road to Denmark Street off the new Charing Cross Road, by a strange accident of geography. For it was there that Lawrence Wright, who had sold songs in Leicester Market, founded his London business on the money he made from a ballad whose copyright he had bought for £5 from an itinerant street singer.

The song, "Don't Go Down The Mine, Daddy", was a hit because publication in 1910 happened to coincide with a disaster in a Whitehaven pit in which 136 men lost their lives; Wright sold a million copies in three weeks and thus raised the capital to rent a Denmark Street basement for £1 a week, the first publisher to do so, but far from the last. Until very recently, when urban redevelopment and rocketing rents scattered many of them, most London music publishers clustered in and around the street, which was known, deservedly, as Britain's Tin Pan Alley.

It would be interesting to conjecture who was the original author of the maudlin song which Wright purchased so cheaply; perhaps he was one of the last of the old balladmongers who had such a thriving business in Seven Dials only fifty years before. Certainly it is interesting that in the pop biz the name for a sentimental song is a ballad, though elsewhere the word's true meaning has always been of a narrative, whether folk or otherwise.

By whatever means, however, the form of British popular music publishing was set for the next forty-four years and was not to change, basically, until 1954 when a young Glaswegian heard Huddie Ledbetter (Leadbelly) sing a fragment about an American railroad, re-recorded it as "The Rock Island Line" and sold 360,000 copies in Britain on the basis of just a couple of airplays, going on to sell a further 700,000 in America. Electronics had entered the scene, and popular music had become almost entirely oral.

COLLECTING – APOLLO DISSECTS DIONYSUS

Though in classical times and the early Middle Ages there had been a clear awareness of the differences between folk and art music, the emergence of popular music tended to confuse the issue – and much of the present-day confusion about which is which stems from this early failure to distinguish between the true composed song and the song ripped off from the community by a cheapjack printer because no one else could lay a better claim to it.

If "The Fair Flower Of Northumberland" is claimed to be the composition of Deloney, and if it is clearly a narrative ballad of a folk type, telling the familiar folk story of the Outlandish Knight who carries a maiden off to the north and is foiled by her, and drowned, does that mean that all his other creations are folk songs (especially since we have learned from the example of people like Woody Guthrie that it is possible for the identity of a folk poet to be known)? And if all the obviously traditional songs in *Pills to Purge Melancholy* are anonymous creations, appearing to emanate from what one might call for want of a more scientific term "the common people", does that mean that all anonymous songs of common origin must be folk songs?

Posed like that, of course, the obvious answers are no and no. But the question would never arise if we did not have to get our understanding of the songs of the period from the printed page, tempting us to regard them as things in a state of stasis (or possibly decay from a once bright original) instead of communications from one generation to another which develop and change as the outside parameters of the message also change and develop.

But the medium of print conditioned and pre-determined the thinking of the collectors, for far from being Dionysian revivalists, they were Apollonians to a man, literate gentlemen attempting to explain to themselves, and each other, this strange phenomenon they had stumbled across, these relics of a bygone age among the lower classes living under their rule, working in their factories, attending their churches, and later even studying in their schools and voting in their elections. Not until folklorists began to use recordings did they begin to appreciate the living nature of the material they were dissecting, and even then only a few did so. Even today, folklorists have been known to express the view that it is only back in the study, and not in the field, that the true significance of their collection can be assessed.

In this sense, the far from scholarly purpose of the compilers of *Pills*, though it tended to confuse the distinction between folk and popular, as we have seen, was closer to the Dionysian spirit. Similarly, the first records of instrumental folk music we have must be extracted from John Playford's *English Dancing Master: or Plaine and easie rules for the dancing of Country Dances, with the tune to each dance*, which was published during the Commonwealth in 1650 – an interesting commentary on the alleged hostility to music of the Puritans. Like D'Urfey in his chosen field, Playford did not distinguish very carefully between courtly rustic dances and the more vigorous dances of the remnants of the folk community, but, like *Pills*, the *English Dancing Master* was an important milestone in the growth of the literate man's appreciation of the unlettered tradition.

Even more important to us now, and possibly the very beginning of folkloristic scholarship, was the work of the anonymous enthusiast who started compiling a manuscript collection of ballads at about the same time. The collection was found a century later by an eighteenth-century antiquary, Bishop Percy, being used by the maidservants of his friend Humphrey Pitt to light his fires. Percy rescued them and, rather heavily edited, they became the basis for his *Reliques of Ancient English Poetry*, published in 1765 with an apologetic preface: "In a polished age like the present, I am sensible that many of these reliques of antiquity will require great allowances to be made for them. Yet have they, for the most part, a pleasing simplicity, and many artless graces, which in the opinion of no mean critics have been thought to compensate for the want of higher beauties, and, if they do not dazzle the imagination, are frequently found to interest the heart. To atone for the rudeness of the more obsolete poems, each volume concludes with a few modern attempts in the same kind of writing..."

In that preface, Percy set the tone for later attitudes to folk song, many of them still persistent today. The emphasis upon antiquity, the reference to the simplicity and artlessness of the contents, and the consideration of them as poems rather than songs continued to hamstring folk-song studies for at least the next century. Only in the past fifty years or so has the music received adequate consideration, and even today the intimate relationship of texts and melodies is not sufficiently well understood. There are too many who refuse to consider the realities of folk culture today, compared with its alleged past glories, and most of all we still hear far too much about the simplicity of the folk technique.

This was excusable when all we had for study were the notes on the stave, for however basic printed music may be to the development of art music, it is a very blunt tool for analysing the infinite melodic shifts of the folk singer, who will employ techniques such as microtonality and polytonality which the art musician has only just begun to discover. (Or, rather, re-discover, for the techniques are ancient, as any student of aboriginal music will tell you.) But with the employment of recording techniques in the field, the true complexity of the folk singer's craft should have become obvious to anyone prepared to listen.

To be fair to the folklorists, they began using recording machines as soon as they became available to them. Some of the very first gramophone records produced by the inventor of the disc method of recording, Emile Berliner, were field recordings of American folk songs. Bartok and other Eastern European folklorists were quick to seize upon recording machines and in Britain both Cecil Sharp and Percy Grainger made early use of them.

It is to Grainger, in particular, that we owe a very carefully documented analysis of the complex craft of one of his informants, George Wray of Lincolnshire. Grainger bought himself an Edison cylinder recording machine shortly after his first visit to Lincolnshire in 1905, and in the *Folk Song Journal* he was able, after playing through his recordings of Wray several times, to publish the most accurate transcription possible within the limitations of conventional notation of one of his songs.

In the first verse of the song, the time signature changes six times: from 5/8 to 3/8 to 5/8 to 6/8 to 7/8 to 3/16 to 7/8 and to 4/4. The next verse begins in 9/8. In addition to these incredibly frequent time changes, which give the song a lively inner pulse, the subtle interplay of rhythms has to be conveyed by such written instructions as "slightly slower" over the fourth, fifth and sixth notes of the song, triplet and couplet marks over specific trios or pairs of notes, and so on. And that was just the rhythm. The musical pitching was equally complex – not because Wray was singing "out of tune" but because the melody he was utilising was not in one of the scales of Pythagoras which trained musicians demand as the norm, though they are so far from being immutable law that a piano tuned to strict Pythagorean principles actually sounds truly out of tune. In addition to these complexities within one rendering of a song must also be considered the fact that, like a jazz soloist, few good folk singers perform a melody exactly the same way two consecutive times. Simple? Not a bit of it! And the "last relics"? What Percy described as "select remains" of an old culture in his preface is always being pronounced dead, but the obsequies were too previous, and like Jack in the old mumming plays the tradition springs up alive again soon after.

Even so scientific a folklorist as Cecil Sharp declared with scarcely any qualification in his *English Folk Songs: Some Conclusions* (1907), still probably the most important publication on the subject nearly seventy years later, that "In less than a decade... English folk singing will be extinct. I have learned that it is, as a rule, only a waste of time to call upon singers under the age of sixty. Their songs are nearly all modern..."

When Sharp wrote that, the singer who was recognised until his death in 1971 as probably the greatest stylist in the English tradition, Harry Cox, was only in his twenties. In fact, he was not to be discovered by the Irish composer E.J. Moeran until long after Sharp's decade was up. Between then and his death, well past the age of eighty, he had supplied over a hundred songs to various collectors, including a treasure like the magnificent "Betsy The Serving Maid" in

5/4 time, a song which he said had been in his family for 200 years, but has rarely been collected in this country.

In fact, obsessive antiquarianism obscures many folklorists' view of what is happening to the folk tradition today. It is a circular argument: by definition, folk culture is the fossilised remains of an ancient culture in a state of increasing degeneracy as the centuries go by, incapable of withstanding the effects of industrialism, education, literacy and mass communication. Therefore, anything which survives these assaults cannot be folk culture, however much it appears to fulfil the other criteria.

This is a familiar problem for anthropologists (and folklore is really only a specialised branch of anthropology), this seeing only what you have been looking for, and excluding anything which does not fit conveniently into your preconceived definition. The real danger is that the folk, not being such simple savages as they are thought to be, quickly become aware of what the researcher is looking for. Recently I was recording in Suffolk and, before he sang, my informant said disparagingly: "What shall I sing? The song I want to sing, you probably wouldn't want to record." I assured him that what he wanted to sing was what I wanted to record, so he gave me a delicious parody of "Among My Souvenirs", itself a variant of the well-known theme of a new-wed husband who discovers that his bride is well-nigh entirely artificial, sung in an earlier age to the tune of "After The Ball":

Last week my honeymoon started:
I like a fool took a wife
But after the guests had departed
I got the shock of my life:
Out came her big glass eye
Her false teeth on the sly
She gently placed them down upon the chiffonier.
She then unscrewed her leg
And hung it on a peg
And oh my eyes were filled with many a bitter tear.
Her beautiful golden hair
She hung upon the chair
And what was left of her
Slipped in between the blankets.
I looked at her and said

I am not coming to bed
I'd rather sleep instead
Among my souvenirs...

THE INSTRUMENTS OF TRADITION

According to Lloyd, legend has it that when Cecil Sharp was collecting in the Southern Appalachians during World War I – coming back with over 1,500 songs, many of them invaluable versions of songs lost to the living tradition in England for centuries – the people sent messengers on ahead of him warning their friends to hide away their banjos and guitars, for Sharp's aversion to accompanied folk song became clear to them as soon as he started work. As a result, Sharp's treasured belief that the English – and Anglo-American – folk-song tradition was largely an unaccompanied one was undisturbed, thanks to the tact of the folk. And the illusion lingers on in the folk revival today; though the popularisation of unaccompanied singing in the folk clubs helped free us of a whole range of unsuitable accompaniments, from the concert-style pianoforte to the wildly thrashed swing guitar, it has held back a really careful understanding of the instrumental tradition, which would have allowed the self-styled purists to welcome the electric guitar as appropriately Dionysian for folk music, and to reject the classically fingered acoustic Spanish guitar as an Apollonian imposition.

The banjo favoured by the Appalachian folk came originally from Arabia, via the slave trade out of Africa, and as played in Sharp's time was distinguished by the constant ringing of the fifth drone string which makes nonsense of conventional tonality, continuing to sound the note of G, even when the fingers fret the chord of F.

The prevalence of the drone in folk music is an interesting example of the way in which the folk will constantly revert to stylistic type, despite what the musical technologists may have put into their hands in the form of instrumentation. Apart from obvious examples like the various kinds of bagpipe, the Appalachian mountain dulcimer, the Jew's harp and the country fiddle, whose practitioners are constantly and deliberately brushing their bows across neighbouring strings to create a drone effect, the drone reappears in a number of unlikely guises: the way pub pianists keep the loud pedal down all the time so that the strings continue to ring long after the fingers have moved on to new notes, making the piano more like its ancestor, the hammered dulcimer or psaltery, the way melodeon-players will sound the tonic and dominant chords over and over with the left hand regardless of what melody is being played with the right, and, in more modern terms, the popularity of open-tuned guitars among electric folk like Sandy Denny, in which an unfretted string rings through all the changes like a true drone.

There are grounds for believing that the double aulos was originally played with one pipe supplying a drone, the other the melody. We have already seen how the cithara ousted the aulos as the accepted instrument with the growth of class society, but of course piped music continued as part of the folk tradition. And it was not merely the similarity of shape which made the pipe a male sexual symbol, cropping up in all sorts of licentious contexts from then to now, for bawdy originally had a magical or religious significance that was never to be bred out of the folk entirely. One of the magical tasks allocated to the hero of "The Elfin Knight" made clear the connection between wind instruments and agricultural, as well as human, fecundity: "And ye maun plow't wi' your blawing horn/And ye maun saw't wi' pepper corn".

The only representative of the pipe family widely played today in the English tradition is the tin whistle, but there were flourishing wind bands in Britain until about a hundred years ago. The instruments included the flute, clarinet, bassoon, trombone, serpent, bass horn, keyed bugle and hautboy or oboe, known in its earlier days as the shawm or waits' pipe, and a direct descendant of the aulos, plus strings such as the viola and cello. In 1870 the band of Brightling church in Sussex included a banjo, made popular in England by the blackface minstrels, while five others included drums, two included accordions and John Robinson, parish clerk of Tyringham-cum-Filgrave in Bucks doubled on clarinet and concertina.

The most famous church bands are those in the works of Thomas Hardy, who had an awareness of the realities of folk culture unequalled by any author, probably, since Shakespeare's time. His story of a band playing the dance tune "Devil Among The Tailors" at evening service by mistake is far from fanciful, for their Sunday work was but the crown of the week's music. And the music was closer to dance music than the hymns we know from today's solemn services: an analysis of nine tune books used between 1750 and 1820 shows 389 out of the 840 tunes were in 3/4 time (46 per cent) while only 14 out of 275 or less than 5 per cent of the tunes in the first edition of *Hymns Ancient and Modern* were in the same, danceable measure.

Meanwhile, the dance music of the English countryside was played on the pipe and tabor – known more popularly as the whittle-and-dub – a three-holed pipe played with a little drum by the same musician in a manner described by Thoinot Arbeau, the sixteenth-century French dancing master in his *Orchesography* of 1588: "And the musician plays whatever songs he fancies on the said flute, holding it in his left hand while supporting the tabor by the same arm." The instrument is said by Frances Galpin to have probably come to England from France about 700 years ago, though it may have been more indigenous. A pre-historic fipple flute similar to the "whittle" has been found in Monmouthshire able to play the four notes of the Dorian tetrachord – the same as the "Phrygian harmony" which, played on the aulos, was alleged to be a cure for sciatica.

The pipe was, as we have seen, a familiar male sexual symbol, but then the drum is a female symbol, so perhaps the two played together became a mimetic sex act – as were many of the dances for which it provided the accompaniment, especially the Morris. By the middle of the nineteenth century, a street musician told Mayhew that no tabors were played in London, though according to a speaker to the Society of Morris Dancers the pipe and drum were still heard all over Oxfordshire as late as the mid-1880s. Mayhew's informant played the pan pipes, an equally ancient instrument (Plato's syrinx), which is interesting, because it was a modern successor of the pan pipes which ousted the three-hole pipe as the favourite instrument of the English musician.

By the end of the century, melodeons were being imported into Britain from Germany at the rate of 25,000 a year and it is easy to agree with Lloyd that there was nothing particularly "traditional" about them then. The combination of free reed and bellows was unknown before they were put together by Friedrich Buschmann in 1822 and the success of the melodeon – or "music", as the country people called them – looks like the triumph of the German genius for cheap toys, instruments and light engineering, coupled with the brief period of rural prosperity at the turn of the century. Harry Cox, who was a competent fiddler and melodeon-player as well as a brilliant singer, recalled to Peter Kennedy: "We had a decent home, we were always welcome there. We crawled in there. We were always happy. When we got a little older and I got a music, and my brother and sister grew up, we used to have many an evening singing and musics and that."

But if, as Mervyn Plunkett has suggested, we consider instruments by their "mode of use" rather than by the technology of their sounding mechanism, so that the violin played as a fiddle is seen as a successor to the rebec and the bowed crwth, and the vamped pub piano the successor to the hammered crwth, psaltery or dulcimer, the melodeon (and its cousin, the concertina) goes back in folk tradition to the portative organ which came into Europe from Byzantium in the eighth century, and through that to the bundle of reeds tied into a cylinder which the Greeks called the syrinx and which in its more familiar trapezoid shape is still called the pan pipes, proclaiming by its link with the great goat god who was the prototype for the witches' horned devil that it was part of the same Dionysian tradition.

So the modernity of the concertina and melodeon does not prove that the folk will play any new thing that comes along; but it does illustrate the way in which they will adapt whatever they find to the needs of the tradition. What are these criteria? We can observe certain characteristics of folk instruments: the penetrating, "vocalised" sound, the use of drones, the adaptation of instruments intended for simple major or minor scales into the unique scales of the folk tradition (which are even more complex than the seven in Glarean's system, still used by most folklorists today), the way in which the mechanics of the instrument are utilised to become an intrinsic part of its sound, so the wheezing in-and-out of the Anglo concertina, which plays a different note as it is pulled out or pushed in, fits more happily into the complex rhythms of the English tradition than the legato tones of Wheatstone's English concertina, playing the same note whether pulled out or pushed in. Dionysian.

The art tradition, in contrast, tries to "purify" the tone of the instrument, to remove it from the voice of which it was originally an imitation and remove it from a human context. (The same process is then turned upon vocal technique so that the communicative content of the voice is gradually removed and it becomes another musical instrument, dealing in abstractions.) Apollonian. The remarkable thing is the way in which this perversion of the instruments' original function is presented as the "correct" way they should be played. When jazz, the first folk-based popular music to be made known throughout the world by use of the medium of electronics, reintroduced the Western world to vocalised styles of playing, the timbre of the New Orleans clarinet, cornet and trombone excited exclamations of wonder wherever they were heard, though if the fashionable young of Paris, London and Amsterdam had bothered to listen to the country musicians outside the cities in which they lived, they would have found the same characteristics at their own back door. Later we shall see how electronics tended to do this, returning people to their own traditions by very circuitous routes which presented what should have been familiar as exotic.

The spread of jazz across the world forces us to take the story of the development of instrumental techniques into a wider context than Europe alone and to see how the polite fingering of the Apollonian acoustic guitar became the howl of the Dionysian electric instrument.

DIONYSUS REBORN

Just when it seemed that the Dionysian strain in Western culture was about to be licked for good, when the triumph of the industrial state was being taken for granted, even by its harshest critics, Marx and Engels, when the last kick of the folk community against the factory system had resulted in harsh sentences of transportation for many Luddites and execution for some, when the new folklorists were really getting down to the job of recording what they were almost justified in considering the last vestiges of a dying culture, Dionysus suddenly came back to life. And, as with so many of the revitalising sources that have prevented Western civilisation from perishing out of sheer boredom with itself in the past hundred years, the revivifying spark came out of Africa.

The conquest of Africa took place when the great non-literate civilisations of the Dark Continent had not developed, technologically, to a level where art music and Apollonian culture generally could serve any useful class function, though there was a very strongly

128

entrenched aristocracy in power. And when the Africans were taken to the New World as slaves, the neglect of their new overlords had the accidental result of preserving the cultural and social patterns of the homeland, so even today it is possible to recognise in the call-and-response vocal pattern of preacher and congregation in a Chicago storefront church similarities to the choral patterns of West African tribes who have never left home.

Also, the impact of African culture, and especially African music, came at a time when the great strength of the industrial state was merely an indication that it had reached its zenith, and only decline could lie ahead. In this period, and especially when electronics had supplied the technological possibility of a new kind of social system superficially similar but radically different in essence from Marx's industrially based socialism, oral cultures that had survived the 3,000-year rule of Apollonian class society began to have a new relevance.

In the search for a cultural equivalent of these developments, modern man has found a useful analogue in the culture of Africa – as well as, to a lesser extent, the other non-typographical cultures of India and Asia – and also in "the Africa within", the so long suppressed Dionysian culture of folk music. This is why, though none of the typographically based folk revivals from Percy to Sharp had much impact on the masses – and, by putting folk music into the school curriculum, Sharp did the cause of revival positive harm, identifying what use in very real terms a subversive culture with the established, Apollonian order – the post-war revival of Lomax, MacColl, Seeger and Lloyd became a very powerful part of the new popular culture being created on the basis of electronics. For like the somewhat analogous rock'n'roll movement of the sixties, with which ultimately it was to live in a sort of symbiosis of which the subject of this book is the interface, the post-war folk revival of the fifties would have been impossible without electronics, without the accuracy of the small portable tape recorder which replaced Sharp's fallible notebook and pencil as a tool for collectors, without the medium of the LP microgroove record and the FM radio station to transmit the hitherto closely guarded secrets of the ethnomusicological elite into the home of everyone prepared to listen.

But all this was to come later. The music the slaves took from America was largely unaccompanied, not because Africa was without instrumental traditions but because they were not allowed the luxury of taking private possessions with them. In fact, what little we know of early African music indicates that its particular richness was in rhythm instruments and it was these which the slaves constructed as soon as they could. African music is polyrhythmic, in which drums played in apparently different tempi establish elaborate cross-rhythms with each other. But a pulse that Western folklorists call "metronomic" in its regularity is always implicit, and it is this feature, the cross-rhythms played across a metronomic pulse or beat, which gives all African derived music, however far from its source, its character. This has got nothing to do with the tyranny of bar lines, of course, which are the creation of visually orientated art music, the product of printed music. The concept of the twelve-bar blues is the ethnologist's attempt to systematise what he hears in terms of his musicological, Apollonian training; many solo blues artists find thirteen- and fourteen-bar blues quite congenial.

The European folk tradition, however, was much freer, though it is doubtful if it always had been so. At an earlier stage in its development, no doubt it was as "metronomic" as African music, but as it freed itself from its association with work and dance, it became much less so. But today the two rhythmic traditions, the ancient, free tradition of Europe and the younger, more metronomic tradition of Africa confront each other whenever a young English traditionalist sings a traditional tune. It is instructive to compare Peter Bellamy's singing of "Pretty Betsy The Serving Maid" with that of Harry Cox, whose version provided the inspiration for Bellamy's. Both could be described as being in 5/4, but while Cox adapts his rhythm to the flow of his narrative so that the actual tempo is shifting constantly and the bar lines cease to have any significance, Bellamy's is clearly 5/4 throughout – actually, alternate bars of 3/4 and 2/4, for Bellamy, like most of us, has been so over-exposed to the simpler time signatures that he tends to break any more complex tempo into more basic constituents, as for instance a jazz musician like Don Ellis will break down a number of his own composition in 7/16 into 2-2-3 when he is phrasing an extempore solo – and with Bellamy the pulse is always explicit. This is not to say that Bellamy is not a fine and sensitive singer but merely to recognise a musicological fact of life resulting from the fact that the contemporary English folk-song revival is rooted in the jazz and blues clubs of the forties and fifties, a fact which Bellamy himself recognised when he recorded a Robert Johnson blues on the last album of The Young Tradition, of which he was then a member.

The other important characteristic of black African music when it first arrived in North America was that it was entirely melodic rather than harmonic. Western harmony, like its wooden tempi and rhythmic simplicity, results from the visual emphasis placed upon art music by the invention of music printing, in which vertical relationships of notes became more important than horizontal sequences of melody. It is not unusual for several voices to sing, apparently in "harmony", in melodic traditions but the resultant polyphony is heard as sequences of notes in individual, interdependent lines, running horizontally, rather than in vertically divided chords.

Another feature of melodic tradition is that there are a multitude of possible scales while a harmonic tradition results in such simplification that to most people there are only two scales today, the major and the minor, though the latter actually has a slightly different sequence when played descending than ascending, a vestige of earlier, more complex systems.

As the more privileged – because musically more talented – black slaves were taught Western instruments so they could entertain their masters, the world heard a phenomenon now so familiar that today it is hardly remarked upon, the attempt to play melodic African scales on instruments that were the creation of the literate, harmonic tradition. The most obvious aspect of this is still the much-discussed "blue" notes of the blues, notes which sound as if they should be played on the cracks between the keys of the piano, as someone once said – an apt simile, because while with the customary agility of the folk artist, black musicians found it possible to play blues on the piano, with its rigidly fixed notes, there could not be a less congenial instrument for folk music. In Britain, the piano's popularity as a folk instrument results from its being played rhythmically, rather than melodically, as black musicians do.

The Africans did bring one instrument with them, the Arabian banjar, which was one side-benefit from the Arab involvement in the

West African slave trade. Few examples of black banjo playing have survived into the age of recorded sound, with the exception of Gus Cannon's jug-band playing, which is obviously something of a digression from the mainstream of black cultural development, and today the banjo, with its fifth string drone which was added after it came to America, is a predominantly white instrument. Possibly the playing of Dock Boggs, who sings in a very "black" fashion, is a clue to what African American banjo playing must have been like, and if so it is hardly surprising to find that it is melodic rather than harmonic: indeed the F#CGAD tuning of Boggs's banjo, miscalled by some musicologists "modal" tuning because it is used to accompany tunes in folk modes far from the conventional major or minor, would be hard to play in any other fashion.

Of course, there has always been a keen interplay between white and black culture on the American continent, in spite of what the bigots of white supremacy or ethnomusicological purity may urge to the contrary, though it must be admitted that the black man has usually given more than he has taken. To hear Huddie Ledbetter sing a Western European ritual ballad like "The Hangman's Tree" to an ostinato twelve-string guitar accompaniment which brings to mind the polyrhythms of African drums, is to hear a rare hybrid in which white and black influences are almost equally balanced. The metronomic regularity of the rhythms against which the Carter Family set their free-ranging vocal harmonies, the jazzy rhythms of bluegrass below the high lonesome sound of the gospel-tinged voices singing the words, even the melodic scales of the Appalachian mountain folk which most folklorists believe to be survivals of European modes in a remarkable state of preservation – all these, in my opinion, represent an African influence long before the worldwide acceptance of jazz and its successors, rock, reggae and the rest.

Before African Americans took it up, the guitar had had little to do with folk music, despite Ewan MacColl's advocacy of its folk ancestry. Henry Mayhew interviewed a street musician who had played the guitar on the streets of London many years previously but we have no information as to *what* or *how* he played, the important things for a musicologist. At that time the guitar was an instrument for genteel ladies.

LeRoi Jones has suggested that African Americans took up the instrument because of its ability to produce vocalised melody and certainly its subsequent development has continued in this direction. He wrote in his interesting but somewhat flawed *Blues People* in 1963: "When Primitive or country blues did begin to be influenced by instruments, it was the guitar that had the most effect on the singers... the blues widened the range of the instrument, too. Blues guitar was not the same as classical or 'legitimate' guitar: the strings had to make vocal sounds, to imitate the human voice and its eerie cacophonies...

As LeRoi Jones put it, "When the Negro finally did take up the brass instruments for strictly instrumental blues or jazz, the players still persisted in singing in the 'breaks'. This could be done easily in the blues tradition with the call-and-response form of blues."

In pursuit of vocalised guitar sound, the technology of guitar-making was developed: the instrument's belly got bigger and fan-strutting was employed inside to give it a bigger sound. The Dobro wooden-bodied and National steel-bodied guitars produced by Ed and Rudy Dopera between 1923 and 1941 allowed white and black musicians to produce notes by sliding a steel bar up and down the strings, imitating the melisma of the human voice. But the need produced the technology: many years before the Doperas made their first Dobro a white boy called Jimmie Tarleton had started using a bottleneck to stop the strings of his guitar, using a comb to raise the strings from the fingerboard. Later, Hawaiian guitarists showed him how to use a steel.

In actual fact, the first electric guitars were Hawaiian, like Gibson's aluminium-bodied EH-120 – though Gibson technicians had been working on electric instruments twenty years earlier, showing their first revolutionary models, including an electric double bass designed by Lloyd Loar, in 1924. Gibson were not to get into proper electrics until the end of the war, with their ES-350, but the early influence of Hawaiian music, coming into rock by way of the Western swing bands of pre-war Nashville, was acknowledged by Chuck Berry, who renamed his version of Floyd Smith's "Guitar Blues" as "Blues For Hawaiians". Smith was a leading steel guitarist of his day.

Quite apart from the use of slide techniques, the acoustic instrument was reaching for vocalised sounds that were to become truly possible only with electricity. Charles Keil, in *Urban Blues*, has pointed out the way in which the single-string playing of a blues pioneer like Scrapper Blackwell led to the horn-like electric music of the white Texan Charlie Christian in the Benny Goodman swing band: it is interesting that the black musician most bluesmen cite as the strongest influence on the development of first amplified and then electric guitar, T-Bone Walker, was also a Texan.

Apart from the Hawaiians, the earliest electric guitars were merely amplified with contact microphones, and the real development of vocalised sound came with the invention of the true electric guitar, in which the metal strings vibrating within the magnetic field of the pick-up created pure electrical impulses electronically much as a microphone or a gramophone pick-up cartridge does. The electric guitar could "sustain" a note long after the last overtones of an acoustic instrument would have died away so soft that even the most sensitive mike could not pick them up. As Keil says: "B.B. King's expressive playing – hit a note, hold it, bend it, quiver it, and slide to the next note – would be impossible without this technical assistance." B.B.'s "Lucille", which makes all this possible, is a solid-body electric such as Gibson introduced in 1952. With the invention of the wah-wah pedal, which altered the overtone frequencies of the note so that the instrument could almost talk, the task of vocalising guitar had reached its present level of advancement.

Put like that, of course, it is hard to see why anyone should be opposed to the electric guitar, especially in blues, where it obviously plays a role consistent with the adoption of the acoustic instrument by black musicians in the first place. But when most European critics (including, I must admit it, myself) first came across the electric guitar in the hands of Muddy Waters during a European tour in the early sixties, we greeted the sound with hostility. This was based partly upon ignorance, for what we knew of the blues was gained from recordings made in the pre-electric era, partly because of a fear of "commercialism", which seemed a greater danger then, when the moribund nature of print-based pop culture was not so apparent as it is now, but also because the very act of criticism is part of the Apollonian analytic tradition, to which the acoustic guitar is naturally more congenial. The Dionysian howl of Muddy's electric guitar sounded less subtle to us than his older, acoustic playing—it wasn't, but the sheer volume and the heavy rhythm'n'blues rhythm section deafened us to the new complexities of what he was doing. Today, the electric guitar is probably the most widely played folk instrument in the world, certainly in the Western world.

So if it has a long and respectable pedigree going back to the Dionysian howl of the original aulos, is there anything else that might make the electric guitar and its associated instruments unsuitable for performing folk material in any way that is relevant to its traditions and continued survival today?

For what makes a music folk is not only how it is played (the style) nor what is played (the repertoire) and is certainly nothing to do with age, anonymity or any of the other shibboleths of the orthodox folklorist: it is the social circumstances in which it is played, the relations between the artists and audience (if, indeed, they can be distinguished in that way) and the relation between performer, listener and the material performed.

To examine how electric folk answers to these criteria − which, ultimately, decide whether it is to be considered as something more than just another form of pop culture parasitical upon the culture of the folk community − it is necessary to compare it with other mass musical movements with a folk base.

FOLK, POP AND THE ELECTRIC AESTHETIC

Though there may be disagreements as to its value, it is almost universally accepted that something has happened to popular music since 1950 and that the change has to do with electricity.

To the lover of folk music, the influence of the folk revival which immediately preceded − but did not at first directly inspire − the rock'n'roll explosion of the fifties is discernible at all sorts of levels, from the wider range of subjects the post-Dylan songwriter now has at his fingertips, to the direct use of traditional repertoire by groups like Steeleye Span and Alan Stivell. There has also been the attempt to create specifically national forms of rock, drawing upon traditions which may not be "folk" in the narrowest sense − The Band's dredgings of American history in songs like "The Night They Drove Old Dixie Down", The Kinks' relation to the music hall, The Who's connection with the mod culture of Shepherds Bush so successfully commercialised in Carnaby Street − an example of how age is not the sole criterion of a viable tradition, for pop culture already has its traditions and even its nostalgias.

But the status of The Who, at least in the early days, was not divorced from their mod audience in the way of most entertainers, and Jon Landau has suggested that the significant thing about rock in the sixties was its analogy with folk music: "Rock, the music of the sixties, was a music of spontaneity. It was a folk music – it was listened to and made by the same group of people. It did not come out of a New York office building where people sit and write what they think other people want to hear. It came from the life experience of the artists and their interaction with an audience that was roughly the same age." (*It's Too Late to Stop Now*, p. 40.)

If true, this estimation may be something rather more to the point than Lloyd's merging of all cultures, art and pop and folk, Oriental and Occidental, ancient and modern, into One (acculturated) Music, and may in fact suggest that Broonzy's "never heard a horse sing" evasion is acquiring new relevance, as all musics strive to become folk in type. For while mass communications in the form of print may have had a stultifying effect upon folk culture, electronic mass media have had the opposite result, closer to (though not identical with) the oral process.

The extraordinary diversity of the modern folk scene, in which doing your own thing under the blanket permissiveness of being part of what is described as the "folk process" has become so much the rule that it is almost a new heresy to suggest that original texts, tunes and interpretations are worthy of any respect at all, can be contrasted directly with the conformism that spread one version of "The Dark-Eyed Sailor" the length and breadth of the land as the result of the sale of printed broadsides in the nineteenth century.

Our folk revival is in such a continued state of flux, however, and its ultimate effects upon the state of our native traditional culture, if any, so much in the balance, that a clearer contrast with the effects of the nineteenth-century broadside might well be the first and still, to my mind, most sensational folk-based pop music of the electric age, the American "hillbilly" string bands of the twenties whose records sold by the million and whose music is regarded today with peculiar reverence by many American revivalists like Mike Seeger and Tom Paley, who appear to treat it as a kind of musical fossil rather than as a fertile and creative source for all that is good in American country music, and thence of today's rock'n'roll.

It is important to realise that the sharp division between written popular music and oral folk music which began to split European popular culture in two soon after the invention of printing, becoming almost schizophrenic in its effect towards the end of the nineteenth century, had not yet struck so deep in America. This was mainly because in Europe, industrialism preceded the development of electronics, so that the medium of mass expression had to be print, while industrialisation and the spread of an electronically based popular culture across the American continent went hand in hand. The black-face minstrel and medicine shows were different from the great tradition of oral balladry that Sharp had uncovered; but they were not so far removed that one couldn't borrow from the other. And even more important, the borrowings did not become frozen in that form so that the living, growing process of variation and selection could not continue, as had happened in Europe.

It is amazing to consider that the records of this traditional and near-traditional music sold in the sort of numbers that we have come to associate with the new pop of the post-Beatles era. And a lot of the songs they recorded were quite ancient. A quick check through the catalogue shows, alongside the modern products, ballads of European origin like "Young Hunting" (number 68 in Professor Child's numbering system), "The House Carpenter" (number 243 in Child, where it is entitled "The Daemon Lover"), "Drunkards' Special" (Child 274, better known as "Our Goodman", and a British charts success in the sixties for the Irish revivalist group, The Dubliners, as "Seven Drunken Nights"), "The Old Lady and the Devil" (Child 278, "The Devil And The Farmer's Wife") and "Little Sir Hugh" (Child 155).

This latter song about a murder, alleged to have been committed as part of a Jewish ritual in Lincoln, England in 1255, was recorded by Nelstone's Hawaiians in 1930; it does not appear in Sharp's *English Folk Songs from the Southern Appalachians*, nor is it on any of the published recordings in the Archive of American Folk Song set up as part of the Library of Congress in 1928. In 1929, the brief period of post-war prosperity came to an end with the Wall Street crash, and things got much tougher. Music became a weapon in the struggle to see who should carry the main burden of economic distress – an association between folk song and radical thought which was to lead, directly, in due course to Bob Dylan and the protest songs of the sixties.

As far as the development of country music was concerned, the rest, as they say, is history. The string bands and radio programmes like the "Opry" developed a stream of music that is with us still today, having created en route such diverse trends as Western swing, Bill Monroe's amalgam of jazzy instrumental solos with the "high lonesome vocal sound" of the mountains that is called bluegrass, the sickly sentimental ballads of Jim Reeves and a whole host of international imitators who mistake the cowboy-hatted shadow of country music for the real substance, the black-influenced country blues of Hank Williams, and of course rock'n'roll – for many of the earliest white rockers like Johnny Cash, Jerry Lee Lewis, Carl Perkins, and of course Elvis Presley, who came out of Sam Phillips' Sun studios in Memphis, Tennessee, in the forties and fifties, were originally (and some would say still are) country artists.

Later, country music interacted with the rock that had developed from these origins, in the following decade and a half becoming a revitalising force which brought the sometimes excessively arty rock of the late sixties back to some sort of roots in the work of The Byrds, The Flying Burrito Brothers and Poco.

At every stage of this development, for good and ill, commercial pressures were at work. But because the medium employed was electronics, each new development tended to increase the diversity of form and content, maximising the benefits of mass distribution and minimising the ill effects. The mass media had similarly beneficial effects upon other branches of popular music, for instance jazz, which nearly died when it was successful in freeing itself from the pressures of the marketplace and became dominated by Apollonian ambitions, only coming back to life when it interbred with the Dionysian influence of rock in the early seventies.

To acknowledge the positive benefits of commercialism in an electronic context, compared with the almost completely negative effects of the print-based profit motive, is not to ignore the fact that big business does these things by accident. But in so many critics, a healthy scepticism towards the motives of the hucksters and the hustlers is used as a cloak for a sort of elitism, a disdain for the tastes of the mass which is really just another side of the show-biz belief that you can sell the suckers anything if you only package it up attractively enough. Of course, it is true that rubbish is foisted on to the public in the name of so-called mass appeal. But The Osmonds, the Cassidys and the Glitters succeed, not because of a manufactured need, but because there is a genuine but unfulfilled desire for something that could have been supplied from more worthy sources.

The real genius of the contemporary entrepreneur is in his ability to tune into that need and when he finds a means of supplying it, to grab it with both hands, regardless of how many of his most cherished musical or business principles it violates. His strength is his amorality, which is why the show-biz power structure was able to make so much cash out of the anti-establishment, anti-money pretensions of the 1960s.

The failure to distinguish between the positive and negative effects of the mass media, and – even more important – to realise how the technology of media dissemination can materially affect the consequences of such massive penetration of the audience, even when the controllers of a medium see it merely as another market, is one of the great failings of many who would comment upon it. Folklorists today are constantly expressing surprise at the fact that, while in the nineteenth and the early twentieth century the mass media were eroding appreciation of folk culture, today they appear to be popularizing it. Dr Maud Karpeles, an old associate of Sharp's, said in a new preface to his *English Folksongs: Some Conclusions* that publication in print or on record crystallised a folk song and inhibited its further development, and went on to remark: "Folksong is taught in the schools, it is to be found on gramophone records, it is a popular item in broadcast programmes. Thus we have the paradoxical situation that those very elements which helped to destroy folksong in the past are now among those that are contributing most efficiently to its revival."

Apart from the school use of folk song, which would be inimical to a true revival unless the educational environment were radically different from the way it is today, all too often, Dr Karpeles' paradox is apparent only to her, for records and radio have never had the deleterious effect she mentions, even when watered-down and sweetened-up versions of the real thing have been foisted on the public for a short while.

The other important thing about electronics is that they return music-making to an oral — or at least an aural — form. Orality has always been regarded as one of the prime essentials of a folk medium. It is this oral basis which creates the diversity of folk, as the folk-tale scholar Stith Thompson showed, in contrast with the set forms of written literature: "The reader... may pause or re-read a difficult passage, or skip one that fails to interest him. But when he is a listener he has only his ears to hear the speaker and he cannot slow or hurry him. What he fails to grasp he loses, and all he can do to recover this is to hear the tale again...

"This process of telling and hearing — and repeated telling and hearing — is the principal characteristic of literature when it is not possible by means of writing to capture and preserve a particular form. Hence oral literature is in continual flux with never exactly the same form manifesting itself."

This creates an incredible variety of interpretations from which, unconsciously, the community selects what it requires and passes on to the next generation. At the same time, the sense of tradition, of a continuity and the conservation of something precious, is strong. A truly living folk culture will function as a sort of triangle of forces, with individual variation, community selection and the sense of continuity operating at right angles to each other, a three-way dialectic from which a new tradition is constantly being forged.

For tradition is not merely what is old. McLuhan has defined it as "the sense of the total past as now" and Professor Harry Levin suggested that tradition ought to be regarded "not as the inert acceptance of a fossilized corpus of themes and conventions, but as an organic habit of re-creating what has been received and is handed on". But perhaps the last word on the subject was the remark of the traditional American singer, Frank Proffitt: "Appreciation for one's traditions and being enslaved by them are two different things."

And it is no one man's property. Proffitt went on to say: "I know I am not being paid for musical talent or for things I have done, but only for what was given to me." And the old cowboy song has the role of the songmaker down to a T: "My name is nothing extry/So that I will not tell."

Anonymity may be an accident, as Lloyd says, but in a situation where all things are in common, communal ownership and, in the sense that as each man changes what he hands on he puts his own individual stamp upon it, communal authorship may make anonymity the very essence. If it is true, as McLuhan says, that "today we come to the oral condition again via the electronic media" then electronic culture ought to satisfy the same criteria as folk culture and, in time, become undistinguishable from it. These are, as we have seen: composition and transmission should be oral; as a consequence of this, there should be a continuous process of re-creation in which the forces of tradition, variation and selection interplay dynamically; consequently, authorship should be increasingly difficult to establish and each member of the "electronic community" (if there is such a thing) should regard the culture as personally his; the composer and/or performer will be regarded as comparatively insignificant, more as the servant of his community than its leader; the distinctions between audiences and artist will tend to blur or break down.

Obviously, the products of electronic culture do not satisfy all these criteria all the time. But it is remarkable how often they satisfy some of them, and sometimes, usually in the most creative stage in a new rock band's development – The Who and the London mods, Slade and the Black Country skinheads who followed them first, Lindisfarne and the Geordie kids of Northumberland and Durham – most or even all of them are satisfied, for at least a short period.

Most popular music is transmitted orally, even if it is written down at some stage. And while many rock musicians now are musically literate – or at least more than formerly – they use notation as a descriptive rather than a prescriptive tool, indicating the sound of music already performed rather than what should be played in future, "ear marks" as the students of the old Hebrew chants used to call it.

Variation takes place all the time, and though the obsolescent process of copyrighting goes on and on, it becomes less and less relevant to the forms of the music and its transmission and recreation. Is Etta James's "Dance With Me, Henry" separable from Hank Ballard's "Work With Me, Annie"? And is there any doubt that "With A Little Help From My Friends" as sung by Joe Cocker is qualitatively different from the chirpy little song on The Beatles' *Sgt Pepper*, or that, conversely, Cocker's "The Letter" is in direct line

141

of succession from The Box Tops' version, though several years separated them?

Of course, if it is true that rock is a folk music (not, it must be repeated, because of its mass following, but because it fulfils these criteria), what does that make a performer who conscientiously sticks to a "folk" repertoire? As we have seen, the true purist denies the description "folk" to any performer who does not stand in a truly folk relationship with the community he serves: in that sense, the young intellectual intoning a classic ballad in a folk club, pint beer mug in his hand, and the traditional folk singer uprooted from his true milieu and presented on the stage of club, concert hall or festival, are both pop musicians. On the other hand, it is possible for a traditional performer to sing songs outside the accepted folk repertoire, usually the pop songs of a bygone age, without damaging his folk status. So it is not the repertoire which makes one performer folk and the other pop.

Indeed, when the folk revivalist adopts an elitist, Apollonian, analytical approach to his material he is less folk than the crowd down in the public bar bawling out the latest song of The New Seekers or David Cassidy. Similarly, a rock band doing its own thing in the conscious certainty that what it plays is art, may be less "folk", in a sociological sense, than a premeditated bid for the Top 40. A band like The New Lost City Ramblers who will play the folk-based pop of the twenties but not the folk-based rock of the sixties puts itself into an Apollonian position if they are guilty of the same sort of archaism that caused Pepys and Johnson to prefer collecting black-letter broadsides and lose interest in the more contemporary white-letter sheets.

Nevertheless, there is still something special about the folk lyric. The traditional singer who has "Lord Randal" and "Keyhole In The Door" in his repertoire knows they are two different types of song, suitable for different sorts of occasion. And the process of variation and selection that has acted on traditional songs over the centuries, wearing away the rough edges of them till they are shaped as smooth as pebbles on a beach, gives them a special character that appeals to the young musician seeking roots for his writing.

This has nothing directly to do with age as such, though it is a consequence of a process which has taken a long time, and is still continuing. Many of the early revivalists, conscious that a living tradition must consist of new additions to replace the old things becoming worn out or non-functional for various reasons, sought models in the old forms and deduced that what made them folk was the employment of certain archaic or time-worn turns of phrase. It is true that these old songs carry along with them the flavour of bygone days but the really significant thing about them is not the detritus of the past that survives, but exactly what is discarded and what is retained – and why.

The folk lyric is a kind of time capsule, preserving only the essentials of its message and hiving off all superfluities. It throws all other lyrics into a new kind of perspective which tells something of the techniques of versification which may be relevant for new songs in a way that the "come all ye" type of pastiche is not. Even the most imaginative folklorists tend to concentrate their efforts on considering the way the folk song is created and is developed; few have a very clear idea of *what* it is that is created and developed as a consequence, for though the word folk describes a process rather than a thing, the collector at any moment of time can cut through the history of a specific communication and should be able to detect certain characteristics in the cross-section which remain constant in kind, even if different in detail from one time to another.

It is easy, sometimes, to forget that folk songs are indeed communication, not so much from one man to another as from one generation to another, part of the great corpus of stored knowledge and custom that tell man what it means to be human, especially in the alienated world of the factory and machine.

The American historian, Oscar Handlin, contrasted the pattern of tradition with the dislocation of industrial life: "The great events of birth, marriage and death, and the lesser ones of sowing and reaping, of digging and building, of contriving and fabricating, were alike governed by a code that was self-validating in that it answered every conceivable question with conviction.

"Folk wisdom and the learning of the authoritative custodian of faith embraced all the accumulated knowledge of the group in a continuum that touched every aspect of knowledge."

In contrast, says Handlin, "the factory regime detached work from nature and from all other aspects of life. The machine disregarded the alterations of the seasons and the rising and setting of the sun to operate at its own pace, winter and summer, day and night... All those who entered the factory did so as detached individuals. Within its gates, they were not members of families or of groups, but isolated integers, each with his own line on the payroll; nothing extraneous counted. During working hours, the labourer had no other identity than that established by the job. From being people who were parts of households, known by a whole community, they had been reduced to being servants of the machine."

The survival of folk culture in these circumstances is thus explained: it is a protective system, essential to our sense of being men. The old songs — and not only songs but sayings, speech patterns, customs and traditional ways of doing things — hand down the community's knowledge of how to survive within an increasingly alien environment. With the growth of industrialism, this wisdom becomes more relevant, not less.

How is this achieved? Often the plots for the old ballads read more like Hammer horror movies than scenarios for action: a young man gets his sister pregnant, kills her and has to leave the community, never to return ("Lucie Wan"), a young man is poisoned by his lover who gives him a dish of snakes (sometimes toads) disguised as eels — as he dies he condemns her to hanging ("Lord Randal"), a lady misbehaves herself with a servant and is discovered by her lord when he comes home early — he slays both of them and buries them in a single grave ("Matty Groves"), or it may be a single incident, a soldier dying of venereal disease, the penalty for a sinful life ("The Unfortunate Rake"). This last song is interesting as an example of the way in which it is not the plot of the story which carries the song's essential message, but certain peripheral detail. Indeed, in all the ballads it is not what happens to the characters but their reaction to the events, which have the predestined inevitability of Greek tragedy, which is important. The story line is simple; the morality is not.

If folk songs are seen as communications from one generation to another, perhaps it is by means of communications theory, that body of learning that has its origins as a statistical tool for the design of telephone and similar electronic equipment, that we may begin to understand how it works. In *On Human Communication*, Colin Cherry describes ordinary conversation in terms which are reminiscent of

Stith Thompson's analysis of the folk tale: "It is remarkable that human communication works at all, for so much seems to be against it; yet it does. The fact that it does depends principally upon the vast store of habits which we each one of us possess, the imprints of all our past experiences. With this, we can hear snatches of speech, see vague gestures and grimaces, and from such thin shreds of evidence we are able to make a continual series of inductive guesses, with extraordinary effectiveness."

To ensure that we are understood, we surround the central message of what we are saying with all sorts of peripheral stuff which is known to communications theorists as redundancy. These may be metaphors, expansions, all the colourful turns of phrase which make all the difference between true human speech and the bald deadpan statement of a telegram – which, incidentally, is the easiest kind of message to misunderstand because it has zero redundancy; the sender relies upon the recipient's ability to guess enough to fill in the gaps in the message from his own experience. The less redundancy there is, the greater is the danger of misunderstanding.

The story of "The Unfortunate Rake" is interesting because it exists in so many different manifestations, but while the central message may change, so that the soldier dying of syphilis in eighteenth-century London crosses oceans, changes sex, becomes a cowboy dying of gunshot wounds on the streets of Laredo, coming to rest finally in New Orleans as the black hero of "Gambler's Blues", more commonly known as "St James's Infirmary", one detail remains constant, a redundancy essential to convey the point of the changing story: the ceremonial funeral at the end, usually with military trappings. Its survival is all the more surprising in view of the folk's tendency to discard anything it no longer requires.

Clearly the funeral is an essential part of the story. The blues version goes:

> Oh when I die just bury me in a box-back coat and a stetson hat,
> Put a twenty-dollar gold piece on my watch chain so that God'll
>   know I died standing pat.
> Six crapshooters to carry my coffin, get a chorus girl to sing me a
>   song,
> Put a jazz band on top of that big black hearse to raise hell as we go along.

When John A. Lomax and his son Alan collected the cowboy song, "The Streets of Laredo" (or "The Dying Cowboy"), the appropriate verses went:

> Get six jolly cowboys to carry my coffin;
> Get six pretty maidens to bear up my pall.
> Put bundles of roses all over my coffin,
> Put roses to deaden the sods as they fall.
> Oh beat the drum slowly and play the fife lowly,
> Play the dead march as you carry me along;
> Take me to the green valley, there lay the sod o'er me,
> For I'm a young cowboy and I know I've done wrong.

If the military music strikes an incongruous note at the cowboy's funeral, it rings even more strangely at the funeral of a young girl in a Nova Scotia version:

> So beat your drums and play your pipes merrily,
> And play the dead march and you bear me along.
> Take me to the church yard and throw the ground o'er me,
> I'm a young maiden; I know I've done wrong.

Harry Cox's version comes closer to the point:

> We'll beat the big drums and we'll play the pipes merrily,
> Play the dead march as we carry him along,
> Take him to the churchyard and fire three volleys o'er him
> For he's a young sailor cut down in his prime.

In 1848 a Mr Aldwell sang one verse of a song he remembered hearing in Cork round about 1790 to the collector William Forde:

> My jewel my joy, don't trouble me with the drum,
> Sound the dead march as my corpse goes along,
> And over my body throw handfuls of laurel,
> And let them all know that I'm gone to my rest.

Though the identity of the hero and the cause of death changes, one thing remains – the triumphant laugh in the face of death, and a horrible death at that – "Tell God I'm standing pat... raise hell as we go along", "We'll beat the big drums and we'll play the pipes merrily". One of the earliest versions says: "Don't muffle your

146

drums… play a quick march" (*not* a dead march). The song is full of scarlet and gold, bright muskets, squealing fifes, gaiety.

All the other details are varied to suit the singer and his community, to help him communicate this basic theme, that life is all there is, that man must die but death is not the end of the story (though there is no suggestion of life, punishment – despite the fact that "I know I've done wrong" – or redemption after death; man has the last word, but on this earth).

This familiarity with cosmic forces is ancient: prehistoric man expected the gods in which he personified the forces of nature to do as he told them. Sir James Frazer's *Golden Bough* is full of accounts of gods and saints insulted and forced to suffer indignities when the rain wouldn't fall or the harvest failed. In earliest times, the god was slaughtered once a year to ensure the fertility of grain; all manner of stories and songs, from "John Barleycorn" to Christ's passion, are rooted in this belief.

Folk lyric is full of these traditional metaphors, which encapsulate whole spectra of experiences: love songs begin in the spring, because it is the season of fruitfulness, but if the outcome is to be tragic then autumn is the setting. Some of the metaphors are mnemonic, the "snow white horse and the dapple grey" that appear throughout the ballads, just as maidens always have either golden hair or coal black, hands are always lily white, especially when death is in the offing:

> He took her by the lily white hand
> And led her through the hall.
> And with his sword he cut her head off
> And kicked it against the wall.

> He took her by the lily white hand,
> He kissed both cheek and chin,
> He took her to the riverside,
> He gently pushed her in.

Once the deed is done, the song ends, without comment; last-verse moralising is usually a Victorian addition, of broadside origin mostly. Such accretions are the first thing to go when the folk process begins its work of whittling down to essentials, resulting in the characteristic sudden end of the classic ballad, which is even more remarkable in the longer stories, packed with illustrative detail: and then they died, it may say, and an end to it.

The stance of the ballad maker, and the ballad performer, is impersonal, which is not the same thing as the pop-song writer of Denmark Street, who is depersonalised because he is trafficking in the chewed-up clichés of art poetry and tasteless traditions of a worn-out form. "Lerve" may make the world go round, but the pop song does not deal in love, it deals with a sentimentality which is the courtly romanticism of medieval chivalry gone to seed. The song does not touch our emotions because we know no one ever felt that way; that is why it goes on so about feelings, manufacturing an ersatz sentiment to mask the absence of the real thing, a monosodium glutamate flavour-enhancer of the emotions.

On the other hand, the ballad maker engages our sense of reality because he deals with the basic facts of human existence, which is why the story has relevance to homespun Aberdeenshire farmworkers even when it is ostensibly about lords and ladies dressed in silk. We don't need to be told how the unfaithful lady's lord felt, because his actions tell us: "with his sword he cut her head off and kicked it against the wall".

The ballad maker is many-faced, but, like Brecht's actor, he never surrenders his own identity for that of the characters in the ballad, though in some traditions he may seek to efface himself temporarily by closing his eyes, or even by singing into the corner of a room. Greek tragedians, whose roots were in the Dionysian rites of pre-historic religion, wore masks for the same purpose.

This is a very different stance from the faceless writer of pop ballads and different again from the highly individualised literary poet whose aim is to convey an experience so personal that it is unique. The folk poet is communicating universal experience, the pop writer is communicating a lowest common denominator of experience that turns out to have no substance at all on close examination; the literary poet, in the end, is talking to himself. While peripheral detail in the folk lyric is *used*, to convey the basic message even when the hard core of the plot is changed, to the literary poet the personalised detail is all there is and nothing "happens" at all. As we saw, this was also true of early pop, like "Sumer Is Icumen In".

The rock poet's break with the forms of printed pop is clear; the influence of the blues and, to a limited extent, folk lyric have created an idiom that inclines towards the impersonality, the universality of balladry. The problem is that, once he starts taking himself seriously, he is asked by society to choose between the archetypes it understands; if he is not to be Denmark Street hack he must be Byronic poet. Despite the early influence of Woody Guthrie, a true folk poet who stands up under the sort of analysis we have recommended very well, most of the solo singer-songwriters from Bob Dylan onwards are Byronic rather than folk, which is hardly surprising when one considers their middle-class, college-educated background. It is this, rather than their closeness or remoteness from traditional forms, which debars them, ultimately, from the "folk" tag, though Dylan's relationship with his audience was for a time that of a folk bard, a role he has tried with some success to escape. The possibility of a third alternative is not considered, though many of the most advanced creators of the electronic age, from Cage to Brecht, from Joyce to Stockhausen, are struggling to adopt a similar stance spontaneously.

This is the true significance of the folk lyric to rock. That rock bands are producing electric versions of the old ballads is less important than that, in the process of re-creating them in an electric context, the habits of versification will become second nature, so that new ballads with the essence rather than the surface appearance of the old tradition are added to the repertoire. This is beginning to happen, though only to a limited extent, with the work of new electric poets like Richard Thompson and Steve Ashley. But in some groups, the emphasis on old ballads at the expense of any contemporary lyric is preventing them from developing creatively and bogging them down in an unreal sort of electric archaism. The existence of electronic media suggests the possibility of a popular music which is an analogue of the old folk forms, but it does not make the development inevitable, just as there is no necessity for Western society to progress beyond the industrial capitalist state that has held it in thrall so far.

Indeed, it must be acknowledged that there are certain factors at work in rock which prevent it from becoming a true folk music and which suggest the value of a specifically folk approach is not yet outmoded, though the "folk" practitioner needs clarity, above all, about what he is doing and why he is doing it. Not the least of the factors preventing rock from becoming any kind of folk music, in the sense that it is the expression of a new kind of community using electronics as the technology of its expression, is, paradoxically, the prohibitive cost of that technology, which ties the rock musician to the money structure of the music business more securely than any of his predecessors.

It is ironic that when so many of the effects associated with rock are actually a consequence of over-driving cheap equipment or using it in ways that were never intended or conceived by its designers, so much emphasis should be placed upon the excellence of the sound in classical terms, with bands like Yes surrounded by ever-mounting stacks of electronic gear of increasing complexity, requiring several trucks to transport and whole squads of roadies to set up and dismantle before and after each concert. In terms of the world energy crisis, of course, the future of the huge megalomaniac touring group may be short; but in the meanwhile such technological overkill tends to separate audience and artist rather than bring them closer together, and it is hardly surprising that as a consequence the music becomes increasingly arty and abstracted in its content.

The volume of rock, which at one point served a positive purpose in bringing musical appreciation back from its cerebral basis into what McLuhan calls an "audio-tactile" relationship, in which all the membranes of the body, not merely the eardrums, react to the sensory stimuli of sound vibrations which are felt rather than heard, has begun to be a barrier between the artist and the audience. The latter has become more and more passive, as can be seen by the decline of dancing at rock events, always an accurate index of the audience involvement. When the audience got up out of their cinema seats to jive to the music of "Rock Around The Clock", they were demonstrating the end of an era, the end of audience passivity. Today, when the derogatory term "idiot dancers" is applied to the few front-row freaks who persist in trying to react to music physically, it seems to have returned again.

Fittingly, the role which electric folk bands may be seen by history to have played in popular music in the seventies has been to reverse this trend as audiences are invited to leap to their feet and dance to the tunes of jigs and reels. At the time of writing, for the most part, the "dancing" is little more than a display of formless exuberance, but

I have seen a Queen Elizabeth Hall audience try to get their feet into this 1,2,3 – 1,2,3 – 1,2 rhythm of Alan Stivell's "plin", and not get too tangled up in it.

This is audience participation of a very primitive kind, but the real problem of electronics is that it tends to restrict the sort of feedback which is an essential part of any information process, which is what music must become again if it is to come down from its ivory tower of art. The money system's involvement in the process sponsors growth towards gargantuanism, in the size of events, in the length of individual items, in the cost of admission, in the numbers of artists participating. Of course, above a certain level, the decentralising impetus of electronics takes precedence over the obsolescent desire to centralise everything which is the way the music business tries to understand the process of which it has become a part, so that throughout your crowds of quarter- and half-million fans at Woodstock and Isle of Wight and Watkins Glen, mini-festivals are taking place, the tiny dot on the distant stage and his disembodied voice is put back into context as a mere accompaniment to what is going on at the periphery.

Size is one enemy of feedback, but so is the present restricted level of the technology. If one looks at electronics as something of wider implication than merely the technicalities of public address systems, instrument amplification and record reproduction, it is obvious that the solution is almost within our grasp. Access to the mass media is one of our most abused contemporary clichés, but never was it more true that man seldom defines a need without having the solution in his hands. Unless the state system breaks down completely in the meantime – something which is far from being a remote possibility – it is likely that the TV set with its yes-no button could oust the ballot box as a tool of participatory democracy before the end of this century. Already this can be seen in embryo form in the escalating popularity of phone-in radio shows. What this will mean to popular music may not be obvious, but its effect could be far-reaching, for if participation were ever to be regarded as every man's right in respect to every decision that affects his life, he is unlikely to accept the role of passive spectator at events designed to entertain him.

The violence that erupts at monster rock concerts, demonstrations and football matches is a consequence of the frustration that the spectator feels today: on all sides the pressures for participation are mounting, but in contrast he begins to feel increasingly remote from the events taking place before him, whether they are musical, political or sporting.

Unlike football or politics, popular music has a primitive feedback mechanism: the charts of best-selling records. Although their results are scorned by the elite among the critics, it is widely acknowledged by the professionals in the business that it is virtually impossible to "fix" them, though occasionally enterprising managements will invest sufficient money in buying copies of neglected singles from the right shops to bring them to the attention of the charts-dominated BBC Radio 1. But though the charts do allow the consumer the exercise of some sort of control over his musical fare, voting with his purse as it were, in effect he is as remote from any real influence as when he puts his cross on a ballot form.

The other means of feedback is the award of applause, or its withholding, during a live performance. But while the effect of electronics *in general* has been to narrow the theoretical gap between the audience *as a whole* and the artists, in specific concert environments the audience's contact is becoming less and less. Not only are they restrained, physically, from contact with the performers by bouncers and barriers, but they are expected to play less and less of a dynamic role. When did you last hear an audience boo an unsatisfactory performance or walk out on a performer who insulted its intelligence? On the contrary, the live performance is becoming more and more an adjunct of the recording; the audience goes to the concert hall knowing what it is to experience, the record made flesh, and it responds accordingly. That traditional accolade of the superlative performance, the encore, has now become a mere formality, and performers come out to respond to a non-existent demand from an audience that is only too willing to declare the evening well and truly over. It is only in the acoustic context, in which size is limited by the carrying power of the human voice and the unamplified instrument, that a performance can become a communication between the artist and audience as equals, with appropriate responses.

Only in this context is it possible to remove the distinction so that, as Pete Seeger once said, the most democratic shape of a gathering is not the face-to-face confrontation of artist and audience but a circle, in which first one person stands out from the crowd to make his contribution, then another. John Lennon once envisaged the entire working class being the superstars of their culture in a socialist society; a Utopian vision, perhaps, but it is the meaning of the folk singer's many-to-many relationship with his audience.

If you go to a country pub in an area where the folk tradition is still alive and kicking, like The Ship in Blaxhall, Suffolk, this is exactly what happens. When Cyril Poacher stands up they all know he will sing "The Nutting Girl" because that is his song. And so with each singer: he has his own song, which is his own and which he knows best. It may be his only one, or it may be one of a hundred like it, but as he sings it he is, in a very real sense, a star. And then the torch is handed on to another who becomes the voice of the community.

The old realities of village life may be on their last legs, or it may be that they offer the only real way forward through the morass of pollution and communications breakdown that lies ahead, but one way or another they provide an analogue for the future of popular music. Electric folk, in my opinion, is only one of many attempts to find a solution to this conundrum. Paradoxically, the more it strives self-consciously to be "folk", the less effective it is; conversely, the more it relaxes and sees itself as just another kind of rock, the closer it is to reaching that goal.

SOURCES

You'll find the originals of many of the electric folk "chartbusters" on albums in the Topic, Leader and Trailer catalogues, sung by country singers, collected mainly in the fifties and onwards, or by various revivalists. The best kaleidoscope of the traditional origins of electric balladry will be found in Topic's ten-volume *Folk Songs of Britain*. For instance, Volume 8, *A Soldier's Life for Me*, includes the originals of Steeleye's "When I Was On Horseback", "The Banks Of The Nile" and "Prince Charlie Stewart". Two failings of this anthology should, however, be borne in mind: the fact that it treats the six or seven separate traditions of this Disunited Kingdom as one (the mythical "Britain" of the collection's title) and the fact that some of the songs are denuded of some of their verses. Though they are printed in full in an accompanying booklet, this truncation encourages the singer to think of all the verses as being sung to the same tune as the first, whereas it is of the essence of folk music that each verse varies, melodically, in keeping with the pace of the narration. Each time the song is performed, of course, a new set of variations occurs.

Other strong traditional influences have been Harry Cox, who appears on several volumes of *Folk Songs of Britain* and has two albums to himself, *English Folk Singer* (EFDSS LP1004) and *Traditional English Love Songs* (Folk Legacy FSB20), which has the original of Steeleye's "Spotted Cow" on it, as well as the rhythmically fascinating "Betsy The Serving Maid" referred to in the text; Phil Tanner (EFDSS LP1005), from whose recording came "The Gower Wassail" for Steeleye; and the Coppers (EFDSS LP1002, Leader LEA 4046/9), from whom stem the glee-type harmonies used by some groups for their ensemble singing. The Coppers' repertoire has more effect in the folk clubs than on the electric scene, though.

Some of Fairport's traditional repertoire is hard to trace: the words of their "Matty Groves" were dictated to them over the phone when they were working on *Liege and Lief*, but the tune is basically similar to that of the American Hedy West, recorded on "Pretty Saro" (Topic 12T146).

The list of songs electric folk has acquired via the redoubtable Bert Lloyd, sometimes passed on more or less as he got them, sometimes extensively reworked, is really remarkable. We would be much poorer without his talent for spotting a good song, for instance "Blackwaterside", "A Sailor's Life", "Reynardine", "The Deserter", "Jack Orion" (the latter more or less an original song on the theme of the traditional "Glasgerion"), and "The Handloom Weaver And The Factory Maid". A fine singer, though very idiosyncratic and less traditional in style than is sometimes believed, he has not always been well served by his recordings, but *First Person* (Topic 12T118) almost does him justice.

Lloyd and Ewan MacColl (aka Jimmy Miller) did an interesting set of recordings of ballads from the collection of Professor F.J. Child for Riverside many years ago which was criticised by musicologists at the time for the rather mannered singing and wayward way with texts and tunes. All singers rework their material, of course, and so they should, but in a scholarly work this is sometimes frowned upon.

MacColl's epic collection of comparative balladry, *The Long Harvest*, compiled with his lady, Peggy Seeger, for Argo, has not yet yielded up many of its treasures to the electric scene. It is more faithful to its sources than the Riverside set.

Instrumentally, English electric folk tends to be over-infatuated with Irishisms, and the flashier aspects of Irish music what's more, rather than the more down-home stuff played in London Irish pubs and available on some records (for instance XTRA 1090, XTRA 5037, 12T123, 12T176, LEA 2004). This Irish music, though a slightly exotic transplant of an immigrant tradition, is closer to the sound of country band than the neo-traditional art music of groups like The Chieftains, Na Fili, Planxty and the other progressives of the Celtic tradition. Reg Hall and Bob Davenport produced a fine album of English Country Music which is long out of print; but I hear rumours that it may be reissued by Topic. A couple of tracks from the same sessions are included on *Boscastle Breakdown* (12T240), an excellent survey of English instrumental music with tracks from Scan Tester, the late, great concertina player. Topic have another more modest collection, *English Country Music from East Anglia* (12TS229) which is a delight, as well as records of Northumbrian music, small pocket instruments like the Jew's harp and piccolo and an increasing number of other instrumental records of great value. Dolly Collins tried to recreate the sound of the old English wind bands on some Shirley Collins albums, and though the rather contrived arrangements were artistically interesting they lacked the lusty vigour one senses in Hardy's descriptions. The fad for crumhorns and similar early English wind instruments has extended the range of instrumental textures available to the modern pop musician or arranger, but the music of bands like Gryphon and City Waites, or the more authentic Musica Reservata directed by Michael Morrow, has more to do with the early history of art music than folk.

Though they are unaccompanied, and therefore hardly "electric", the influence of powerful-sounding revivalist groups like The Watersons (Topic 12T142, 12T136, 12T167) and The Young Tradition (Transatlantic SAM 13, SAM 30) on the vocal ensemble sound of many electric folk groups would be hard to over-emphasise.

FOUR

Folk-Rock in Britain

ROBIN DENSELOW

A TALE OF TWO CULTURES

Just after midnight on New Year's morning, a few minutes into 1973, a curious incident occurred at a club called The Howff in London's Primrose Hill. The place was packed, celebratory drinks were flying to and fro, and an exceedingly good band up on stage was improvising around the statutory "Auld Lang Syne". They called themselves The Albion Country Band, and their line-up included two ex-members of Fairport Convention. They had just finished a show which included contemporary songs by their guitarist, the brilliant Richard Thompson, and a revolutionary sequence in which a team of Morris dancers suddenly emerged on stage and performed their symbolic ritual to the highly effective backing of the appropriate dance tunes played on rock instruments – electric guitar, bass and drums.

Particularly through the alcoholic haze it seemed a glorious mixture of old and new, and a culmination of the battle between the rival schools of "folk" and "rock" that had ludicrously managed to grow further apart during the cultural revolution of the sixties. Here were musicians spawned during the confused "underground" days of UFO and Middle Earth, back in 1967, at last putting the pieces together.

Or rather, some of them. "Auld Lang Syne" ended and one of the band – probably Richard Thompson – responded to the audience's not unnatural wish to start dancing by blasting into some old Chuck Berry. Ashley "Tyger" Hutchings, the man who founded both Fairport Convention and Steeleye Span on his way to creating the Albions, reacted in a most unexpected way. He ripped out the plugs from the band's equipment and stormed off with them into the night.

The bemused audience had to wait while replacements were found. Later, one of the band explained what had gone on. "It wasn't that Tyger was against people hearing Chuck Berry or enjoying themselves. But he thought it blasphemous that anyone should use The Albion Country Band and all it stood for to play that stuff." It was obviously irrelevant that Tyger himself had recorded Berry's "Nadine" for a jokey album earlier in the year. He was acting here on behalf of an intellectualised folk ideal. He had decided that English traditional music, however played, should not be mixed with good-time rock.

I start with that story not to spite the highly imaginative Tyger, but because it sums up the whole confused musical mess of the folk-rock relationship. In brief, the problem was, and is, this: during the sixties British musicians played a major part in a revolution that transformed the musical taste and standards of the Western (and quite a lot of the Eastern) world. The decade started with Cliff Richard and Billy Fury, and ended with The Beatles, Van Morrison, The Who and The Pink Floyd. Rock'n'roll, the vibrant fusion of two all-American styles (black American rhythm'n'blues, white American country music) was transformed. In an extraordinary, rapid and contradictory artistic flowering, rock music emerged in myriad forms, some important, some very important, and others merely mediocre. At the end of it all, rock had grown up. Dylan mixed strong lyrics with amplification; The Who wrote about their own backgrounds in extended "rock operas"; the Floyd emerged from the underground to fuse electronic lyricism and technological stagecraft; and The Kinks even merged rock with music hall.

All of that provided a problem for folk music. Folk started the decade at the top – almost anyone with any serious popular musical interests in 1960 frequented folk clubs – but it gradually lost out in popularity to rock. The folk clubs were normally in upstairs rooms in pubs or in student common rooms, and to start with, at least, they provided an important forum. Nothing too expensive could ever happen in them (the normal entrance fee would be a couple of shillings, and a normal club crowd would rarely be over 300), but within those limits anything was possible. Mostly this meant that a bearded man in jeans would bash out three chords on an acoustic guitar and sing a ballad about the Oklahoma dustbowl – oblivious to its lack of direct relevance to South Croydon – or a look-alike Joan Baez would warble through "Wildwood Flower". But it was possible for solo guitarists or singer-songwriters to break in and establish their own local reputations. And alongside all this, the admirable ideals of the Ewan MacCollites and the Bert Lloyds were disseminated: the main idea in setting up the network of clubs was to make sure that as many people as possible got to hear British traditional material, and that there were venues where traditional singers could operate.

All of this was quite admirable, and I don't want to appear anti-folk in the criticisms that I make of the way the scene developed. Much of the music is, was, and will remain, of enormous importance. It deserves to survive first and foremost because it is good – because it is a store of fine melodies and strong lyrics, because it can be appreciated on the level of a "good story", before any interest – academic, sociological or Marxist – is added.

What eventually went wrong was the limited presentation of this music to the public, and the lack of interest and awareness shown by those in the clubs towards the developing music scene outside. The clubs started with an open attitude and gradually became narrow-minded. Many folk musicians found they were being stifled, that while barriers outside were being lifted, barriers in the folk world were coming down. Some clubs became "purist", only accepting singers who sang traditional material in the prescribed manner, and discouraging a broader outlook.

Tim Hart, once part of an acoustic duo with Maddy Prior and now part of Steeleye Span, described the scene he left like this: "It's petty-minded and it's done nothing for folk for the last eight years, apart from keeping it within the folk clubs and trying to make sure nobody else ever heard about it." Dave Swarbrick, once the leading instrumentalist on the folk circuit, and now with Fairport Convention, is even more bitter. "I didn't like seven-eighths of the people involved in the scene. They made it insular, they made their own laws and they were so strict that you couldn't go outside them."

This is a study of those who did break the laws, and those contemporary songwriters who have attempted to assimilate something of the feel of English traditional music within a rock context. But before looking at those who attempted to straddle the two cultures, it's necessary to look at why such action should be necessary and important. After all, why not just let the folk purists play folk, and the rock revolution rattle away without them? There are surely two answers to that. First, with a popular music revolution sweeping Britain, it would seem ridiculous that Britain's native music should be left out in the cold. Likewise, with a new popular culture of singer-songwriters tackling personal and contemporary problems, it would seem right that they should be at least aware of predecessors in the field – whether anonymous industrial balladeers or music-hall artists.

Some purists object to a marriage of folk and rock on the grounds that it wrecks the songs by giving them entirely alien accompaniments and connotations. Two comments, again from Tim Hart and Dave Swarbrick, give the folk-rockers' answers. Swarb, sitting in a hotel bedroom at London Airport at the start of the Fairports' 1974 World Tour, treated the electrification of the tradition with a characteristically colourful outburst: "You know, if you're singing about a bloke having his head chopped off, or a girl fucking her brother and having a baby and the brother getting pissed off and cutting her guts open and stamping on the baby and killing his sister – now that's a fantastic story by any standards, whether told in a pub or on Broadway. Having to work with a story line like that with acoustic instruments wouldn't be half as powerful or potent, dramatically, as saying the same things electrically. Because when you deal with violence, when you deal with someone slashing with a sword, say, there are sounds that exist electrically – with electric bass, say – that can very explicitly suggest what the words are saying." Tim Hart was a little more academic. "My personal philosophy is that most English traditional song is unaccompanied song, and the only argument is – should you or should you not accompany it at all? After that, I'm not interested in any argument as to what degree you can go to. To me, it's equally outrageous to accompany a traditional song on a Spanish guitar or an American instrument as it is to accompany it with an electric guitar and a Moog synthesiser – in fact you could be a hell of a lot more sympathetic to a traditional song with a Moog or an organ than you can with any stringed instrument, because they work around drones…"

BEGINNINGS: SKIFFLE AND DEM EAST CROYDON BLUES

The confused relationship between folk and rock, and the attempts to bring the two together, are now a world away from the man who launched pop music in Britain, and is largely responsible for the growth of both. I last saw Lonnie Donegan in the spring of 1974 in the unlikely setting of London's Penthouse Club. For his after-dinner cabaret turn he followed the busty Pets onto the stage, and when they had finished an uneasy section from *Cabaret* he shook hands with the few diners (mostly businessmen and elderly couples) and announced "You don't know me. The name's Donegan." It was indeed clear that they didn't know him, but he put on the sort of show that goes down well in such places. He rattled through a selection of old hits, put on a straw boater for a dance routine and spent ten minutes on off-blue wisecracks. Afterwards he complained to me of the limitations of the cabaret scene, commented unfavourably on rock audiences, and showed right-wing leanings when the subject turned to politics.

Twenty years earlier, in July 1954, the same Mr Donegan had started a revised revolution. He was then the banjoist with the Chris Barber Jazz Band, and the trad jazz movement was gathering a highly enthusiastic cult following. The band reverently played the New Orleans classics, but during the intervals Donegan and a small splinter group bashed away at "skiffle" versions of American folk-songs and blues. The Barber Band's album *New Orleans Joys* happened to include two of these "skiffle" songs – "Rock Island Line" and "John Henry" – and a full eighteen months after the album's release (in 1956) they were put out as a novelty single by Decca.

The reaction was quite extraordinary. All Donegan did on "Rock Island Line" was to lay down a rhythmic acoustic shuffle, with guitars, bass and drums, and over it to drawl and then sing the story of the train driver fooling the man on the toll gate outside New Orleans by claiming to have "pigs and all livestock" instead of "all pig iron", and then speeding up down "the road to ride", the Rock Island Line. It started slowly, and built up to a break-neck climax with Donegan whooping and hollering as the train gathers speed. The sheer vitality and earthy simplicity knocked British kids sideways. The lyrics may appear curiously transatlantic for Britain's first home-grown pop breakthrough, but no matter. The music had unheard-of guts (this was before the days of rocking with cavemen and Tommy Steele, remember) and anyone with a cheap acoustic guitar and able to strum three chords could imitate it.

"Rock Island Line" sold well over a million copies and became the first British pop record to get into the American Top Ten. Donegan went on to notch up an incredible twenty-six hits in the next six years, and spawned an army of imitators across the country. By mid-1956 there were 600 skiffle groups in the Greater London area alone.

Although the music was embarrassingly simple compared to what was to follow, skiffle soon began to break down into two schools (though this was not so obvious at the time, and there was great overlapping). On one side there were the blues-influenced skifflers, mostly men from jazz bands who found they were instinctively drawn to black music, even when bashing out three chords on a guitar. In this category was Ken Colyer (who can claim to have invented skiffle – for his original skiffle group contained both Barber and Donegan, along with Alexis Korner). He went on to record songs like "Midnight Hour Blues" and "Take This Hammer". Then there was Alexis Korner, who left Colyer to record songs by the great bluesmen – skiffle versions of anything from Leadbelly's "Sail On" to Sleepy John Estes "I Ain't Gonna Worry No More". "Sail On" makes particularly fascinating listening now: instead of strumming, Korner picks his way finger-style through the guitar parts, and only a thumping skiffle backing stops this from being a straightforward blues revival number.

Korner was later to progress through skiffle to become the father of the British blues revival, and arguably the single most important figure in the history of white rock music in Britain. He moved from the skiffle clubs to the amplified blues clubs (and across to the folk clubs if an acoustic bluesman needed encouragement), and in the process he gave a hand to many of Britain's greatest rock musicians. He helped bring The Rolling Stones together, and among the dozens of musicians who played for his Blues Incorporated were Mick Jagger, Ginger Baker, Jack Bruce, Paul Jones and Phil Seamen.

On the other side, skiffle also led the way for the folk clubs. The skiffle style could be readily adapted to many American three-chord folk songs, and Lonnie Donegan was to popularise the ballads of Woody Guthrie. "The Grand Coulee Dam" and "This Land Is Your Land" may, again, appear to have no direct relevance to a kid from Liverpool or London, but these were songs with something to say, and often with radical overtones. They were a world away from the dance-band pap that made up much popular listening.

So skiffle united and launched the two cultures of folk and rock-rhythm'n'blues. The interest in Guthrie songs was to open the field for singer-songwriters in the folk clubs, while the interest in the blues led both to the establishment of amplified blues clubs, and the growth of rock. Most important of all, skiffle gave music back to the people and started a popular revolution. If it hadn't been for Donegan, a skiffle band called The Quarrymen wouldn't have been formed in Liverpool. The Quarrymen never achieved anything extraordinary, but two of its members were John Lennon and Paul McCartney.

Donegan's own subsequent history is one of limited commercial success and artistic suicide. Having launched a popular, unified British culture, he chose to follow neither of the two musical paths to which it led. Instead of folk or blues, Donegan went for cabaret. After the success of such lyrical breakthroughs as "Does Your Chewing Gum Lose Its Flavour" and "My Old Man's A Dustman" it probably seemed the obvious thing to do. He's made a good living at it, and can't be blamed for that, but it's astonishing how totally he has rejected the musical revolution he started (in complete contrast to his former colleague Alexis Korner). "Skiffle was my floor but also my ceiling," he told me. Now he prefers to wear expensive suits and warble trivia to rich diners.

FOLK CLUBS, UP AND DOWN

As skiffle faded out, the folk clubs faded in. From the late fifties through to the mid-sixties, they sprung up and flourished across the country. Joined together in the upstairs rooms of thousands of pubs were those who had moved from folk to skiffle, the genuine revivalists (followers of MacColl and A.L. Lloyd), those who were interested in acoustic blues, and those just generally interested in anything that was likely to be the new fad.

To start with, American music predominated – Woody Guthrie ballads, and the songs of his followers from Ramblin' Jack Elliott to Tom Paxton. There were harmony trios, copies of The Kingston Trio and Peter, Paul and Mary, and there were the post-Baez crop of Appalachian balladeers. During the years of CND and the Aldermaston marches, there were dozens of home-grown "Ban the Bomb" protest singers, followed by imitators of the early Dylan.

Most clubs had their own crop of singer-songwriters. They didn't rush off tapes to the big record companies, simply because life wasn't like that. It was not until relatively late in the development of the clubs that Donovan became a star – much to the amazement of his mates back at The Cock in St Albans. Until then he had been typical of the writers that folk clubs produced – he'd simply written about his friends. The "violent hash smoker" who "kicked a chocolate machine" in "Sunny Goodge Street", for instance, was a guy well known around St Albans.

In the early sixties, a folk club was an exciting place to be. The music was varied, and so were the characters involved (you might meet anyone from the hearty Redd Sullivan to the avant-garde Ron Geesin). There was a feeling that this was where things were happening, and as the emphasis shifted from American to British traditional material, there was no hint of the cultural claustrophobia that was to follow. The fact that British folk was becoming increasingly popular rightly seemed the most encouraging trend of all. After all, unaccompanied revivalists like The Watersons and The Young Tradition were young, dressed in pop clothes, and were far from being musical isolationists.

But the growing success of British traditional music led, ironically, to the eventual paralysis of the folk scene, the phoney "battle" between folk and rock, and the furious rejection of the scene by musicians like Hart and Swarbrick.

The reason was this: clubs started to take on specific characteristics. Some became exclusively traditional, approving only of hand-on-the-ear unaccompanied singers. Others concentrated on blues and singer-songwriters. Gradually, the easy-going acceptance of different forms of music broke down. The traditionalists created a ghetto, and a host of excellent musicians were trapped inside. The efforts of the best and most broad-minded traditionalists – The Watersons, The Young Tradition, Anne Briggs and Martin Carthy – seemed to have backfired.

The blues and contemporary clubs were somewhat less rigid in their attitudes, but the situation was such that they too suffered, cut off from hearing many of the fine traditional singers. With a stalemate like that, and rock music roaring over the hill, gathering intelligence and respectability, it was no surprise that the folk clubs went into a period of slow decline.

Apart from the "folkier than thou" problems, there was another drawback. Being small – and making little effort to expand – the clubs could only afford modest fees for outside artists who appeared. Anything larger than an acoustic duo became uneconomic (even The Young Tradition, a trio, found this); amplification was also quite out of the question. The clubs, and those who played them, hadn't the space or the money for electric instruments, speakers and roadies – even if amplification of folk had been tolerated in the first place.

So the folk scene began to get a little worrying – though not all the talent and excitement disappeared at once, and the clubs remained the one opening for brand new performers. On the one hand, worried revivalists like Hart and Swarbrick kept playing the trad clubs, wondering what to do next. On the other side, bluesmen and songwriters sat in their clubs, pushing their music as far as they could but looking with increasing envy at the concert opportunities that began to open up outside.

FOLK BLUES IN GREEK STREET: GRAHAM MEETS COLLINS

The best club in London to gauge the head of steam building up on the blues and contemporary side was Les Cousins, in Soho. It consisted of a small, desperately hot and overcrowded basement in Greek Street. Across the way was a pub called The Pillars of Hercules where many of those propping up the bar tended to be musicians. It was here, in the mid-sixties, that one came to hear the best folk-blues artists and songwriters – many of whom were to move on to national success within a few years.

The father of the folk-blues (as well as the R&B) scene was Alexis Korner. Following closely after him was a remarkable guitarist called Davy Graham. Long before anyone else was thinking of mixing styles or inventing "folk-rock", Graham was playing the most extraordinary fusions. He stuck to acoustic guitar, and with that instrument alone he broke down the barriers. He started mixing blues with Eastern styles, and jazz and folk. His record *3/4AD*, made with Alexis Korner in 1961, went unnoticed by the general public because it was so advanced. Two later albums, *Folk, Blues and Beyond* and *Folk Roots, New Routes* (both released in 1965) were rather like delayed time bombs; their initial impact was not enormous but the long-term effect was devastating.

Graham became one of folk music's great practical academics because he lived out the experiments that he played. He could talk of the similarity between an air and a raga, and elaborate on his theories of gypsy migration and its effects on Irish and Hindustani music, because he has made those journeys himself. He was born in England in 1940. His father was a Scottish Gaelic teacher, and his mother was from Georgetown, Guyana. While at school, he was partially blinded in his right eye. As soon as he left he became an itinerant musician, first playing around Europe, then North Africa.

The *Folk, Blues and Beyond* album, which consists of Davy singing and playing solo guitar, backed by an unnamed bass player and drummer, sums up his catholic influences and the way in which he put them together. The first track starts with a wailing Indian-sounding theme that gradually turns into a spirited version of Leadbelly's "Leavin' Blues". It's followed by an elaborate, bluesy accompaniment to an English song, "Seven Gypsies" (the beginning of a style that was to be known as "folk baroque"), an instrumental from Morocco, versions of contemporary songs by Cyril Tawney and Bob Dylan, and even excursions into jazz – Bobby Timmons's "Moaning" and Charlie Mingus's "Better Git It In Your Soul".

The next album, *Folk Roots, New Routes*, broke even more ground. This time Graham didn't sing, but his guitar accompanied one of Britain's best-known traditional singers, Shirley Collins. It was a shot-gun marriage of folk songs from Britain and America and accompaniments with blues, jazz or Indian overtones. And it worked remarkably well. Shirley was one of the more broad-minded of the folk "establishment". She had first learned folk songs from her family, in her native Sussex, had taken an early interest in Appalachian music, and went there on a long song-collecting tour with Alan Lomax. She followed that up by playing American instruments like auto-harp, five-string banjo and mountain dulcimer to accompany British folk songs. British folk material was traditionally unaccompanied, so some folk purists were startled by her actions. To such eyes, the fusion with Davy Graham was even worse.

The record still stands up well. Shirley's gentle, clear and sensual voice, and Davy's understanding, daring playing, bring together black and white, East and West, as if no clash existed. On one record there's the variety that it was impossible to hear in the clubs – Monk's "Blue Monk" and Bobby Timmons's "Grooveyard" next to an unaccompanied "Lord Gregory", and the medieval "Cherry Tree Carol" played on five-string banjo.

Shirley and Davy came together for one record and a concert or two, then went their separate ways. Shirley went back to the clubs, but her position there was now an enigmatic one. She was a straightforward English traditional performer who treated her repertoire of largely medieval songs with no greater gimmickry than to accompany them on banjo, guitar and dulcimer. But there was a fine, trance-like quality about her performance that made her well respected with the folk avant-garde, and this aroused the suspicions of the sterner folk academics.

Shirley never received mass acclaim outside the folk circle, but she produced a string of highly original albums. For years she played with her sister Dolly, a trained musician who accompanied Shirley's voice and banjo with a flute organ. This was an electric-powered reconstruction of a medieval hand-pumped instrument, and had a delicate breathy tone that admirably matched Shirley's voice. The sisters used it to good effect on two albums – *The Sweet Primeroses* and *The Power of the True Love Knot* (the latter produced by the King of London's musical underground, Joe Boyd, with The Incredible String Band banging drums and finger-cymbals on one track).

Later, when the so-called "underground" emerged blinking from the all-night sessions at UFO to be gobbled up by the record companies, Shirley found herself on EMI's "underground" label, Harvest. In 1969 she recorded *Anthems in Eden*, which was both the first folk "concept album" and the first on which she used the "natural orchestra" for her traditional material. The orchestra included David Munrow and the Early Music Consort, and to settings by Dolly Collins they played sackbuts, viols, rebec, cornett, recorder, crumhorn, sordun, and other such unlikely-sounding instruments. (The crumhorn is a relative of the bagpipe chanter, the sackbut is an early small-bore trombone, the cornett is a wooden ancestor of the trumpet, and the rackett is described as "a wooden pipe with a curly pipe on top".)

All this gave the songs a toughness, a vitality and an element of surprise that literally shook them into life. The album's "theme", a thin one of love, death and re-awakening, could have sounded fey, but the overall effect of the album was anything but.

Shirley's experiments up to this point were largely influenced by her husband, producer John Marshall. His final production for Shirley was her second and last Harvest album *Love, Death and the Lady*. Again, early instruments were used and Dolly provided the arrangements, but the mood was blacker. The opening track has sparse, bleak backing, and in its chilling treatment of death it displays what Shirley once described to me as "the black horror of medieval song behind all the trappings". Shirley was to emerge again, at the other side of a divorce, married to Tyger Hutchings, and involved in his experiments after he had launched electric folk.

Davy Graham had a more chequered history. Since the mid-sixties he has sporadically turned up to play in clubs, made occasional albums, and sporadically disappeared again. He had personal and serious health problems, and his followers often seemed unsure whether he was alive or dead. In 1969 I found him living off London's Ladbroke Grove, in a flat with hippies downstairs and a rock band practising upstairs. "I'd really like to hear Ravi Shankar and Chico Hamilton play Ravel's 'Bolero'," he said, "wouldn't that be fantastic?"

FOLK-BLUES 2: JANSCH TO GROSSMAN

Graham started the folk baroque guitar school, but the man who was to popularise it was born of Scottish-Austrian parents and started work as a gardener in a plant nursery in Edinburgh. Bert Jansch then moved to London, became a professional musician, and was soon a regular at Les Cousins. Jansch was influenced initially by Big Bill Broonzy, Lightnin' Hopkins and other American classic bluesmen. Unlike Graham (who just wrote a few instrumentals) he then applied his blues technique to song-writing, and the result was the highly personal collection that appeared on his first album, *Bert Jansch*, in 1965. His voice was weak, but delicately propped up by the intricate accompaniment. The songs were for the most part introspective and quietly melancholy, and the best known, "Needle Of Death" (which he soon disowned) was one of the first successful songs to be written on the drug problem.

By the time the third Jansch album, *Jack Orion*, was released, he had become exceedingly fashionable in London, and his records were outselling even Dylan in the Charing Cross Road folk shops. But his interests were beginning to change. "I'm definitely not a blues singer and I'm not really a writer," he told me in 1966, and this was becoming clear from his music. He cut back on writing, and on *Jack Orion* he applied the folk baroque style to British traditional songs like "Blackwaterside" and "Nottamun Town". In the same year he recorded an album simply called *Bert and John* with his only active rival in the "folk baroque" field, his friend John Renbourn. It consisted mostly of jazz-tinged instrumentals that the two of them had composed, along with a Charlie Mingus piece "Goodbye Pork Pie Hat". It's highly inventive, free-flowing music that shows the enormous scope that is possible with just two acoustic guitars. For me, this is the best example of folk baroque in captivity, and the best album that either Jansch or Renbourn made.

As for John Renbourn, he'd made his own first solo album a year earlier, in 1965. Renbourn was a Londoner, a veteran of a Guildford R&B band (if you can imagine such a thing) who had drifted up to the clubs, and ended up sharing a flat with Jansch. He wrote a few songs, did versions of a few traditional songs, but his main interest was the blues – his first album included selections from the Reverend Gary Davis and Blind Boy Fuller. He and Jansch seemed incredibly similar (and both were identically scruffy), but differences gradually emerged. While Jansch stuck to blues and English "folk baroque", Renbourn gradually developed an interest in early English music, modal styles and early classical work.

I once met him on a train, on his way to a gig somewhere, immersed in the medieval romance *Sir Gawain and the Grene Knight*. He wasn't exactly sure what he was going to do with it, he said, but he wanted to use it as the basis for an album. In due course it appeared – *Sir John Alot of Merrie Englandes Musyk Thyng and Ye Grene Knight* was his first excursion into the folk/medieval field. One side of the album contained a piece by William Byrd, an arrangement of a traditional song and two instrumentals in similar style. Just to prove that he hadn't given up his earlier interests, the flip side was all blues. Two years later (in 1970) Renbourn returned to these ideas on his most academic and serious album *The Lady and the Unicorn*. This was a collection of medieval pieces, early classical pieces and English and Italian tunes, immaculately played on guitar and sitar, with viola, violin, concertina and flute backing.

Jansch and Renbourn toured the British clubs, made solo albums, and both got restless. They started their own club at the Three Horseshoes pub in Tottenham Court Road and they thought about expanding their music. In 1967 – the year that rock finally gained respectability with The Beatles' *Sgt Pepper* and The Who's *Tommy* – they formed a band, Pentangle. It consisted of Jansch and Renbourn, singer Jacqui McShee (who had begun her career in the south London folk clubs), Danny Thompson on bass and Terry Cox on drums (both coming in from the jazz scene). Pentangle were not an electric folk band, for (to start with at least) they only played acoustic instruments. But they played directly into microphones and so the sound was always amplified – particularly when they moved from the Three Horseshoes to the Albert Hall.

For the five years of their existence, Pentangle were a considerable commercial success, and were the first progressive folk-based band to win international acclaim. They gave concerts all over the world, recorded a steady flow of albums, but were, I felt, consistently depressing. Not that they could ever be bad – all five are excellent, highly professional musicians – it was just that they were never exciting. They played traditional songs, jazz instrumentals, blues and occasional contemporary songs, and they all came out smoothed down with the same approach. At its best, such music was pleasantly mesmeric. At worst, it became high-quality folk muzak. The soporific approach eventually appeared to rub off on the performers themselves, who seemed less and less animated with each appearance. Towards the end, on the *Cruel Sister* and *Solomon's Seal* albums, they introduced muted electric guitar, but this didn't change the band's sound or approach.

Eventually, and not before time, the band broke up. Jansch and Renbourn returned to solo work. Danny Thompson demonstrated at long last that he could actually sound exciting, as well as being a technical wizard, when he toured the country backing Ralph McTell and John Martyn. Martyn doesn't fit into any folk category, but he deserves a brief digression here: he started from bluesy roots to develop a quite unique guitar style. On stage he performs a mixture of his own songs, with nasal buzzing vocals, breaking away for anything from "Singing In The Rain" to a one-man imitation of The Pink Floyd on electric guitar.

Martyn kept going, and kept progressing, but he was an exception. The British acoustic blues boom started with a flourish, and gradually ran out of steam and interest. Other classy guitarists and blues enthusiasts came out of the clubs – from Wizz Jones to Mike Cooper and John James – but the British blues scene cooled somewhat until a young American turned up at Les Cousins in the summer of 1967.

Stefan Grossman is not, I suppose, strictly eligible for inclusion in the story of British folk-rock. He deserves to be mentioned because he has become one of the best-loved performers on the British circuit, and has carried out the ideals and promise of the folk-blues revival with greater success than anyone else.

Stefan comes from New York, where he had the luck to meet that guitar genius, the blind Reverend Gary Davis, in Harlem. Davis had the luck to find a student who, though only 15, would study and learn his techniques, and later help his career. Stefan learned to play Reverend Davis's blues, and also met and learned from Son House and other early bluesmen, and fast became one of the leading authorities on their work. With all that behind him, he managed to get thrown out of architectural school, play with the highly entertaining Even Dozen Jug Band, travel to the Virgin Islands, play with the first outrageous underground heroes, The Fugs, get out of the draft, and eventually end up playing solo guitar to the delight of London's folkies. The folk scene liked Stefan, and it suited him too.

For a while he was based here, then he moved to Rome (his wife is Italian), but he keeps returning to Britain for regular visits.

What Stefan achieved with the blues is a musical ideal that other folk musicians, working in different fields, might have followed if they'd had the skill or the imagination. From his base in Rome, he spends part of his time writing books on the early blues and guitar technique, part of his time touring, and part of his time writing. His songs are "totally blues–influenced", he insists, "though some may not sound like it. Some may sound like jazz or Bach, but it's blues-influenced, because that's my base, that's where I learned about music."

At a Stefan concert, one might hear John Hurt's "Satisfied And Tickled Too", Rev. Davis's "Candyman", medleys of ragtime styles, all mixed with Stefan's highly individual compositions. He's written everything from children's songs to bleak, surreal ballads, and a whole variety of instrumentals. He moves from the traditional to the experimental, and back again, in a way that British traditionalists, with only one or two exceptions, find quite unthinkable.

POETS AND ONE-MAN BANDS

Another variety of songs that could be heard in "progressive" clubs like Les Cousins were the works of the singer-songwriters – mostly soloists, singing to guitar accompaniment. Such people emerged through the folk clubs because this was the only outlet they had, though most of the songs that these "folk singers" produced had nothing to do with "folk song" proper.

The singer-songwriters mostly saw themselves as following in the tradition of Woody Guthrie, whose songs had been popularised in Britain (albeit in a sing-along form) by Donegan. Guthrie was a migrant worker and radical who roamed across America in the twenties and thirties, writing songs about what he saw and extolling the virtues of the unions. He was a great humanitarian, his writing was simple, clear and powerful, and he became the ideal hero for a generation emerging from the growing affluence of the fifties and sixties, and beginning to question the society in which they found themselves. Bob Dylan visited Guthrie in hospital, where he was dying of Huntington's Disease, and saw himself – to begin with – as carrying on the grand Guthrie tradition. So "folk singing" meant dirty denims, hard travelling, crashing out on the floors of friendly strangers, and a bucketful of unspecific left-wing idealism. It may seem corny now, but its heart was in the right place.

Britain soon developed its own singer-songwriter "folk singers", and they tended to be in the American style. Ewan MacColl may have written his remarkable radio ballads, using the style of British industrial folk song to deal with the lives of fishermen or train-drivers – but fashion was in America's favour. Another factor helped swing the balance. One of the best singer-songwriters to be heard around the clubs in the early sixties happened to be American. He was called Paul Simon. In the summer, when he wasn't at college, a friend called Art Garfunkel would come over to join him.

Originally influenced by Dylan, Simon wrote introspective, personal, rather clever songs, and so broadened the scope of what was considered possible as "folk singing". *The Sounds of Silence*, which he wrote in 1964, was revolutionary for the time, for its self-consciously poetic lyrics about alienation. The same song caused a greater revolution when a producer back in America added soft-rock backing and it became a hit. Simon and Garfunkel left the British folk scene to become superstars, and later to record that best-selling album of all time, *Bridge Over Troubled Water*.

Bob Dylan himself even appeared in the British clubs – just. In 1963 he was flown to Britain to appear in a television play, *Madhouse on Castle Street*, and he stayed on to play in a club or two – with some apparently chaotic results. He, like Simon and Garfunkel, was to re-appear only for triumphant concerts – triumphant, that is, until 1966, when he brought on The Band to back him at the Albert Hall and a London folk audience booed in horror at this sign that their hero had moved across to the rock camp.

Britain soon had its carbon copy. Donovan – a performer of some charm but limited talent – moved from The Cock, St Albans, to television's *Ready, Steady, Go*, singing pleasant, Dylanish songs like "I'll Try For The Sun", "Josie" and "Catch The Wind". He summed up the public image of a "folk singer", and found it a hard one to shake off. He did change styles to make a couple of enormously successful pop singles, "Mellow Yellow" and "Sunshine Superman", before disappearing from the front ranks. At his 1973 concert at

London's Rainbow he sat cross-legged on an artificial rock in front of a Japanese screen, and sang a new collection of twee, pleasant, unexceptional songs. One was about spacemen's toilet arrangements.

Other denim-clad guitar-toters followed Donovan. From the Olive Tree Folk Club, Croydon, came Ralph McTell, who had a good line in Blind Blake rags and blues (many learned from Wizz Jones) and became very successful as a songwriter. He moved from the clubs through to the concert circuit, and was soon rightly insisting that he was not a "folk singer" but a contemporary songwriter.

The quality of his songs has varied enormously as he has become more successful. The best known, "Streets Of London", is folksy and friendly, with a strong tune and agreeably English-based lyrics (one annoying habit of English writers was that they felt they should sound American). It also balanced dangerously on the edge of sounding twee – one of McTell's constant problems. At times he has gone over the edge, as with "Old Brown Dog", but at other times he has produced thoughtful, intelligent and humanitarian songs, with an apparently genuine concern for the underdog and loser. From "Michael In The Garden", a study of madness and reality, through to "Maginot Waltz", a simple, cheerful and doom-laden cameo of a coach-load of seaside trippers just before the First World War, he has kept the ability to produce a really fine song among the plain and the commercial.

McTell has survived, but other of the singer-songwriters who inhabited the folk clubs have had varied fortunes. David Campbell, for instance, a Scottish-Guyanese singer who made two very strong albums in the early sixties, seems to have disappeared completely. Leon Rosselson wrote a batch of witty, socially committed songs, received only moderate recognition, and remained a teacher, though he still makes club appearances. And on the other side, Harvey Andrews wrote some of the best "post-protest" songs of the mid-sixties, but never emerged from the folk circuit until he happened to get signed by a rock-orientated record company in the seventies. His ultra-honest, somewhat old-fashioned style was suddenly heard by rock audiences, and he had an unexpected burst of popularity.

Particularly after Dylan had appeared in London with The Band in 1966, many singer-songwriters developed dual styles, playing solo guitar in folk clubs but adding rock backing for records and for occasional prestige concerts. Al Stewart tried to achieve this rather harder than most. He arrived in London from Bournemouth in 1965, and then did penance for once having backed Tony Blackburn by going off to Paris to starve in the traditional way. Back in London he moved into the flat where Simon and Garfunkel were staying and got a weekly spot at Bunjie's Coffee Shop, off the Charing Cross Road.

His first album *Bedsitter Images* had orchestral backing and a selection of pleasant soft-rock songs with London-orientated lyrics. So far so good, but there followed a grand attempt to "launch" him, with a prestige concert at the Festival Hall, where he was backed both by a rock band and an orchestra. It was every struggling folkie's dream of escaping from the clubs to the big-time rock circuit, and the result was a spectacular mess of styles. Back to the clubs he went, though he has continued making acceptable albums (five by 1974, each containing two or three good songs), and he's made regular forays into the concert scene. His 1974 album, *Past, Present and Future* was a noticeable step forward, a concept album, concerned with the passing of time, with a song for every decade of the twentieth century. Maybe he'll still make it.

CRAZY BRITISH INDIVIDUALISTS: HARPER

Roy Harper managed the "dual styles" (playing solo, then adding a band for occasions) the best of all. He is also – though he could be rivalled here by the excellent Pete Atkin – the most successful of the new singers whose work had nothing to do with folk music, but who used the clubs as a training ground and fall-back, before leaping off into the rock concert circuit.

He is an unusual, difficult and (when he wants to be) highly talented man, and it has taken many years for his talents to be appreciated by the public. The fault is largely his own, for he has been consistent only in his unpredictability. He was born in 1941 in Manchester, the son of a long-distance runner. His mother died in childbirth, and he was brought up by his stepmother, a Jehovah's Witness, who, he claims "drove me mad and filled me with a lifelong hate for any form of religion". In order to get away from home he joined the Air Force at 15, then found that he wanted to get away from that too. He feigned madness, got his discharge, but ended up under electric shock treatment (which made him "start throwing darts across crowded rooms") and then locked up in a group therapy centre in Surrey. Next came the Lancaster Moor Mental Institution, an escape from there, drifting around Blackpool, three years' probation, and a year in jail.

Mr Harper, you may deduce from this, was something of a mess. Physically weak, mentally chaotic, socially unacceptable, the only thing he had going for him was music. He had started playing skiffle at 13 and had played Leadbelly numbers at Air Force camp concerts. Once released from jail he started street singing, and he made enough to set off on the statutory wander around Europe in the summer of 1964. He bought a guitar, sang blues in Scandinavia, and then started writing poems. Soon he was pouring out his hang-ups, problems and philosophy into some of the most original, powerful songs that the "folk singer-songwriter" school was to produce. By 1965 he was back in London with a residency at Les Cousins. The following year he made his first album.

It took eight years from then for Roy Harper to get mass recognition and there's still the constant danger that he'll do something so outrageous or disastrous that his reputation will collapse and he'll go sliding down a snake, back to Square One. For his great strength is also his great weakness: he is almost terrifyingly honest, and just as unpredictable. He is also vain, self-obsessed, and can be as dull as he can be fascinating. He can play brilliantly, or he can drive the audience to the point of despair or departure with rambling monologues, but he often saves his more outrageous acts for the more important concerts. His first solo concert at the Festival Hall was one of the worst he has given; only when most of the audience had left did he start to play well. His first (and only – so far) American tour was undertaken in much the same vein. Playing his first night at the Troubadour in Los Angeles he threatened to pee over the first row. He then decided to abandon the tour, and disappeared to a beach hut at Big Sur. Here – predictably – he got raided by the police and locked up.

To compensate for this sort of behaviour, an artist must have something going for him to win the praise that Harper has picked up from the music establishment (fellow musicians were faster to realise his worth than the general public). Ian Anderson of Jethro Tull has called him "a great acoustic player who wipes the floor with all your James Taylors, Gordon Lightfoots, Dylans", while Led Zeppelin's normally reticent Jimmy Page paid him the compliment of backing him on record and on stage. Harper himself, with characteristic modesty, explains it like this: "I have more than one song. The average guy has one or two songs – like Woody Guthrie had one song all the time; Jagger's got two, 'Moonlight Mile' and 'Brown Sugar'." Harper says he's got about seven. "Five of them make people say 'he's not a folk singer, is he?', and two of them make them say 'yes he is'." When I commented on his conceit, Harper readily agreed. "Jimmy Page said to me 'if I'd made the records you'd made and only had the amount of success that you've had, I don't know what I'd do', and I replied 'well, I exist on ego these days'."

Harper got the opportunity to develop his "seven songs" thanks to the tolerant audiences in the contemporary folk clubs. He's one of the folk scene's finest products, although – as he points out – there's little that's obviously "folk" about his material. He's more a rock singer who happens to play acoustic guitar. The best of his songs, like "McGoohan's Blues" (on the *Folkjokeopus* album), and "Me And My Woman" (on his best album to date, *Stormcock*) are a barrage of stream-of-consciousness self-revelation, with the blackness lifting occasionally and unexpectedly to reveal a gift for lyrical descriptive writing. Another of his styles is straightforward and emotional ("I'll See You Again" and "Forever" on the *Valentine* album) but Mr Harper is determined to shock if he feels he's getting too friendly and accessible. Quite often, it would seem, just for the sake of shocking.

What happens to him now depends largely on his capacity for self-destruction. He has become a minor cult figure, particularly since he gave a concert in early 1974 to promote the *Valentine* album, and was joined on stage by The Who's Keith Moon, Zeppelin's Jimmy Page and ex-Face Ronnie Lane. It was, by all accounts, a pretty disastrous show musically compared with the excellent concerts Roy had given in earlier months. But it did launch him into the big league. I, for one, think he deserves to stay there.

CRAZY BRITISH INDIVIDUALISTS 2: THE STRING BAND

Harper was one major talent that the contemporary clubs produced, and The Incredible String Band was another. Like Roy, they used the clubs as a launching pad for talents that only obliquely reflected folk proper. Unlike Roy, they peaked after a couple of years, after a period in which I felt they could match even The Beatles in writing ability and sheer inventiveness, and then went into a slow and unsteady decline.

The String Band came from Scotland. They started as a three-man jug band in 1965, playing in Glasgow at Clive's Incredible Folk Club, from which they took their name. Their first album was so un-incredible that at least one folk-orientated record company turned it down, and it was not until Clive Palmer left that the other two members – Robin Williamson and Mike Heron – suddenly blossomed out to produce some extraordinary music. With their second album *The 5,000 Spirits, or the Layers of the Onion* they virtually invented a new, global folk form that made use of instruments and musical styles from anywhere. Both were excellent guitarists, but they embellished with any interesting sound they came across – gimbris, whistles, harpsichords, drums, fiddles or mandolins. More surprising still, they played them bafflingly well; the result was no weak imitation of alien material, but a completely new, fresh fusion.

In 1967, when the String Band's *5,000 Spirits* leaped up the folk charts, there were new and powerful influences at work in the music world. For many people 1967 was the golden year, when the new form of rock finally flowered. It was the year of unspecific hippy idealism – San Francisco, flower power, drugs, psychedelia, *Sgt Pepper* and the Beach Boys' *Good Vibrations*. A year of the underground, free concerts and a sudden apparent rejection of the affluent society by thousands of middle-class kids. It didn't last partly because there was no coherent philosophy, and partly because drugs didn't help at all. Haight-Ashbury moved from love to squalor. And partly it was because "the underground", being popular, was ripe for straightforward commercial exploitation.

Now it may be unfashionable to say so in the cynical seventies, but there were some admirable idealistic sides to "flower power". The Incredible String Band summed them up. Their albums mixed an Eastern sense of awe of being alive with a Western dry humour. On *The Hangman's Beautiful Daughter* they managed to combine such oddities as a wailing chant in honour of the powers of water with a Gilbert and Sullivan spoof, "The Minotaur Song". Their music was constantly surprising, moving through changes of idea, instrument and influence. The songs showed a mystical, pantheist involvement in a very live universe. It was neo-Wordsworthian imagery drawn not from a Cumberland vale but the world at large. "A Very Cellular Song" (again on *The Hangman's Beautiful Daughter* album) sums it up. It starts with a gently swinging version of the Pindar Family spiritual "Bid You Goodnight", moves away from the Bahamas to harpsichord and fiddle, wittily explains the inter-relatedness of matter in terms of a splitting amoeba, to a West Indian ska beat, and ends with a repeated universal benediction: "May the long-time sun shine on you, all love surround you, and the pure light within you guide you all the way on."

For a time the String Band managed to straddle both the folk world and the underground. In one memorable week in 1967 they appeared alongside Shirley Collins at a folk concert at London's Queen Elizabeth Hall, and alongside The Pink Floyd at one of Brian Epstein's heavy rock concerts at the Saville Theatre. But it was just a matter of time before they moved completely to the rock concert circuit, when the clubs could no longer afford them or give them the necessary scope.

Their fourth (double) album, *Wee Tam and the Big Huge*, showed them extending their range yet again, this time to jug band and country material. It included "Air", a simple, gently humorous anthem to the life-giving union of blood and oxygen, set to a murmuring calypso, and "The Circle Is Unbroken", one of Williamson's most eerie, haunting hymns. It was all a long way from traditional music, but the influences were still there.

After releasing this remarkable album in 1968, the String Band's fortunes began to slide just a little. In the public eye they did well – there were more albums and tours of Europe and America (they first played at the legendary Fillmore West in San Francisco in May 1968), while new members of the band came and went. For a long while it included two girls, Rose and Licorice, then in came a dancer, Malcolm Le Maistre, and a solemn-looking clarinet player, Gerard Dott. Thankfully, he didn't last long, and in came yet more members.

The band's ambitions also changed. Their most adventurous, and disastrous, scheme was launched in 1970, when their musical, U, ran at London's Roundhouse and then toured America. It was described as "a surreal parable in song and dance", and consisted of boy losing girl because he can't see what she can see, and then eventually getting her back, after being told "you're one of my kind, you're an infinite mind". It flopped largely because it was a mess – Williamson and Heron produced more than adequate music, but the dancing, acting and choreography was that of an amateur pantomime.

Musically, too, the String Band failed to live up to their early high standards. They continued to give some fine concerts, and some of their album tracks remained impressive. But the spark of enthusiasm, excitement and idealism in their work gradually dimmed. In place of exotic instruments they moved to a more conventional rock line-up of electric guitars, bass and drums. In place of the unspecific romanticism they became Scientologists.

There's still, I suppose, a chance that Williamson and Heron will write something startling to match their early work. They were, after all, once songwriters of an equal stature to Paul McCartney, and he managed a comeback. Heron, I suspect, will eventually produce something outstanding within the rock framework. He's always been the more rock-orientated of the two, and his one solo album, *Smiling Men with Bad Reputations* (1971), was an impressive departure. On it he was backed by everyone from John Cale to Pete Townshend, with chunks of Fairport Convention and Fotheringay added. It may be a long way from folk-rock, but anyone who has not heard the album should at least listen to "Warm Heart Pastry" for the best track The Who never put their name to.

FOLK-ROCK IN MUSWELL HILL

Back in the traditionalist camp, the situation was getting decidedly uncheerful. In 1967, while The Incredible String Band roared out into the underground, Harper spat away in the contemporary clubs, and rock was adding intelligence and respectability to its initial excitement, a folk club no longer seemed such an attractive place to be in. The music was as valid as ever, but the "folkier than thou" purists now seemed a world away from the very real, and very popular, revolution that was going on outside. Somehow, the two worlds needed to be brought together.

The group that first achieved the fusion did so in such a carefree, haphazard way that they never seemed to fully appreciate the significance of what they were doing. The Fairport Convention – whose name has become synonymous with folk-rock – have remained that sort of a band. Despite the folky image that they have attracted, these modernisers of Britain's musical heritage started off with no connections with the folk scene. They came from London's Muswell Hill, had just left school in 1967, and could be heard at weddings and youth clubs playing "the usual sort of juggy band thing with one amplifier between three guitars and half a drum kit". The band consisted of Richard Thompson, who also had a job making stained-glass windows, Simon Nicol, who was cinema projectionist at the "Highgate Odeous", and Ashley "Tyger" Hutchings, who had already chucked in his job in publishing for music. "It was", Simon recalls, "a nice summer, and Tyger had left home and moved into a flat in the house where I lived and was born. It was called 'Fairport'..."

The Fairports played their first gig in a church hall in Golders Green. It ended with Martin Lamble emerging from the audience and asking to become the drummer. He stayed. Judy Dyble, a local librarian, was also added "because we decided we should get someone who could sing". With a repertoire of the latest West Coast American, Dylanish, Byrdish, Butterfieldish songs they descended on the newly flourishing underground scene, the shades and incense of the Middle Earth and UFO clubs. It was at UFO – a dancehall in the Tottenham Court Road that was home for underground heavies like Pink Floyd – that the Fairports got their break. They were signed up by a tall, soft-spoken, highly talented American called Joe Boyd, who was something of an underground hero because he also ran The Incredible String Band. Boyd took the Fairports into the studios, where their carefully studied scruffiness startled even the engineers.

Now the Fairports – just like their American counterparts, The Byrds – have been plagued with a long and baffling series of changes in their line-up, with members coming and going, forming offshoot bands, and then offshoot bands from them. In the process the entire folk-rock scene became entwined around them.

The first changes went like this: the band became worried by Judy Dyble, so they augmented her with a sixth member, Ian Matthews (then known as Ian MacDonald). He had an "experienced pop background" (which meant he had once played in a band called The Pyramids), and a good voice. Judy Dyble finally left, after appearing on the first Fairport album. The band carried on as a five-piece, but audiences were unhappy. Fairport had acquired something of a Jefferson Airplane image for having a girl singer up front, and a new girl was needed. Auditions were held in the unremarkable surroundings of the Eight Feathers Boys Club in Parsons Green, and here a great new English music style was born.

Sandy Denny, the lady who got the job, says she had no idea who the Fairports were, but she thought they were American. She had already made something of a name for herself on the London folk scene, which she'd gone into after leaving art school because "I liked singing, though I was frowned on by the ethnics". She sang at clubs like the Scots Hoose and Les Cousins, performing "the usual mixture" of Dylan, Scottish, American and Irish folk songs. From the start, while she was still developing her clear, exquisite voice, she was happy to experiment. She joined the Strawbs for a while, and recorded an album with them (only just released, years later) before returning, solo, to the clubs.

She went along to meet the Fairports because she was bored with being a folk soloist "flitting round the country by myself, finding my way to obscure pubs". Not that she was immediately impressed by her new band. "I listened to their first album and thought it terrible," she says, "but thought I'd see what happened." It's as well that she did, for the first album she made with them, *What We Did on Our Holidays*, was a breakthrough. It contained the statutory songs by Dylan and Joni Mitchell. It contained a slow, moody song, "Fotheringay", by Sandy. And it contained the catchy and thoughtful "Meet On The Ledge", the first recorded solo composition by Richard Thompson (later to prove an exceptional songwriter). All these were fine, but in retrospect none were quite as important as the tracks on which Sandy's folk repertoire was given a rock backing. No one thought much of it at the time. "We just asked Sandy to sing some of her favourite songs," says Simon, "and we tried to follow her." "We were sitting in a dressing room before doing a gig somewhere," says Sandy, "and we thought 'what can we do that's different'. So I sang them some songs."

The first known examples of Folk-rock Britannicus were "Nottamun Town" (which had already been orientalised and jazzed up by Davy Graham and Bert Jansch) and "She Moves Through The Fair". The Fairports treated the former with harmonies and a Graham-influenced Eastern instrumental break, and the latter with muted drums and electric guitar in the background. Sandy sang both as she would in a folk club, and the band filled in and improvised discreetly around her. It was all very tasteful, and – to a listener now – excellent but unremarkable. But those two tracks were the new move that British folk badly needed.

The Fairports were obviously pleased with them, for on the next album, *Unhalfbricking*, there was a folk-rock track included, along with the expected Dylan, and new songs by Sandy and Richard. This was another excellent, varied album that still stands up well. It included Sandy's "Who Knows Where The Time Goes" (the song popularised by Judy Collins), a great Thompson rocker, and an oddity track "Si Tu Dois Partir", a Dylan song in French that got the Fairports a surprise hit single. The one traditional track, "A Sailor's Life", was particularly impressive. It starts with Sandy singing quietly against a wash of drums and guitars improvising around a couple of chords behind her. Then gradually a rock riff is introduced on bass, and the song continues with the vitality of any rock piece, without the amplification in any way detracting from the melody or the story line of the ballad. It ends as an improvised jam session, and one of the instruments joining in is electric violin. It was played by the folk scene's leading instrumentalist at the time, Dave Swarbrick.

Soon after *Unhalfbricking* was recorded, but before it was released, a tragic event occurred that was to suddenly change the emergent folk-rock scene. Several of the Fairports were travelling back to London after a concert when their van crashed on the M1. Martin Lamble, the drummer, was killed, and others were badly shaken. It was an event they still find difficult to talk about, but all agree that it affected the personalities of some of the band quite considerably – and also affected the music.

Almost as a therapy to recover from the crash, the Fairports threw themselves into the next project, a complete folk-rock album. Before work on it started, a couple of new members joined the band: a drummer, Dave Mattacks, coming in from dance combos, and the folk instrumentalist hero himself, Dave Swarbrick.

Swarbrick's move caused a mild sensation. Here was a leading member of the folk establishment, with a history of playing first with Ian Campbell and then with Martin Carthy, suddenly giving it all up to join a rock band. And why did the wily-looking man with the disarming grin do it? Because he liked amplified music, and had thought long and hard about what was going wrong on the folk scene.

A lot of his criticism of the folkies centres around that misused word "ethnic" (which, loosely translated, means "genuine as regards the folk tradition"), and the difference between "traditional" singers and "revivalists". A "traditionalist" is a "real folk singer", that is to say someone who has learned the songs as part of an aural, parent-to-child tradition. A "revivalist" is someone who only learns the songs by going along to a folk club or listening to records. Now the true traditionalists, says Swarbrick, have not become professional musicians, have not intellectualised the music or worried about what's ethnic and what's not, and wouldn't object if it were amplified. The revivalists, on the other hand, did become professional "folk singers", and worried about "whether Tin Pan Alley would get hold of these songs and ruin them", because – according to Swarbrick – "they were dealing with a minority cult and wanted to keep it minority". And worse than that, he says, "it turned into a real back-biting, rat-snapping scene. I didn't like seven-eighths of the people involved in it, and it was exceedingly opportune to leave. I was suddenly presented with the possibilities of exploring the dramatic content of the songs to their full."

So Swarbrick teamed up with Richard Thompson, Sandy Denny, Simon Nicol, Dave Mattacks and Tyger Hutchings. Hutchings had now decided that he preferred British folk to The Byrds, and was later to react in the most dramatic way, switching from dark glasses and boots to the English squire look. Trevor Lucas, now Sandy's husband and a member of Fairport, describes the symptoms as "a great attack of 'galloping folk' that can strike at rock musicians". The new line-up disappeared to Farley House, a Queen Anne mansion in Hampshire, to rehearse. Three months later they emerged to record the *Liege and Lief* album and give the first series of folk-rock concerts that Britain had heard, starting off at the Festival Hall. "We just treated it as a project," says Sandy, "though everyone thought we had gone completely mad just doing folk songs. We really channelled our minds to it, and excluded everything else including other people's reactions. Then, just as we went on stage we were very, very nervous…"

Both the Festival Hall concert, on September 24, 1969, and the *Liege and Lief* album were milestones. The old songs were made to crackle with a new vitality, and that vital element in each – the story – was not lost in the process. On stage, the small, bearded and genial Swarbrick looked like a delighted weasel. "I'm still a folk fiddler," he told me just before the Festival Hall concert, "and maybe this is the folk revival. Or maybe it's the story revival, which comes to the same thing."

The Fairports played very loud and with extraordinary intensity that night. I particularly remember guitarist Simon Nicol launching into the robust tune of "The Deserter", drums, fiddle and bass crackling out through the amplifiers, and over the top of it all, Sandy's clear voice re-telling the old story of the young man walking through Stepney, who has too many drinks with the recruiting party, finds he's enlisted, deserts, and is re-captured: "the guns were presented, a cruel sight to see, for now the Queen's duties lie heavy on me."

The Fairports also applied their electric folk to the ever-popular "Matty Groves", a song that A.L. Lloyd has described as "among the grandest of romantic ballads". It was an obvious choice – a highly dramatic, fast-moving and bloodthirsty tale of a lady seducing a commoner, the two of them being discovered by her lordly husband, and the ensuing fight and death of the two lovers. The lady naturally gets buried on top because "she was of noble kin". The Fairport version has a robust urgency, with Swarbrick adding dramatic fiddle embroidery for the fight sequence, and the whole thing ending with a cathartic instrumental workout when the tension finally breaks. On another long track the "Tam Lin" ballad is successfully re-told, with Sandy's strong voice carrying the narrative over verse after verse of bass riff and crashing amplified chords.

The next few months, when Fairport toured playing the *Liege and Lief* material, were what Simon now calls "the real magic period". It wasn't to last long, though, for the band contained so many strong personalities, songwriters and ideas that it was almost immediately beset with problems. Once again, Fairport began to split up.

First to go were Tyger Hutchings, the band's unofficial boss, and Sandy, the band's best-known personality. The reasons were the usual ones – personality clashes and differences of musical policy. Tyger had become an all-out electric folkie, determined to stick with traditional music, while for Sandy the folk side had been "just a project", and she wanted to develop her own writing.

So Tyger went off to found Steeleye Span. Sandy went off to follow her own musical interests, and also to spend more time with Trevor Lucas (now her husband). They were to found their own band, Fotheringay, and eventually both joined a later Fairport.

The two departures were a shock, but the band kept going. A new bass player, Dave Pegg, came in from the Ian Campbell Folk Group, and soon looked like a veteran rocker. The new five-piece produced yet another excellent Fairport album, *Full House* (1970), though it showed a slight move away from folk-rock. Only half the tracks were traditional, but they included two sets of jigs on which Swarbrick could demonstrate some pyrotechnics on mandolin and fiddle. These dance tunes responded easily and admirably to amplification, and soon even the hip audiences at London's Roundhouse were leaping around to old folk tunes. The Fairports also recorded yet more songs by their ever-improving writer and guitarist, Richard Thompson.

This was another good Fairport line-up, if a little weak on vocals. They toured America, gave the Fillmore its first taste of British folk-rock, and exuded an air of the good-time rather than the experimental. But it all collapsed when managerial wizard Joe Boyd quit to take up a prestige job on the American West Coast. Richard Thompson decided to leave ("though I never knew he was so impressed with me," says Joe, "he never did what I suggested"), and disappeared to absorb folk influences and eventually to reappear with his own band.

From here on in the Fairports' history gets yet more confusing, and the standard of their output begins to sink. After Richard left, the band thought about new members – A.L. Lloyd was even considered at one point, astonishing as that may sound – but in the end they took the easy way out and continued as a four-piece. Simon's bitter about that now: "The inspiration for the group was merely to carry on being successful, and make some money in America. As for musical direction, I don't think we had one."

This line-up recorded *Angel Delight*, a lightweight and cheerful mixture of old and new, and then embarked on what was conceived as a really major work – the first "folk-rock opera". *Babbacombe Lee* was a crusading project for Swarbrick and Pegg, who wrote it, and it almost came off. The entire album was taken up with telling the story of a man sentenced to death for murder, who protests his innocence, and escapes death because the gallows trap-door fails to open on three occasions. It was not a total success because neither the story nor the music were quite strong enough, but it was an admirable near miss. One folk-song, "A Sailor's Alphabet", is introduced a little spuriously, just because Lee was once a sailor, and clashes with the best parts of the album, a folk-rock update of the Victorian penny-dreadful. There are good dramatic sections, as on the aftermath of the murder, and Lee's prison lament. Just a touch of Richard Thompson, and it could have been the folk world's *Tommy*.

It was followed by yet more changes. Simon left – to join The Albion Country Band and later team up with Richard again – and a new guitarist, Roger Hill, joined for a few months before being replaced by Jerry Donahue and Trevor Lucas. Drummer Dave Mattacks also disappeared to the Albions, then came back. The Donahue-Mattacks-Lucas-Pegg-Swarbrick line-up then actually managed to stay together for some time. They made a dreadful album, *Rosie*, an excursion by Swarbrick into writing pop drivel. Then, in 1973, when all but their most stubborn fans must have given them up, they brought out *Fairport Nine*, which showed them to be back on the up again. The folk numbers on the album's first side had all the old verve and enthusiasm – with Swarbrick's concepts of "dramatic story telling" coming through well on "Polly On The

Shore". The new songs on the second side showed how Trevor Lucas, in particular, had improved as a writer.

But nothing ever goes smoothly for the Fairports. This excellent album was followed by a world tour that went fine musically, badly financially. They returned with business affairs apparently in a mess, and they sacked their manager. For a while it looked as if the band would break up, then suddenly the bad news turned to good. In the spring of 1974 it was announced that Sandy was rejoining Fairport – which may have seemed a natural move (she wanted to be with Trevor), but was still surprising. How would her solo career fit in with that of the band, and how would her song-writing flourish against whatever they wanted to do? Had the old personality clashes also been ironed out? First impressions of the new line-up were that the best qualities of those involved had been remarkably well married together. With the Fairports it has proved unwise to predict the next move, but it seemed they were firmly on the way back up.

STEELEYE: THE FIRST FOLK SUPERGROUP

While the Fairports were launching off into folk-rock, the folk world looked on, bemused. Some of the more far-seeing members of the folk establishment, like A.L. Lloyd, approved. Many others didn't. Even so, some folk musicians started to get worried. In 1969, just before the Fairports released *Liege and Lief*, an impromptu late-night meeting took place at the Keele Folk Festival. Discussing the possibilities of amplification were Tyger Hutchings (still with the Fairports), Bob and Carole Pegg, Dave and Toni Arthur, and Tim Hart and Maddy Prior. Tim says he took part because "I'd been walking around the festival, and everyone was doing the same thing. The new singers were imitating the older singers, there was no drive and it was all very complacent." The meeting between Tyger, Tim and Maddy, and the discussions that night, were to lead eventually to the most successful folk-rock band of all, one that was to bring a highly amplified version of British traditional material into the vast rock shows in the American stadiums and into concert halls across the world. The band was to be called Steeleye Span.

As with Fairport, Steeleye's members have come and gone. The two constants are Tim Hart and Maddy Prior, so their story is really that of the band. Tim and Maddy started as typical revivalist singers. They come from St Albans, where they used to play along with Donovan in the local pub, though Tim also played in the school rock band, The Ratfinks (the school's second-best band, actually, after the rather more famous Zombies). Tim became a professional musician after six months working behind a dole desk in Kings Cross. Once he proved he could hold down a job his father agreed to help him become a musician. Maddy had meanwhile been making ends meet by acting as driver for the folk duo, Sandy and Jeanie. They did her the invaluable service of persuading her to stop singing American songs like everyone else, and stick to English traditional.

Tim and Maddy set off in a Ford Anglia to conquer the British folk scene, and they amazed themselves by doing so in a very short time. They avoided over-exposed songs, and dug around to find good obscure ones, pillaging collections and libraries. And the combination of Maddy's exquisite, crystal-clear voice with Tim's guitar playing and harmonies soon established their reputation on the club circuit.

They turned professional at the beginning of 1967, and gradually realised that "the crock of gold at the end of the rainbow on the folk scene wasn't that difficult to achieve". Two years later, "We were up with your Martin Carthys and your Alex Campbells, and there was nowhere to go. Once you get £25 at clubs and headline at occasional festivals, that's it. You either become a folk intellectual or you become an alcoholic. Just to work around the clubs over and over again is totally boring."

Tim, like Swarbrick, began to rebel against the way the folk revival had gone. "It built its own limitations within itself. It came out of skiffle – a popular movement – and popularised traditional music for a while, but then went backwards." Tim thinks that the revival "could have opened out a bit, musically" and should have done more than setting up a string of folk clubs. "No one said 'let's glamourise it a bit, let's do a bit of publicity, let's really try to sell folk records, let's try to sell a folk act to a larger market'."

So when Tyger turned up, fresh from the Fairports and wanting to start a new band, Tim and Maddy were quick to join in. Martin Carthy gave the new band their name, Steeleye Span, after a character in the song "Horkstow Grange". Tim and Maddy backed his suggestion, though Tyger wanted "Middlemarch Wait", and the other two members, Terry and Gay Woods, wanted to call it "Iyubidan Waits". I can't imagine anyone going into a shop to ask for that, so it's as well that Steeleye won.

They all set out to be different from the Fairports in one important way. Fairports were a rock band that drifted into folk music, but Steeleye wanted "not to be a rock band but traditional musicians working with electric instruments". The first Steeleye line-up made one album, *Hark! The Village Wait*, and then broke up without giving a concert. The cause was apparently friction between the two duos, Tim and Maddy and Terry and Gay, though this was in no way reflected in the album, which is restrained, slightly formal, with amplification added sparingly and tastefully.

Steeleye Mark II really shook the folkies, because ethnic guitar superstar Martin Carthy took the place of Terry and Gay. Martin had played for years in a duo with Dave Swarbrick but was such a dedicated purist and traditionalist that no one expected him to turn to amplified music. The band also acquired a (then) unknown fiddle player, Peter Knight. This line-up did tour, and made two albums, *Please to See the King*, and *Ten Man Mop*. The first, in particular, was a minor masterpiece. Traditional songs were dressed up with slightly solemn, highly elaborate arrangements, all immaculately performed. Unfortunately, Steeleye couldn't reproduce all this on stage, for in one important sense they were not a true band. Both Martin and Maddy and Tim continued to do solo work, and so were not fully committed to Steeleye. On stage, they looked more like a collection of individuals than an integrated unit. As an extra problem, the ethnic Martin played very loud, and the sound balance was sometimes extremely strange.

Even so, this line-up was a decided success. Keith Dewhurst wrote a play, *Corunna*, for them and it had a successful run upstairs at the Royal Court. Folk fused with rock was now fused with drama – an experience that was to help enormously in the band's later success. *Corunna* was an important step, but it helped break up this line-up. The play was going to move to the Young Vic, but one spanner got in the works. Tyger said he didn't want to do it any more, and soon after this announcement he again apparently made himself unpopular by deciding that he didn't want to go on an American tour. Once again the band broke up.

There followed a major policy disagreement between Tim and Martin (Tim wanted another bass player brought in, Martin wanted a multi-instrumentalist), and after Tim, Maddy and Pete had done an experimental gig with bass player Rick Kemp, Martin decided that he too would leave. He went back to solo work around the clubs – still playing amazingly, but now heard by relatively few people – while Steeleye marched on to become the first folk-rock supergroup. Rick Kemp came into the band, and was followed by another "unknown", Bob Johnson, who had once played in a duo with Pete. There was another round of rows ("the usual stuff – the threatening stuff, the banging on the table stuff"), at the end of which the band had a new manager, and a new record company. From then on in – as they say – they didn't look back.

I remember visiting them when they first started rehearsing, among the stately halls of the Irish Club in London's Eaton Square, and it was immediately clear that there was a new enthusiasm, and purpose. Steeleye was a band now – no one was rushing off to pursue a solo career on the side – while the two "unknowns", Rick and Bob, had brought in a whole new area of experience. Rick is a highly imaginative bass player who worked for a long time with the underestimated Mike Chapman. Bob had already combined his experience playing as a folk duo with Peter Knight with a weird rock career – he had backed everyone from P.J. Proby to an early incarnation of Gary Glitter. Both of them knew about amplification, rock and production, and both helped to transform Steeleye from a serious electric folk group to an outfit that could appear alongside the best rock bands, and still stay true to its original ideals.

It couldn't have happened to a nicer band, but then it could have happened to other folk bands if they had been as daring or well managed. Steeleye were the only good band in Britain that concentrated entirely on folk material, and everything they did was handled with complete professionalism. They chose their material well, played it well, and blended in the rock influences gradually and tastefully. By the time that the winning line-up made their third album *Now We Are Six* (produced by Jethro Tull's Ian Anderson and with David Bowie playing saxophone on one track), a sixth member, drummer Nigel Pegrum, had been added. The result, on "Seven Hundred Elves" and "Thomas The Rhymer", was sparse, aggressive rock backing, but even at this stage the overall effect of the music was far from "heavy". The Fairports back in 1969 had been far noisier and brasher.

There was another side to Steeleye's success, and that had nothing to do with folk, but an awful lot to do with the study of how some of the world's greatest rock bands became successful. Throughout the seventies, as rock moved from being a trendy minority cult to the largest growth area in the entertainment field, audiences got vaster and vaster, and in America they began to regularly pack the vast basketball stadiums. In Britain, huge concerts were held in exhibition halls or football stadiums. The music was embraced by the establishment, and by a vast new following. To get across to these audiences, an element of large-scale theatre began to creep into performances. Once The Who had wrecked their guitars and exploded smoke bombs, but now bands invested in expensive and subtle lighting, plus elaborate stage clothes, and even experimented in mixing music and drama. Steeleye were well prepared to play in the vast American stadiums because they alone of the British folk-rock bands really cared about presentation, and had experimented with introducing theatrical elements into their act.

Tim, Maddy and Pete already had some experience of theatre, through appearing in *Corunna*, and in Steeleye Mark III they began to put some unusual ideas into practice. They caused considerable amazement in the vast auditoriums of the American West in the summer of 1973; thousands of kids were waiting to see Jethro Tull when on came a support band bathed in blue light and dressed in mummers' costumes that covered them in ribbons from head to foot. When they started singing, it was the eerie, haunting chant "The Lyke Wake Dirge", an unaccompanied tale of the soul's journey from the corpse to purgatory.

Mixing rock-show technique with theatre and the English folk tradition involves walking a thin and dangerous line. For their 1974 world tour, they took it a stage further. Their concerts included a ten-minute mummers' play in which the band wore costumes and masks, and acted out Tim Hart's re-write of a medieval story. It involved authentic characters like Little Devil Doubt and the King of Egypt's Daughter, and was an amusing electronic knock-about (voices pre-recorded, booming out through the speakers). Despite the rather academic explanations, it's doubtful whether many of the audience appreciated that they had been watching an allegory on winter and the rebirth of the year – but no matter. It worked, just about, and was yet another sign that Steeleye were ahead of the field, and still gaining.

But then, by the summer of 1974, there wasn't all that much of a field still running. The Fairports had regained Sandy and re-found their form, but other English folk-rockers? There were few in sight. Fascinating Frenchmen, interesting Irishmen and stirring Scotsmen, yes, but that was about it. Tim Hart could make an arrogant claim on behalf of Steeleye: "We are the first people to come out of the folk club scene since Ewan MacColl to actually do something to English folk music." And he was absolutely right.

So where did all the competition go? Very simple, and very depressing. It simply didn't come, although the success of the Fairports and Steeleye showed both that it was possible for a style like this to develop, and that the audience was there for it. And apart from a few curiosities like the unhappy and short-lived Trees, the handful of folk-rock bands that did appear had Fairport connections.

FAIRPORT CONNECTIONS: SANDY

For a start, there was the band that Sandy Denny formed after leaving Fairport, before making her solo albums, and before re-joining Fairports. The band was called Fotheringay, and it also contained Sandy's husband-to-be Trevor Lucas, plus Jerry Donahue, Gerry Conway and Pat Donaldson. The band was a vehicle for Sandy's writing and performing, which was moving away from folk to a distinctive, highly personal form of chanson. Many of her songs were slow, drifting ballads, which were backed with a mixture of electric and acoustic instruments ("We were the first group in England to use acoustic instruments in an electric band," claims Trevor). When the mixture worked, as on the band's one album, *Fotheringay* – which I can't recommend too highly – and on their farewell performance at London's Queen Elizabeth Hall, it was very fine indeed. They could sound delicate and subtle on Sandy's songs, then break away to a rousing country-influenced piece from Trevor. The band as a whole had a relaxed, West Coast-ish feel, which could be both very good and very bad. When it was bad they spent what felt like hours tuning up, were hopelessly untogether, giggled, and got the balance wrong.

It was no surprise when Fotheringay broke up in February 1971. They left behind an album that, as I say, is excellent. As well as the expected songs by Sandy and Trevor, it contains a Dylan track (echoes of the early Fairports) and just one folk song. It's ironic that it happens to be one of the very best folk-rock recordings of all. It's a version of "Banks Of The Nile" that has none of the strident Fairport quality, and a mellow introspection not found in Steeleye. Sandy sings it exquisitely, as a quiet and private piece of lover's plotting (it's another of the old stories of a girl dressing up to be with her man in the forces), and as a heartfelt indictment of the meaninglessness of war. The backing is a delicate backdrop of acoustic guitars, punctuated sparingly and thoughtfully by bass and drums. If ever an old song was given new life and emotional force, it's in this track.

After Fotheringay, Sandy made three solo albums before returning to the Fairports, and they all continued her move away from folk, and the development of her own song-writing. By the time the third came out she was also taking an interest in the fringes of jazz, and Fats Waller's "Until The Real Thing Comes Along" appeared alongside classic new ballads of her own like "Solo". Only in the first of her solo albums did a token folk song appear, and that was the now predictable "Blackwaterside".

FAIRPORT CONNECTIONS: TYGER

With Sandy following her own song-writing career, the main hope for a third folk-rock force in Britain to match the Fairports and Steeleye came from none other than Ashley "Tyger" Hutchings. Seeing that he had founded both of them it seemed only reasonable to expect his next creation to be just as fruitful. But alas, The Albion Country Band proved to be rather the reverse. It was in existence for three years, never released an album, and didn't enamour its record company towards folk-rockers.

The sorry saga went like this: in 1971 Tyger master-minded an "electric folk" record for Shirley Collins, to whom he was now married. The album – which turned out to be another neglected

Collins classic – was called *No Roses*. The backing was provided by every folk-rocker in the business, and Tyger blessed them with the witty title the "Albion Country Band". He went on to form an "Albion" of his own – though Shirley was not a member.

He recruited Simon Nicol and Dave Mattacks from the Fairports, Royston Wood (ex-Young Tradition), an excellent American fiddle player, Sue Draheim, and a singer-songwriter guitarist-harmonica player, Steve Ashley. Their record company gave them a nice advance, and they set out to rehearse, and eventually give concerts. From what I remember of them they weren't bad, but (rather like Steeleye Mk II) they sounded like a collection of individuals, not a band. The two least-known members, Sue and Steve, seemed the most dominant (Steve's harmonica, and songs like "Fire and Wine" were particularly impressive).

But this line-up broke up after predictable personality clashes. It was replaced by a temporary group that included Richard Thompson, and finally a new band of Tyger, Simon, Sue, John Kirkpatrick and Roger Swallow. They eventually recorded an album ("and it wasn't that bad", said Simon), but by the time it was finished this line-up too had split. Without a band there to promote it, it wasn't worth bringing out.

So on the face of it, the Albions achieved nothing. It's ironic that the one recording of the band (and line-up Mk I at that) that was released[1] can be found on the solo album of someone the band chucked out. Steve Ashley's long-delayed *Stroll On*, which eventually appeared in the summer of 1974, contained one cut of straight Albion. It's called "Lord Bateman", and it's long, but imaginatively treated, with an instrumental section in the middle where the story leaps seven years. Steve sings well, the always self-effacing Simon plays extremely fine guitar, and Sue's fiddle-playing is silkily smooth. Not an amazing track, maybe, but it shows what the Albions could do.

They did achieve one breakthrough, though, and that was to drag that much-satirised part of the folk tradition, Morris dancing, into the twentieth century. The Albions' set always included a series of Morris

---

[1] Until now, that is. It is hoped that some of the Albions' tracks will be released as part of an album set issued to coincide with this book.

dance tunes, and a team of Morris men would leap on and perform to an electric folk accompaniment. Audiences were favourably amazed at the sight of grown men performing ritual prancing and banging sticks together. As an exercise in both rock theatrics and popularising a tradition, this was just as important a move as Steeleye's mummers' play.

The shame of it all was that the Albions could never stay together or produce a record on time. A shame too that Tyger got so involved with it all that he wouldn't let his band play other music (I recounted earlier the incident at The Howff). But he did manage to bring out two albums of dance music without the Albions. *Morris On* (1972) was, as the title suggests, a selection of Morris tunes. They were played on electric and acoustic instruments by the old team of Richard Thompson and Dave Mattacks, with John Kirkpatrick on accordion and concertina, and Barry Dransfield on fiddle. The dance tunes were reinforced with the occasional clash of Morris men's sticks, and the odd combination of concertina and electric bass sounded happily unremarkable after the first few bars.

Tyger returned to his fascination with English dance in 1974, with the release of another album, *The Compleat Dancing Master*, an ambitious compilation of readings on dance (everyone from Chaucer to Dickens), and folk-rock or acoustic dance tunes. By now he had formed yet another group, The Etchingham Steam Band, an acoustic outfit that was largely an outlet for Shirley. But the architect of British folk-rock seemed likely to bounce back somewhere.

THE CELTIC INVASION

By 1973, a potential audience for folk-rock was there and waiting, but even the staunchest fan must have been bored with the lack of choice. England didn't deliver the bands, and so − with mild irony − a Frenchman and a group of Irishmen moved in. The Frenchman − or rather a Breton nationalist − was Alan Stivell. The Irish band were Horslips. The two were poles apart in their style and treatment of essentially Celtic material, but both showed what was possible.

It took Stivell just a year to build up a following in Britain that was only surpassed by that of Steeleye, though on the face of it he was a highly unlikely figure to become the first new folk superstar of the seventies. He played the harp (and who has ever played the harp recently and been taken seriously?), spoke only halting English, and approached his work with a mixture of academic solemnity and campaigning zeal.

Stivell is the son of a Breton music teacher who had built his own Celtic harp as the first step towards reviving traditional Breton music. Alan learned to play it, playing mostly classical pieces, and with his father's encouragement set out to explore the whole field of Celtic music – that is, the songs of Brittany, Ireland, Wales and Scotland. After spending his childhood in Brittany, Alan moved to Paris, where he began playing in small clubs, sometimes just on solo harp, sometimes with fellow Breton Dan Ar Braz on guitar. He recorded a solo album, then began to add an electric backing band. He packed Paris's famous Olympia, and became something of a French national hero before moving on to conquer Britain.

Stivell's concerts contain a little of everything. He begins with solo pieces and explanations of the songs – enough of the "correct" approach to satisfy any purist – and then starts embellishing the music with a rock backing. He has a drummer, an organist, a fiddle-player, and a still-outstanding guitarist in Dan Ar Braz, but he uses them not so much as a band but as backing musicians. Stivell is always the focal point, whether singing, plucking his harp through sweet or stirring ballads, or explaining the musical history of the Celtic countries. He is the only academic I know who can suddenly march on stage playing bagpipes, with a rock band in full cry behind him, and reduce a solemnly attentive concert hall to a rocking and reeling shambles. It's a rare and glorious talent.

Horslips, from Ireland, have a somewhat less exotic history (they met while making a commercial for Harp lager), but in their glittery, pop-world way they've also done a great deal to popularise Celtic music and keep folk-rock going. They were residents on an Irish television show in 1971, started touring and recording in 1972, and the next year their album *Happy to Meet... Sorry to Part* was released in Britain. It was a pleasing, if slightly wishy-washy mixture of Irish airs and rock, played by a band who were now expert at bashing out rock tunes around the tough Irish dance-band circuit, and were likely to unwind after a gig with a heavy session of drinking and playing folk tunes on pipes or concertinas. Their second album, *The Táin*, which they released in 1974, finally established them. It was a "concept album", based on the pre-Christian Celtic saga "The Cattle Raid of Cooley". The music was mostly a rock interpretation of traditional Celtic melodies, and was part-brash, part-traditional linked with echoes of Jethro Tull. Like most Irish music, it was gloriously tuneful.

These two bands – with support from a handful of others, like the energetic Scottish J.S.D. Band – made sure the folk-rock kept moving, and broadened its base. But the Celtic bands, in a way, had an easier task than the English folk-rock bands. Celtic music has an accompanied tradition, while most English folk does not. It is easier to play an Irish air, with accompaniment on pipes and fiddle, and then to add bass and drums, than it is to invent a new folk-rock backing for a song that previously had none. In that way, Irish music has similarities with American folk. Both slid easily into rock, when pushed.

THE NEW ST GEORGE: MORE FAIRPORT CONNECTIONS

In the sixties, singer-songwriters accompanied themselves on solo guitar, and mostly followed transatlantic musical styles. In the seventies, a few folk-rockers tried to take song-writing a stage further and produce something that was new, but with English roots. It was about time. Throughout the sixties' rock revolution Britain had produced great music by aping and transforming American styles. It wasn't surprising, as rock was an American invention. But what was needed was a way of blending it with English influences.

Was new English song-writing possible? Ewan MacColl, in the folk field, had thought so when he used the influence of industrial folk song in his remarkable radio ballads. In the very different rock field, Ray Davies of The Kinks had thought so when he mixed rock with music hall and English nostalgia in albums like *Arthur* and *The Village Green Preservation Society*. A few folk-rockers followed on with their own experiments.

The first, most original, and most disastrous of the studiedly English folk-rock writers were a couple from Leeds, Bob and Carole Pegg. They were hard-core traditionalists who had spent some time wandering around the Yorkshire vales and moors, collecting songs and local stories. Then, with a barrage of quasi-academic explanations and attacks they rounded on the folk scene and started a rock band, Mr Fox. The band was mostly a disaster – its members simply weren't good enough – and this obscured some of the extremely fine songs that Bob, in particular, was writing.

Mr Fox made two albums – *Mr Fox* and *The Gipsy* – that still stand up well. The songs were mostly Yorkshire nostalgia, all about the closing of lead mines and village bands, but with a black, creepy edge behind the sturdy tunes. "The Hanged Man", a gory tale of a hiker who slips to his death, and Carole's supernatural "Gay Goshawk" both hinted at something nasty out there in the English countryside. Bob and Carole both had harsh, unusual voices, and played guitar, whistle and fiddle. Bass and drums completed a band that when on form – as on their two albums – was compelling listening. But live, as at the Cambridge Folk Festival, it was too often a different story.

Bob and Carole's marriage broke up, and so did the band. Both have since followed solo careers, but neither has yet produced anything to match the first *Mr Fox* album. Carole came quite close, changing her name to Carolanne, and recording an excellent solo album, backed by leading session musicians. Her interest was moving towards country and rock, though, and her best song, "Winter People", was hardly folk-orientated. Carolanne later formed a short-lived band, Magus, with Graham Bond (just before his death), and then returned to solo work. Bob meanwhile teamed up with Nick Strutt as an acoustic duo, and produced a surprisingly quiet and melodic album. Pleasant, but no match for his earlier songs.

The real success story in this musical category is, believe it or not, yet another ex-member of Fairport Convention, and a name that's cropped up a few times already. You may remember that guitarist Richard Thompson left the band after the *Full House* album, at the height of the band's creative and popularity peak. He then made the extraordinary move of going into the folk clubs – and as far as I can recall he's the only artist to have done such a thing at the height of his success. Plenty of up-and-coming singers have moved from the clubs to the concert circuit, but doing it the other way round, and moving from the Festival Hall and the Fillmore West to pub back-rooms in Wandsworth or Hull? It was unheard of.

Imagined Village, WOMAD show, Tower of London, 2009. *Tom Oldham/Shutterstock*

June Tabor and Oysterband, The Orangery, London, 2011. *Judith Burrows*

Home Service, Cropredy Festival, Oxfordshire, August 2011.

Fairport Convention, Union Chapel, London, 2012. *Judith Burrows*

Jim Moray, fROOTS concert, Roundhouse, London, 2012. *Judith Burrows*

Sam Lee, Greenwich, 2012. *Judith Burrows*

Bellowhead, Northampton, 2014. *Judith Burrows*

Billy Bragg, Hoxton, 2013. *Judith Burrows*

Olivia Chaney, Chelsea, 2013. *Judith Burrows*

Eliza Carthy and Martin Carthy,
Scarborough Beach, 2014.
Judith Burrows

Shirley Collins and Martin Carthy, 'Bobstock'
tribute to Bob Copper, London, 2015.
Judith Burrows/Getty Images

Jon Boden and The Remnant Kings (original line-up), Sidmouth Festival, 2010. *Judith Burrows*

Richard Thompson, Liverpool Philharmonic Hall, September 2015. *WENN Rights Ltd/Alamy*

Steeleye Span, Cropredy Festival, Oxfordshire, August 2016. *MusicLive/Alamy*

Show of Hands, Snape Maltings, Suffolk, 2016.
Judith Burrows

Eliza Carthy and The Wayward Band, Bristol, 2017.
Judith Burrows

Offa Rex (Olivia Chaney and The Decemberists), Grammy Awards, New York City, January 2018.
Angela Weiss/AFP via Getty Images

The Rails, Cambridge Folk Festival, August 2019.
Richard Etteridge/Alamy Live News

Stick in the Wheel, Finsbury Park, 2020.
Stick in the Wheel

But Richard knew what he was doing. He wanted to get real contact with audiences for the first time, and he wanted to immerse himself in English traditional music, so that it would rub off in his own writing. So that's exactly what he did, first solo and then with his wife, singer Linda Peters. There were breaks, of course, when he became session guitarist on other people's albums and when he joined up with The Albion Country Band, but for a couple of years he travelled up and down the country, giving the folk circuit its biggest treat in years.

Musically, as well as socially, it all paid off. Richard's first solo album, *Henry the Human Fly*, was slightly marred by a curious mix (Richard is unnecessarily modest about his singing and kept the vocals too far back), but it contained good new songs influenced by everything from the English tradition through to Phil Spector. The title of one track, "The New St George", summed it all up.

By the time he recorded the second album, *I Want to See the Bright Lights Tonight* (a joint effort with wife Linda taking many vocals), the problems had been ironed out. This was one of the best albums of 1974. The influences were Victorian ballads, music hall and industrial folk song; the songs were sturdy, stirring and eerie, and performed with a bleak intensity. They had a strange timeless quality, and were unmistakably English, without sounding in the least bit folksy. Despite Richard's reputation as an ace guitarist, he allowed himself no ornamental flourishes, but carved the arrangements down to the essentials. The one embellishment was as English as it was original – the introduction of a silver band playing on the title track. Musically, this album was the work of a painstaking craftsman; as for the lyrics, they were almost all chillingly black – tales of loneliness, disillusion and despair – but with no mawkishness, no excess of sentiment, and just enough hints of hope and nobility for the effects of this strange, compelling album to be far from depressing.

With the album released, Richard returned to the rock circuit from the clubs. He formed a band Sour Grapes, which included yet another ex-Fairport and Albion veteran, Simon Nicol.

SO WHAT?

In terms of the numbers of people involved, and the numbers of records produced, British folk-rock may all seem pretty small scale. Yet in terms of the significance and quality of the music produced, it has been of considerable importance. English traditional music has not been swept away by the rock'n'roll landslide, it may have been saved by it. Steeleye Span really have done more for folk than anyone since MacColl, as they outrageously boast. There may be no directly socialist overtones to Richard Thompson's work, but he has done as much for English writing as the famous radio ballads.

What's more, the folk-rock bands even carried interest in traditional music across to the rock bands proper. Traffic recorded an excellent version of "John Barleycorn" (breaking away from jazz-rock to play it "straight", with guitar, piano and flute backing), and even named an album after it. Over in the States, no less a band than The Byrds recorded "Jack Tarr The Sailor" on their *Ballad of Easy Rider* album, and behind the smooth West Coast harmonies it sounded quite uncannily like A.L. Lloyd singing "The Whaleman's Lament". And for the most curious example of the rock world taking an interest in folk, there's the bass line on Cream's "Pressed Rat And Warthog". If Tim Hart hadn't pointed it out, I confess that I wouldn't have noticed that Jack Bruce is playing "The Cutty Wren".

And the folk world, as I say, hasn't responded with the same interest and sympathy. Folk had its golden age in the early sixties, followed by a decline and fall in which some of the best musicians got fed up with it all. But the clubs are still there, and still provide one of the few openings for new performers. The audience for folk and folk-rock is still there. And so are the songs. Like rock, the folk revival could go almost anywhere next.

SOMEWHAT POSTSCRIPT

... and to prove that very point, it's necessary to add a tailpiece, just a few months after writing the above. The British folk-rock scene has, as I've said, become famous for its instability, and for the way the same handful of musicians keep shuffling around, joining and leaving bands. That process has continued.

Fairport Convention are – inevitably – one band involved. At the time of writing, Dave Mattacks, the drummer, has left. This latest change – equally inevitably – comes at a slightly awkward time for the band. With Sandy Denny now back with them, they have just completed a world tour followed by a British tour, and they are playing better than at any time since the great heyday of the Denny-Swarbrick-Thompson-Hutchings band. They have moved slightly away from folk-rock, and now play the free-wheeling mixture that characterised their early albums. Sandy's slow and moody ballads are interspersed with Swarbrick's fiddle jigs, old Dylan songs and old Fairport favourites like "Sloth". The band that even their record company were beginning to despair of has leaped right back. So another change of personnel, just as the audiences are rediscovering Fairport, is unfortunate. But the band has now survived so much for so long that they are bound to survive this change, too.

The Incredible String Band haven't managed as well – in fact they split up in the autumn of 1974. They had fast been losing the qualities that made them the most magical musicians of the late sixties, and after their record company had given them the push it was only a matter of time before they gave up. Despite their decline, I still regard Robin Williamson and Mike Heron as major songwriters, and it's still possible that they will produce important work. Williamson has left for the American West Coast and unspecified musical plans, while Heron has remained in Britain and already formed a new band, "Mike Heron's Reputation". They'll begin performing in early 1975, and if they follow up the promise of Heron's first solo album, four years earlier, they'll be more rock-influenced, highly original, and good.

One other band has folded – though this one scarcely got off the ground. Richard Thompson's Sour Grapes played a few gigs then disbanded, amid rumours that Richard was about to quit and return to his original interest, stained glass. Thankfully he hasn't: he is still playing as a duo with his wife Linda.

Finally, the biggest and most pleasant surprise of late 1974 – the return of Bert Jansch. Earlier in the year there had been confused stories of his retirement, and then non-retirement, so it was quite unexpected that he should release one of the freshest, most pleasing albums of the year. His new record company introduced him to Mike

Nesmith, the ex-Monkee turned country hero, and Nesmith in turn introduced Jansch to a musical style he knew nothing about. "I'd been to America a lot with Pentangle," Jansch told me, "but we were so close we never let ourselves be influenced by other styles." Nesmith brought a gentle country backing to Jansch's guitar work, and without fundamentally changing Jansch's style he gently nudged him into a new field. *L.A. Turnaround* was an encouraging sign that folk-rock wasn't finished.

SOURCES

Steve Ashley: *Stroll On* (Gull). The only captured track by The Albion Country Band, and some of his own very good songs.

Shirley Collins and Davy Graham: *Folk Roots, New Routes* (Decca). The original folk/blues fusion.

Sandy Denny: *Like An Old Fashioned Waltz* (Island).

Fairport Convention: *What We Did On Our Holidays* (Island). The first "folk-rock" and a lot else besides.

Fairport Convention: *Full House* (Island). Without Sandy, but still with Richard Thompson.

Incredible String Band: *Wee Tam and the Big Huge* (Elektra).

Bert Jansch: *Bert Jansch* (Transatlantic). His first album.

Bert Jansch and John Renbourn: *Bert and John* (Transatlantic). "Folk-baroque" guitar instrumentals.

Mr Fox: *Mr Fox* (Transatlantic). Terrible band, great record.

Steeleye Span: *Please To See The King* (B & C). Their best with Martin Carthy.

Alan Stivell: *Chemins De Terre* (Fontana).

PART TWO

The Electric Muse Revisited
Folk into Rock – and Beyond

ROBIN DENSELOW

FIVE

THE GREAT SURVIVORS

STEELEYE SPAN

Richard Thompson's 70th birthday concert at London's Royal Albert Hall in 2019 was a historic gathering of veteran folk-rockers and later generations of musicians equally determined to keep traditional music alive and show how it could be successfully fused with other musical styles. It was a night that proved that folk-rock lives on, in new and different forms, and a night of memorable performances.

From the newcomers (those whose careers started after the folk-rock glory days in the seventies) there was Olivia Chaney with her exquisite revival of Sandy Denny's "Who Knows Where The Time Goes", and Eliza Carthy with a glorious solo a cappella version of Richard's song "The Great Valerio". And from the veterans, there was Richard himself, of course, showing once again why he is one of the finest songwriters and guitarists of his or any generation, as he revived his back catalogue, folk songs or pop songs in the company of everyone from David Gilmour to Martin Carthy and his old colleagues from the first great English folk-rock band, Fairport Convention.

And then there was Maddy Prior, another triumphant survivor from the seventies as the leader of that other great English folk-rock band, the massively successful Steeleye Span. Her voice was still as fine as ever, as she proved with a powerful treatment of the traditional "Sheath And Knife", in which she was backed by Olivia Chaney, and then the Cyril Tawney lament "Grey Funnel Line", which she had once sung with June Tabor in Silly Sisters. Richard and his son Teddy now provided the backing.

Maddy also had an anniversary to celebrate in 2019. In December there would be a major concert at the London Barbican to mark the 50th anniversary of Steeleye Span, a band that never veered from the original ideas of folk-rock. After all these years Maddy still insists that traditional songs, not self-written or new material, should still mostly dominate the band's output. The line-up may have changed many times over the years but their 2019 album, *Est'd 1969*, was a classic Steeleye collection of ancient Child ballads and new songs, including one by Maddy's daughter Rose-Ellen. And it included a flute solo from Jethro Tull's Ian Anderson, who had produced and appeared on Steeleye's first album with a drummer, *Now We Are Six*, back in 1974 – the set that had also included David Bowie playing saxophone.

When I met her the morning after the Albert Hall show, Maddy drew me a diagram. In the centre was a planet, representing success and popularity, and around it circled a satellite, Steeleye Span. There were times when they were far apart, and others when they were closer together – though they never actually touched. She explained that the seventies and today were the times where mass popularity and Steeleye Span came closest together.

The year 1975, when *The Electric Muse* was first published, was an extraordinary one for the band, who had by then become the first British folk-rock supergroup. Thanks largely to the suggestions of Tim Hart – the one member of the band who seemed to cherish a rock-star lifestyle, and who most enjoyed dealing with record companies and marketing ideas – Steeleye Span had acquired a rock manager, Tony Secunda, and a successful pop producer, Mike Batt.

Batt is a songwriter, musician and producer who was most famous at the time for having created the successful pop act The Wombles, in which musicians dressed up as characters from the children's TV show, and he notched up an impressive series of hits. Maddy and the rest of the band understandably needed to be convinced that he was right for a folk band like Steeleye, but then they agreed that "he's such a good producer". The result was the band's biggest hit single, "All Around My Hat", which broke into the Top Five of the British singles chart in November 1975. The album of the same name reached number 7 in the charts. It was an extraordinary achievement for a band playing traditional songs that included "The Wife Of Usher's Well" and "Hard Times Of Old England", the latter taken from the repertoire of those celebrated singers of unaccompanied traditional songs, The Copper Family from Sussex.

Watching them on stage that year, it was hard to imagine that Maddy Prior and Tim Hart had started off on the folk-club circuit. They had moved on to become an electric guitar band of fine harmony singers, complete with a drummer, and to add folk-rock theatre to their repertoire. One of the BBC TV shows they hosted during the year included their updated treatment of a medieval mummers' play. And as their status grew, so did their reputation for decidedly unfolky stunts.

While they were on tour in Australia in 1975, their manager Tony Secunda devised an unusual sales technique. Any girl who turned up at a concert in Sydney holding a copy of Steeleye's current album could enter a contest to win twelve hours with a male member of the band. There was outrage from the press, the church and even the government, though the stunt turned out to be entirely innocent. The winner took her boyfriend along for a chat with Bob Johnson, the band's guitarist. Steeleye had acquired unexpected notoriety, and publicity, in Australia – though most of the band didn't know about the stunt in advance.

The following year Steeleye gained more press coverage in England, when the entire takings for their headline show at Hammersmith Odeon – some £8,500 – was dropped from the roof of the auditorium during the encore of "The Mason's Apron" (a stunt that would be impossible to repeat now that punters pay by card rather than in pound notes). "I found it vaguely embarrassing," said Maddy, "but we laughed all the time. It was just very funny and unexpected. When we went into folk music we weren't expecting to have an exciting life in that sense. But I'm pleased that we did *Top of the Pops* and got chased across an airport in Australia with things over our heads because the paparazzi were chasing us…"

But did all of that promote the cause of traditional music? "Oh no, it was just silliness. But you have to do it once. I'm pleased we had that moment. When I see people playing big stadiums I understand it because I've been there."

Steeleye would never be as commercially successful again, for musical tastes were changing. A second Mike Batt album, *Rocket Cottage*, only reached number 41 in the charts, though it was followed by a world tour. In 1977, after the band had taken a six-month break, both Bob Johnson and Peter Knight announced they were leaving.

They went off to record the folk-rock concept album, *The King of Elfland's Daughter,* which would feature an extraordinary cast including Christopher Lee and that glorious soul singer P.P. Arnold, and might have sold far better if it had not been released in the late seventies. Folk-rock was now falling from fashion, as younger audiences – and the record companies – were far more excited by the advent of a new musical style, punk.

But Steeleye kept going for a while, and now reverted to a more traditional folk approach, with the return of that brilliant guitarist and folklorist Martin Carthy. Known for his adventurous acoustic guitar playing, and his work with the celebrated folk family band The Watersons, he had been a key member of Steeleye's second line-up but had left the band back in December 1971.

So what was the attraction of Steeleye for Carthy? Simply that he liked the idea of playing the traditional songs he loved in different ways. As he put it, "I found my mind was open, and I was very happy about that. And you can't hurt this stuff [folk music] by messing with it. The idea of trying to freeze it is nonsense. It's not an edifice, it's a process." When he first joined the band, Carthy had startled the purists by playing very loudly – which he continued to do. "I was doing the right thing. I refused to turn it down to lounge because it was boring. It's huge fun to do, it's great being noisy – and the material loved it, it seemed to me!"

The new Steeleye line-up also included John Kirkpatrick, an enthusiast for Morris tunes and Morris dancing and a fine player of squeezeboxes of all kinds, from accordions to concertinas. A folk-rock fan who had "fainted with delight" when he first heard the Fairports' *Liege and Lief,* he had worked with two of Fairport's founding members, Richard Thompson and Ashley Hutchings, and (unknown to John at the time) had been suggested for Steeleye membership when Carthy had first joined the band.

Now he finally was a member, Kirkpatrick said it was "a fantastic opportunity. I did enjoy it. But we felt we had to fit into a bit of a formula. They had had their epic hits by then, so we were slightly tail-end Charlies..."

Even so, the band continued to experiment and record new material. Their album *Storm Force Ten* (1977) included a folk-rock treatment of "The Black Freighter", a song from Bertolt Brecht and

Kurt Weill's *Threepenny Opera* that had been suggested by Martin. "So it was different and interesting," said Maddy. But the album failed to chart, and the following year it was announced that Steeleye Span would break up.

Their farewell tour included a concert in Bournemouth, in March 1978, that was recorded as Steeleye's farewell – and their first live album. *Live At Last* included a new treatment of "The False Knight On The Road", originally recorded on the classic *Please to See the King*, back in 1971 when Martin was first in the band. And on the back sleeve of this 'eleventh and final album', Tim Hart summed up Steeleye's achievements like this:

> Eight years ago a collection of musicians formed a group called Steeleye Span with the intention of taking this well-preserved music, revitalising it and putting it back into the world of popular song. We were told it couldn't be done: that traditional songs and ballads, mummers' plays, sword dances and Morris dances had no place in the world of rock; that they were relics of the past with no relevance outside of folk clubs and universities. We proved them wrong with a gold album, five silver albums, two hit singles and concert success in America, Australia and Europe as well as Great Britain.

The apparent demise of Steeleye was no real surprise. After all, Martin and John had only joined on a temporary basis, and the late seventies British music scene continued to be shaken up by the arrival of disco and punk. Looking back now, Martin Carthy says "it had a lot to do with the Pistols. The Pistols changed everything – because the audience changed." Steeleye may have been a major force in the mid-seventies, but punk audiences wanted something very different.

Steeleye and punk were, on the face of it, light years apart, but – as the folk-punk bands were soon to prove – the two styles had much in common. And there was a Steeleye–punk connection that their audiences didn't know about. Like all major bands, Steeleye sold T-shirts, albums and other merchandising when they were on tour, and in charge of the merch stall were two brothers, Colin and Stewart Goldring, who were also actors, musicians and comedians, whose sales techniques were so good that John Kirkpatrick said "I used to go out and watch them. It was the best part of the evening!" The Goldrings had played in the early seventies prog-rock band Gnidrolog (which had also included Steeleye's drummer Nigel Pegrum and bass player

Rick Kemp), but were also part of a mysterious punk band, The Pork Dukes, that involved Steeleye drummer, Nigel Pegrum, as well. Their identities were supposed to be kept secret (they wore pig masks on stage) and their songs were so outrageous that John Peel said that they would be hits if they were not so "manifestly un-broadcastable".

When Kirpatrick left Steeleye, he invited them to join him on a unique solo album, *Going Spare* (1978), which included Morris tunes alongside wild squeezebox experimentation. On some tracks the backing is credited to the Goldring Brothers and Pegrum, while The Pork Dukes are credited with playing on the frantic, funny and bitter "What Do You Do In The Day?", the lament of a working musician, "because it's in their style". It's a limited field, I know, but the song is still an accordion-backed folk-punk-rock classic.

John Kirkpatrick had other musical plans. While they were in Steeleye together, he and Martin Carthy had begun considering a band of their own. According to John, "we were chatting about the idea of having a big band, but without the electricity... using some sort of percussion and bass, but without a rock rhythm section." After Steeleye they both worked for a while at the National Theatre, joining the Albion Band musicians for the *Lark Rise* and *Candleford* productions in a line-up that also included trumpeter Howard Evans, whom they knew well. He had played alongside Kirkpatrick on Martin's 1979 solo album *Because It's There*.

So when Carthy and Kirpatrick started playing together, they invited Evans to join in. Then they added trombone and percussion to the line-up, and formed a new folk brass band, Brass Monkey. The five of them gave their first performance at a Sussex pub, The Black Horse at Telham, without having had time to rehearse. "And we started laughing once we began playing," said Martin, "because it was the greatest noise we had heard!"

Brass Monkey were unique, with their combination of squeezebox and brass instruments, and often featured Martin playing mandolin. He decided that he had "run into a brick wall" playing the electric guitar and decided to switch to the mandolin, an instrument that gave him "tremendous release". He "then came back to the guitar and found I could play it properly again".

He can be heard playing both mandolin and guitar on the first Brass Monkey album in 1983, which he rightly pronounces to be "still bloody good". It includes a powerful version of "The Maid And The Palmer" which he recorded on Steeleye's *Live at Last* album, and which he has continued to perform when he works as a duo with Kirkpatrick.

Brass Monkey were never as massively commercial as the old Steeleye, but they toured America and the Far East (with help from the British Council), and would keep working together, sporadically and with different line-ups, for the next thirty-five years, and would have a major influence on the folk big bands that followed.

Kirkpatrick meanwhile continued to be involved in other ventures, including his folk-rock project, The John Kirkpatrick Band in the nineties, when the time was not yet right for squeezebox backed by electric guitar, drum and bass. "I thought people would be gagging for it," said John. "But they weren't."

And as for Steeleye... well, they had officially broken up in the late seventies, but then they started again. Their record label Chrysalis wanted another album and the old, hit-making line-up including Bob Johnson and Peter Knight got together again, this time working with producer Gus Dudgeon, who had been responsible for hits by Elton John and Gilbert O'Sullivan, on the album *Sails of Silver* (1981). The aim, Tim told me at the time, was to be "more rock-oriented and even more commercial. Gus said he didn't want to do the album unless he thought there were two or three hit singles there." The band tried hard to be commercial, with Knight now playing keyboards as well as fiddle, but there were to be no more hit singles.

Explaining what happened next, Maddy referred me back to that diagram of Steeleye circling around success. The eighties and nineties were decades when the two were furthest apart. Tim quit the band in 1982, Rick Kemp (who was now married to Maddy) left in 1987, and drummer Nigel Pegrum left in 1989, to be replaced by Liam Genockey, who is in the current band. Steeleye still toured at home and internationally from time to time, and in 1986 released their first album in six years, *Back in Line*. It was released on Flutterby, a label owned by the band and their new manager Adrian Hopkins (the man who had physically dropped the money onto the Hammersmith crowd back in 1976, after being told to strip to his underpants to make sure he didn't take any). According to Maddy, "Adrian always said that he took us from success and built us into obscurity – that was his phrase."

But in 1995 Steeleye were suddenly back, celebrating their 25th anniversary with a lengthy and rousing charity show at London's Forum, featuring a reunion of each of the band's many line-ups. Tim Hart and Martin Carthy were on stage, and the one absentee was Terry Woods, from the first-ever Steeleye – the band that had recorded but never performed live. The following year Steeleye were back playing stadiums, this time in the UK as the unlikely support act for Status Quo, who released their own, unlikely version of "All Around My Hat", featuring Maddy.

But Maddy's interests had begun to change. She already had a solo career outside Steeleye, working and recording with The Maddy Prior Band, The Carnival Band and later with the duo she formed with her husband Rick. And she "now had a family and didn't focus in the same way". Gay Woods, who was part of the first-ever Steeleye line-up, was now back in the ever-changing line-up and Maddy decided to leave: "I felt that I wasn't really there any more." And so she quit Steeleye in 1997.

The idea of Steeleye Span without Maddy now seems unthinkable, but the band continued without her, with a line-up that initially included Gay, Bob Johnson and Peter Knight, who recorded the more acoustic-sounding *Horkstow Grange* album. Then came yet more personnel changes, and a major crisis for the band – and at one point Peter Knight was the only remaining member. But in 2002 a new 'classic' line-up was announced, with Maddy (now Maddy Prior MBE) returning, joined by Peter, Bob Johnson, Liam Genockey and Rick Kemp (despite the fact that he was now Maddy's ex-husband).

"I didn't like leaving it the way it was," said Maddy. "I didn't want it to fall apart, so I said I would join again, even though Rick and I had split up... but we are back being good friends. He's a great musician and a great person. And since then we have made albums and people have come and gone..."

The first major change was the departure of Bob Johnson later that year. It was, said Maddy, "a big miss because he brought in a lot of traditional stuff, the big ballads". But Steeleye Span survived, with Maddy now firmly in charge. The new century saw the growth of a new folk revival, and the band have kept touring and recording.

In 2007 and 2008 they hosted their own festival, Spanfest, and in 2013 they broke away from their standard folk-rock formula and emphasis on traditional songs by recording their first self-written concept album.

When the author Terry Pratchett appeared on the BBC radio programme *Desert Island Discs*, one of the records he chose was "Thomas The Rhymer", from Steeleye's 1974 album *Now We Are Six*. "And so," said Maddy, "we invited him to a gig in Salisbury, near where he lived, and we became friends and played at his 60th birthday party. He was brilliant, so astute. You didn't talk any bullshit around him because he would call you on it..."

As a result of those meetings, Steeleye recorded *Wintersmith*, a double-album concept set inspired by Pratchett's book and the related Tiffany Aching stories. Steeleye wrote the music, with Bob Johnson, a big Pratchett fan, adding two songs and also credited as guest vocalist. The other guests were that fine Northumbrian piper Kathryn Tickell and melodeon player John Spiers, with Pratchett himself credited as 'voice' and co-writer of all the songs. On the sleeve he described how he became "hooked forever" on Steeleye. "When I was an adolescent young man, my mate Dave put me between two huge speakers and turned everything up to eleven. He played 'Boys Of Bedlam' until the chimney wobbled."

The album brought Steeleye a welcome burst of publicity, including a coveted appearance on the BBC TV show *Later... With Jools Holland*. A rare occurrence for a folk band, it featured an interview with Maddy and Terry and a video of the band playing the stomping "Dark Morris Song".

Peter Knight, who had first joined Steeleye back in 1970, now left the band to concentrate on his Gigspanner project, and the current violin player, the classically trained Jessie May Smart, took over. Further changes included the departure of Rick Kemp, another great Steeleye veteran, and the arrival of Benji Kirkpatrick, the son of former Steeleye squeezebox player John Kirkpatrick. A singer and a bouzouki, mandolin, guitar and banjo player, Benji had previously worked with the massively successful folk big band Bellowhead, recorded an album of Jimi Hendrix songs, and in 2019 launched his own "power trio", The Excess. Maddy Prior now fronted a line-up that included impressive young players who helped bring the band back into fashion – their 2019 shows included the Glastonbury Festival.

As they prepared to celebrate their 50th anniversary, Maddy considered the band's history. They have survived a ridiculous number of personnel changes, and continue to match rock riffs against distinctive harmony vocals, while always concentrating on traditional songs. "We are based in the hard tradition, if you like – not the nice Victorian stuff," said Maddy. "We met the Queen at a charity do and she said 'such jolly tunes', and I thought 'that's not how I see us at all'. Because I'm singing 'Long Lankin' or 'Blackleg Miner' and 'Tam Lin'. They are really profound ballads about our society. I always say that the only thing that changes is the transport system and the togs – otherwise people do the same stuff. It's not that people back then were different – they are not..."

Maddy paused. "It's been great. I couldn't have hoped for a better life in music."

FAIRPORT

"There's loyalty, and then there's Fairport loyalty," said Simon Nicol, as he contemplated the fans who flock to Fairport Convention's Cropredy Festival, held in August every year out in the north Oxfordshire countryside. "You look at this crowd who have come from all over the world, literally, and the only single common factor is that at some point, Fairport's music has got under their skin and into their lives."

If Steeleye's survival for over half a century feels like a well-deserved miracle, then Fairport's continuing history is perhaps even more remarkable. Here, after all, is a band that is even older – it was co-founded by Ashley Hutchings two years before he moved on to Steeleye – but within months of releasing *Liege and Lief*, the most-praised album in folk-rock history, it had already lost two of its most celebrated members, Sandy Denny and Hutchings himself. When Richard Thompson also left it seemed the band could be in trouble.

But by 1975, when *The Electric Muse* first appeared, Fairport's fortunes were on the up once again. Founder Simon Nicol may have quit to join Ashley in The Albion Band, but the great Sandy Denny was back, in a line-up that also included her husband Trevor Lucas, fiddle virtuoso Dave Swarbrick (who had shaken up the acoustic folk scene in the sixties thanks to his work with Martin Carthy), guitarist Jerry Donahue and the distinctive rhythm section of bass player Dave Pegg, who had joined Fairport after the release of *Liege and Lief*, and that fine drummer Dave Mattacks. Their 1975 album *Rising for the Moon* showed a change of direction, with all of the ten songs written by the band, Sandy writing or co-writing seven of them. It was an uneven, but often classy set, thanks to Sandy's distinctive, brooding ballads "Stranger To Himself" or the piano-backed "One More Chance". Trevor's American-influenced "Iron Lion" and "Restless" sounded as if they belonged to a different band.

The album was well received but never sold as well as the band had hoped, and led to yet another Fairport crisis, as Sandy, Trevor and Jerry all quit the band. Sandy continued with her solo career, releasing one more album, *Rendezvous*, before her tragic and untimely death in April 1978. She fell down the stairs at a friend's house, struck her head and never regained consciousness. At her funeral a lone piper played "The Flowers Of The Forest". I was among the small group of friends and fans who stood by her grave that day, wondering how she would be remembered.

Sandy was the finest female singer that the British folk and rock scene had produced, a woman who was droll and sometimes unconfident offstage, but once she started singing she displayed an emotional intensity that was applied to anything from ragtime tunes to traditional ballads or her own haunting songs. It took time before her brilliance was fully appreciated. A box set of her work was released in 1985 but it took twenty years for her record company to finally release *Gold Dust* – a live recording of her last concert. She is now regarded, rightly, as a music legend who played a crucial role not just in the Fairport story but also in British music history.

Sandy's departure, for the final time, could easily have meant the end of Fairport. It was followed by another period of uncertainty and personnel changes, and by the *Gottle O'Geer* album, dominated by Dave Swarbrick. But then founder member Simon Nicol returned after four years away. "Which was easy," he said. "I'd been working with the Albions and then Gerry Rafferty, and – unofficially

– I had been working in the folk clubs for cash with Peggy and Swarb. And once I was back there was a very stable line-up – for nearly four years!"

This was a good, solid folk-rock band who produced a couple of good, solid albums, *The Bonny Bunch of Roses* and *Tipplers Tales*, mixing their arrangements of traditional songs and tunes with new material, including a song from Ralph McTell, a close friend of the band.

But musical tastes were changing, and Fairport, like Steeleye, were to suffer. "It was the post-punk reaction," said Simon. "The music business had no interest in anything that had been around before... and everyone was a dinosaur if you weren't big enough, like the Stones. Record companies weren't interested in signing us, and at that time, if you weren't signed to a label, there was no way of getting a record out. The independent system didn't yet exist..."

Audiences had also changed. "Our bread and butter was the university circuit," he said, "and they turned their backs on us. They wanted pogoing and spitting, which we weren't very good at. Amphetamines were their drug of choice, and ours was real ale – a world apart." There was another major problem. "Swarb had been going deaf, and was told not to play electric violin any more."

And so Fairport Convention officially split. Their lengthy farewell tour ended on August 4, 1979, an emotional and busy day for the band. First they performed before a vast crowd at the Knebworth Festival, where Led Zeppelin were also playing a farewell show (for very different reasons). And then they headed to Oxfordshire, for their own farewell show at Cropredy.

It's a village that has played an important role in the Fairport story. "Peggy and Swarb both lived there," said Simon, "and I was not too far away, in Abingdon. Peggy's children went to the village school and we were integrated into the community. We borrowed the village hall for rehearsals. Three years earlier, back in 1976, we had been asked to play in the hall after the village fête... I think we got free beer." The following year they repeated the exercise, and the crowds had grown. By 1978 they had moved to a field outside the village, where they played from the back of a flat-bed truck.

Some 3,400 people attended the Fairport farewell in 1979. And then, said Simon, "we went our ways". He went back to playing with both the Albions and Richard and Linda Thompson, while Pegg joined Jethro Tull, and Swarbrick returned to acoustic work in the folk clubs.

And that should have been that, but of course it wasn't. "There had been four Cropredys, so there was a certain momentum…" said Simon. "So 1980 came round and we thought 'let's run it up the flagpole one more time, and see if there's a possible reunion here' – which there was. We had more people than at the farewell." The band's 'Special Guests' that year included Richard and Linda Thompson and Dave Mattacks.

The following year, 1981, there was another reunion, this time at Broughton Castle, near Cropredy. It attracted an even bigger crowd, and a cast that again included Richard Thompson, who also made an appearance alongside Ralph McTell, Pegg and Mattacks in a band who called themselves The GPs and played old Hank Williams and Jerry Lee Lewis songs.

And since then… Cropredy continued as an annual summer festival, always starring Fairport Convention in the eclectic line-up. It moved to its current location, in a field outside Cropredy, in 1982 and has now become an institution, part of the British summer season, attracting around 20,000 music fans a year. And would Fairport Convention have survived without it? "No, it wouldn't," said Simon. "Particularly when the band was not touring, between 1979 and 1985. We weren't in the studio, there was no new product, and we weren't appearing at other peoples' festivals… Fairport wouldn't have survived without that reminder every August that there were a lot of people out there for whom the band meant something."

The Fairports gradually recovered as a still-evolving band. In 1985 they at last released an album of new material, *Gladys' Leap*, the title taken from the story of an athletic postwoman that had appeared in the *Guardian*. It was recorded for Dave Pegg's DIY Wormwood label by the trio of Simon, Dave Pegg and Dave Mattacks. They then acquired new members, with Ric Sanders, formerly with Soft Machine, taking over from the departed Swarb, and recorded their first all-instrumental album, *Expletive Delighted!* It was mostly self-written but included an exquisite treatment of a seventeenth-century tune by Irish harpist Turlough O'Carolan, with fine violin work from

Sanders, along with a twanging burst of The Shadows' "Apache", with Richard and Jerry Donahue both playing lead guitar.

The new band were clearly having fun, and for a while there were two Fairports. In the nineties they launched a second version of the band as a four-piece acoustic line-up, while the electric folk-rock Fairport Convention still continued.

There were, inevitably, further personnel changes, but in 1998 the unthinkable happened. Fairport acquired a stable line-up that would remain the same for over twenty years. It's still unchanged at the time of writing, with the veteran duo of Nicol and Pegg joined by Gerry Conway on drums, Ric Sanders on fiddle and keys, and Chris Leslie on guitar and fiddle.

And the music has continued to evolve, with the emphasis on new songs and story songs. "We haven't taken a traditional song and made it afresh with this line-up," said Simon. "Trad has never been a big part of what we do since the Swarbrick era, though traditional songs occasionally make a reappearance, and there are Richard's songs like 'Now Be Thankful' that sound traditional. I don't want us to be a tribute band to ourselves and new records are important to refresh the repertoire."

That new repertoire has included songs by the Fairports' old folk-scene friends Ralph McTell and Steve Ashley; much of it is suitably concerned with history, but with many of the new songs written by the band. One of my personal favourites, Chris Leslie's "The Festival Bell", honours the bell in Cropredy village church that was cast to celebrate the Cropredy Festival.

But Fairports' grand folk-rock history is always in the background. At the BBC Folk Awards in 2006, *Liege and Lief* was named the "Most Influential Folk Album of All Time", after a public vote. Sandy's daughter Georgia Lucas collected the award, and the 1969 line-up of the band reassembled to play the album's best-known song, "Matty Groves", with Chris While taking Sandy Denny's role. The following year, Fairport's 40th anniversary, that line-up reassembled at Cropredy to perform *Liege and Lief* in its entirety.

The festival remains the highpoint of the Fairport year, with Richard Thompson making regular appearances (most recently in 2019). It always ends with a Fairport set, of course, and has attracted an extraordinary diverse range of guests, described by Simon as "people we like or with whom we have something in common". The list has included everyone from Bellowhead and Oysterband to Alice Cooper, Petula Clark and Robert Plant. In 2019, when Plant wanted to play some warm-up shows with his latest band Saving Grace, they toured with Fairport as the support act.

"We are part of the establishment now," said Simon. "We don't want to trade on that history but we are proud of it."

ASHLEY HUTCHINGS

So what then of the man known as "the Guv'nor", the co-founder of Fairport and Steeleye, described by Bob Dylan as "the single most important figure in English folk-rock"? Well, Ashley "Tyger" Hutchings kept working on new ideas. A restless, wildly inventive if not always commercially successful musician, he had quit Steeleye "because I wanted to be more English and Steeleye were getting more Celtic... and I had just married Shirley Collins, who was very English."

And yet in the summer of 2019 he could be found on the Isle of Wight cheerfully bashing out Bob Dylan songs in a band that included his son Blair Dunlop. He was there as Creative Director of a festival that marked the 50th anniversary of Bob's celebrated appearance at the same festival. Ashley explained, "I was always a big Dylan fan. I bought his first two albums, and it was shortly after that the Fairports were formed, influenced by Dylan and The Byrds. Without Dylan there would have been no Fairport – or most of the intelligent music of the last fifty years."

Back in the mid-seventies, when *The Electric Muse* first appeared, Ashley was in a difficult position. The passionate convert to English traditional music had recorded a classic album with Shirley Collins, *No Roses*, backed by an array of folk-rock friends he called The Albion Country Band, but the follow-up album took some time coming. Live Albion shows had been bravely original affairs, with folk-rock backing matched against Morris tunes and Morris dancing, but record company bosses were not impressed when the band finally recorded an album but then broke up. *Battle of the Field*, which was described on the sleeve as a "now legendary" album, included traditional songs and a "Morris medley" performed by an impressive line-up including Martin Carthy, Simon Nicol and John Kirkpatrick. It was released in 1976, three years after the recording, "though Island hadn't wanted to put it out. They didn't think it was worth it. But then there were petitions. Loads of people wrote to them. So there you go..."

By now, Ashley had moved on, of course. Along with Shirley Collins he formed The Etchingham Steam Band, a small acoustic group in which Shirley's singing was backed by Ashley's bass and squeezeboxes. They started out playing the folk circuit, but the band expanded when they were invited to larger venues or ceilidhs. "It just grew and grew," said Ashley, and it included several of the musicians who had appeared on yet another Ashley project, *Son of Morris On* in 1976. So the Steam Band became the eleven-piece folk-rock big band The Albion Dance Band, which featured Shirley on vocals, along with singer/melodeon player John Tams, electric guitars, two drummers, concertina, crumhorn and bagpipes. The emphasis of their elegant 1977 album *The Prospect Before Us* was, of course, on dance tunes, which ranged from Morris to polkas and Purcell.

It was an intriguing album, but the timing was, of course terrible. The seventies folk-rock era was now nearing its end and musical fashions were changing. Fairport would survive the onslaught of punk thanks to Cropredy, while Ashley and the Albions were saved by being offered regular work at the National Theatre in London.

Ashley says it was "the most important phone call in my whole life, without a doubt. Bill Bryden, a director at the National, asked if I would like to bring The Albion Band to the theatre to do music for a new play. Wow! It would change my whole world, my attitude to everything." He had first met Bryden during his time with Steeleye Span, when Steeleye (then including Ashley and Martin Carthy) played in the foyer during his production of *Pirates* at the Royal Court, and then acted and sang in another play, *Corunna*.

Ashley and the Albions would remain at the National from 1977 to 1981, with the band initially taking part in *The Passion* and later *The Nativity* – both "medieval mystery plays put into modern dress" – as well as two other successes for the theatre, *Lark Rise* and *Candleford*, adapted from the books of Flora Thompson about Victorian rural life. The band, which included brass as well as electric guitars, "played with the actors, in costume", said Ashley. John Tams and Martin Carthy were among those credited both as members of the cast and as musicians.

Somehow, The Albion Band managed to record a memorable studio album between their theatrical engagements. *Rise Up Like the Sun* (1978), which Ashley understandably rates as his favourite Albion album, was a bravely varied affair that he describes as "more rock than folk". It included a powerful version of Richard Thompson's "Time To Ring Some Change", along with the thoughtful "House In The Country", a song about the persecution of Travellers, written by Scottish singer Maggie Stewart with vocals from co-producer John Tams and that fine Canadian singer Kate McGarrigle. Guests joining the nine-piece band included Andy Fairweather-Low as well as Richard and Linda Thompson. But there was no Shirley Collins.

Shirley's marriage to Ashley had come to an end. He had left her for an actress who, said Shirley, took to showing up while she was on stage, with devastating results. In the middle of one performance of *Lark Rise* she found she could not sing. She was suffering from a severe type of dysphonia triggered by her emotional crisis. Shirley can be heard on the *Lark Rise* album (1980), providing fine, ghostly lead vocals on "Witch Elder", but after that our finest female folk singer would not be heard again until her remarkable comeback album, *Lodestar*, in 2016, over three decades later.

There were further dramas at the National. Ashley Hutchings went off on tour with a new version of The Albion Band, while the earlier band kept working at the theatre before deciding to break with Ashley and branch out with a new folk-rock outfit, Home Service. Led by John Tams, it featured both electric guitars and brass – including trumpeter Howard Evans and trombone-player Roger Williams, who also worked with Kirkpatrick and Carthy in Brass Monkey. Musically, their brand of guitar folk-rock may have suited the seventies more than the mid-eighties, despite the added brass, but their political stance and songs like "Alright Jack" reflected the angry era of Thatcher and the miners' strike.

As is the way with folk-rock bands, Home Service had a complex history. Tams left soon after they had released their *Alright Jack* album in 1986, and the band made only sporadic appearances before he re-united Home Service twenty-five years later (only to leave and then join again). He became as well known for his acting and music for TV as for his singing, thanks to the *Sharpe* TV series and the massively successful *War Horse* play and film, but also recorded a series of solo albums including *The Reckoning* (2005), which won him a batch of Folk Awards.

And as for Ashley Hutchings, he had been transformed by the experience of working at the National Theatre. He wrote and performed in a one-man show about the great song collector Cecil Sharp, in which he rode a bicycle on stage and appeared as both Sharp and himself. And he released his most adventurous solo album, *By Gloucester Docks I Sat Down and Wept*. An autobiographical concept work, telling the story of a doomed love affair from the viewpoint of both partners, it mixed spoken passages and poetry (including a burst of Shakespeare) with songs that matched grand, folk-influenced melodies against folk-rock. He says modestly that it is his "best album… there was only one other album like it, and that was Springsteen's *Tunnel of Love*".

Well, the album was certainly good, though completely wrong for 1987. It was largely ignored at the time, and had far greater impact when it was re-released in 2013 after being unavailable for years.

Since then, Hutchings has continued to experiment with new ideas. There was *Street Cries* (2001), a collection of "dark traditional songs re-set in the present day", written by Hutchings and performed by a cast that included John Tams and June Tabor. Then there was a new line-up of The Albion Dance Band, and an acoustic line-up of The Albion Band that included Simon Nicol. After ending the Albions in 2003 he handed the band to his son Blair Dunlop, who would run it with a younger line-up from 2010 to 2013. Ashley spent years with the less successful Rainbow Chasers, "who wrote fabulous songs but never got recognition. Not folky enough, I suppose…"

There were yet more projects. The Lark Rise Band, formed in 2007, paid tribute to the memory of Flora Thompson, who wrote the stories that had inspired the National Theatre productions of *Lark Rise* and *Candleford*. *My Land Is Your Land* (2008) was "a celebration of English and Italian cultures in music and words", a collaboration with Italian musician and DJ Ernesto De Pascale, "the John Peel of Italy". And *Paradise and Thorns* (2018) was an even more ambitious follow-up to *Gloucester Docks*, mixing new love songs with poetry and even dialogue taken from films.

And from 2001 to the present day he has toured every year in December with The Albion Christmas Band, along with an unchanged line-up of former Albion members, Simon Care, Kellie While and Simon Nicol – who always takes time off from Fairport to join them. It's different every year as they mix anything from obscure poems to dance tunes or Jackson Browne.

"I can't emphasise enough what a force Ashley was," said Simon, looking back to their early days together in Fairport. "He'd never say he was a virtuoso player, but his strength has been looking at how we could create music – what is interesting source material, where can we take it? And I still see him doing that on the Christmas tours. He's a very clever chap!"

RICHARD THOMPSON

And then, of course, there's Richard Thompson, the one member of Fairport's *Liege and Lief* line-up who has gone on to develop a large and still growing following both here and in the USA, where the *Los Angeles Times* hailed him as "the finest rock songwriter after Dylan and the best electric guitarist since Hendrix".

Richard has been a remarkable musician since he was a teenager. Simon Nicol remembers that when he first met him "he was a great guitarist from the start. It was down to what he listened to – he tried to incorporate Jimmy Shand and John Coltrane. Because he listened to that... and to Edith Piaf, French melodies... and Dylan." In Fairport Convention he also become fascinated by English traditional music, and had a clear aim of what he wanted folk-rock to achieve. "We thought, we are never going to be as good as The Band at playing American music, we are never going to be Buck Owens or Howlin' Wolf, but if we take things in this British direction we can be leaders in our field... if we are in the charts and it's taken seriously it could change people's attitudes to British music."

After leaving the Fairports he played on the folk circuit, worked with Ashley at The Albion Band, then recorded a solo album of his own material, *Henry the Human Fly*. It was not a critical success, but it marked him out as a distinctive, folk-influenced songwriter, thanks to songs like "The Poor Ditching Boy". And it featured an impressive band including Ashley Hutchings, Sandy Denny and another fine singer, Linda Peters – who would soon become Linda Thompson.

The first Richard and Linda Thompson album, *I Want to See the Bright Lights Tonight*, is now rightly regarded as a folk-rock classic, thanks to songs like "Withered And Died" and "The Great Valerio", and the interplay between Linda's cool, haunting vocals and Richard's guitar work and often bleak, memorable songs. Linda says it didn't feel that special at the time. "We had just two grand, maybe £1,800 to make the album. We just went in and did it. I wish I had paid more attention."

Linda had been playing the folk-club circuit before marrying Richard, "and it was all good fun and chugging along nicely. I did lots of adverts... Ski yogurt and 'flour so fine it flows and flows' – do you remember that?... but then Richard said 'you can't do adverts any more – it's dreadful'. So stupidly I listened to him and stopped... it had been so profitable!"

Marriage changed her life in other ways. The duo recorded a second studio album, *Hokey Pokey*, filled with such fine, typically bleak songs as "I'll Regret It All In The Morning", but the third album, *Pour Down Like Silver* (1975), would be very different. The album cover showed Richard and Linda both wearing headscarves. At the age of 23, Richard had become a Muslim, and says he has "been one ever since".

He had discovered Sufism, the mystical branch of Islam, after he had visited "a very old, esoteric bookshop, Watkins in London's Covent Garden, and started reading about it". Several of the songs on the album, including the exquisite "Dimming Of The Day" – which would later be covered by other artists from Emmylou Harris to David Gilmour – were seen as being inspired by his new faith. And for the next three years the couple largely disappeared from the music scene, spending their time in Islamic communities in London and then Norfolk.

Linda hated it. "Sufism had appealed to me but the guy who ran it was a bit of a tyrant. There was lots of praying and guilt... it's a control thing... and women were so subservient. It was terrible." Richard, who had been attracted to Sufism by "the nobility of being – it seemed like the way human being should be", agreed that the commune had faults. "It was full of human foibles... people are lustful, jealous. God knows what." He was far more impressed when he went to visit a sheikh in Morocco "and it was wonderful".

Richard and Linda left the commune and continued recording. It wasn't easy. The *First Light* and *Sunnyvista* albums both included some strong songs but failed to match their earlier work, and a third album financed and produced by singer Gerry Rafferty failed to interest the record companies. There were further problems – Linda was pregnant and their marriage was falling apart. Despite – or perhaps because of – these pressures they now produced their last and finest studio album together, after their manager Joe Boyd suggested it must be recorded in just a matter of days. The result – *Shoot Out the Lights* – was an album of furious, spontaneous-sounding songs matched against equally angry, thoughtful and furious singing and guitar work.

It was very well received and sold well, especially in the USA, and though their marriage was over, Richard and Linda were under pressure to set off on what became an infamous farewell tour, even by rock'n'roll standards. Simon Nicol, who was in the backing band for the three-week American tour, said it was "not a time I would care to re-live. It was like being on a survival course."

Linda said she was "mad and off my head. I was living on booze and anti-depressants, and was so angry that I was kicking and hitting Richard on stage. I trashed a dressing room, stole a car and got arrested. At one venue they said that the Sex Pistols had been there earlier and didn't make as much mess as you..."

Linda was suffering from dysphonia, though her condition was unlike that of Shirley Collins in that it hadn't come on suddenly and was progressing slowly (and so far has sadly not been reversed). She said that her anger on tour "made Richard play better and me sing better! I was singing really well. I guess because I was so heartbroken it freed me up. The dysphonia was not too bad in those days. It's much worse now..."

After the tour was over, and Richard and Linda had split up, Richard rang her with some dramatic news. "He said 'Bruce Springsteen is male singer of the year and you are female singer.' Was it in *Time* magazine or *Rolling Stone*? I think it was in both!"

Linda had returned to London to join John Tams and the other folk-rockers at the National Theatre, where she appeared in the

Mystery Plays trilogy. But she was now a star in America and was given "a huge advance" to make a solo album. *One Clear Moment* was a disappointment – it was pleasant enough but lacked a sense of identity. Linda didn't care. She was travelling the world with her new husband, a successful agent. Her voice caused her increasing problems, but later albums were far better. *Fashionably Late* (2002) included a fine tragic folk ballad, "The Banks Of The Clyde", written by Linda, and the lament "Weary Life", co-written by her son Teddy, who had been born in 1976 during the commune days and would prove to be an increasingly impressive singer-songwriter.

Two great albums were to follow: *Versatile Heart* (2007) included songs by Teddy and by Linda's daughter Kami, along with songs by Rufus Wainwright and Tom Waits and with her own tribute to one of the great veterans of the English folk scene, on "Whisky, Bob Copper And Me". *Won't Be Long Now* (2013) included a powerful, unaccompanied live treatment of "Blue Bleezin' Blind Drunk", a reminder that she could still be a remarkable performer, on a good night. But time was running out. In 2019 she told me that she was writing an album of new songs – but would be unable to sing on it herself. Dysphonia had robbed us of one of the great English folk voices. "It's tragic," said Richard. "Such a voice and you lose that voice. It's very tough."

And as for Richard himself, he stayed in America, where he re-married and kept playing and writing. Punk may have damaged the careers of his folk-rock friends back in England, but he had no such problems working from his new home in California. "In the States I got treated as a new artist," he said. "At aged 33, when I went solo, they put me on college radio – so my audience was ten years younger than me in America. It still is. And very, very slowly I did well. It was word of mouth. I toured America relentlessly, and I still do. And it's still growing, which is amazing. Without having a hit record or any of that stuff, more people come to the shows now than they ever did!"

He succeeded both because of his guitar work, and because of his powerful and distinctive songs, which ranged from the bleak and lyrical ballads that are regularly heard in folk clubs (where some singers probably think they are performing traditional songs) through to upbeat rock songs like "Tear-Stained Letter", where a cheerful melody is matched against a typically un-cheerful chorus: "cry, cry if it makes you feel better, write it all down in a tear-stained letter". Elsewhere, his song-writing includes Scottish influences, dance tunes or the edgy and pounding stories of foreboding on his 2018 album, *13 Rivers*. "I write fiction," he said. "I think it always reflects your own experience and feelings but it isn't always in a way that's clear. If you find something honest enough in yourself then it will be universal, it will appeal to other people as well."

There is enormous variety in his work, and it's reflected in his live shows. Sometimes he plays electric guitar and tours with a band and sometimes he gives solo acoustic shows. "I love doing both," he said. "And switching it from year to year is kind of refreshing for me and maybe for the audience – because the repertoire is slightly different."

And as for those celebrated, often blistering guitar solos, he insists that they are only there to emphasise the songs. "Most of what I do revolves around the song. I'm not interested in playing instrumentals. I like accompanying a voice, or if there is a solo, then extending the narrative of a song. To me that's the interest in being a guitar player."

And as a songwriter, he has shown remarkable consistency. His followers all have their own favourites, and mine would range from "1952 Vincent Black Lightning" (on *Rumour and Sigh*, 1991) to "Razor Dance" (*You? Me? Us?*, 1996), the rocking "Cooksferry Queen" (*Mock Tudor*, 1998), that bitter Iraq story "Dad's Gonna Kill Me" (*Sweet Warrior*, 2007), and the recent brooding "The Storm Won't Come" (*13 Rivers*, 2018).

Aside from his solo albums, he joined singer Judith Owen on the *1000 Years of Popular Music* project, in which they covered anything from "Sumer Is Icumen In" to Britney. And along with his ex-wife and children he of course contributed to the 2014 *Thompson Family* album, which starts with the title track by Teddy and the lines "my father is one of the greats to ever step on a stage, my mother has the most beautiful voice in the world". As for Linda, who also sang on the album, she has now forgiven Richard. "I have. It was a bad time but it was forty years ago. Forget it!"

Increasingly, other artists wanted to record Richard Thompson's songs, and in 1994 he was honoured by a tribute album, *Beat the Retreat*, which featured new versions of his work by a remarkable array of artists. American heroes R.E.M. covered "Wall Of Death", indie rockers Dinosaur Jr. played "I Misunderstood", Los Lobos revived "Down Where The Drunkards Roll", and there was a fine new treatment of "The Great Valerio" by English folk stars Martin Carthy and Maddy Prior. Since then his songs have been covered by everyone from Emmylou Harris to David Gilmour.

Richard Thompson is special. His music includes an array of varied influences but much of it is still rooted in the Fairports' early experiments in creating a distinctively English style of folk-rock. He may be based in the USA (he has now moved from the West to the East Coast) but he has retained his English (and Scottish) influences, and there's no hint of an American accent. He returns regularly to Britain to perform, and of course, is a regular visitor to the Fairports' Cropredy Festival where he continues to play with his old band. "I have never wanted to be culturally absorbed by America," he said. "I like British culture. But I work a lot in the States. I'm based there – until Trump kicks me out."

SOURCES

Author Interviews

(All 2019)
Martin Carthy
Ashley Hutchings
John Kirkpatrick
Simon Nicol
Maddy Prior
Richard Thompson

Written Sources

Cath Clarke, "The Ballad Of Shirley Collins", *Guardian*, October 12, 2017.

Tim Hart and Robin Denselow, *The Complete Steeleye Span* (Boyesen Enterprises Ltd, 1978).

Patrick Humphries, *Richard Thompson: Strange Affair, The Biography* (Virgin Books, 1996).

SIX

FOLK INTO PUNK

THE POGUES

Richard Thompson was one exception, of course, but punk – and then the Two Tone movement that followed – badly damaged the folk-rockers of the seventies. Record companies were no longer interested in a style that suddenly seemed outdated compared to The Clash or The Specials. Here, after all, was a relevant and new and exciting DIY style that reflected the new multi-cultural face of Britain and could be seen as an updated form of folk, with its reflection of social and political issues. Certainly the two were not as far apart as it may initially have seemed, but the more conservative elements in the folk clubs may not have acknowledged any such similarities at the time.

But there were artists combining these different influences. Billy Bragg, one of the most original and influential singer-songwriters to emerge in the eighties, says that "the thing that attracted me to punk that was similar to folk is the authenticity. This was real music and not stuff that was going to be on the mainstream, on telly. Folk pokes its head up and people remember it when the New Romantics come along and it becomes about syn drums and haircuts again... and becomes about style over content. Folk is almost all content – and I have always been a content over style man."

Punk helped, he said, "because it cleared the way – it cleared the space for the likes of The Pogues and me to come along", in what became a new post-punk amplified folk scene that often included strong Celtic influences.

Initially, the London Irish band The Pogues would prove to be the most successful and exciting of the bunch, after a remarkable transformation. They may have started out as something of a drunken shambles, back in the early days when they were known as Pogue Mahone and were bashing out "Paddy Works On The Railway" in an Islington cellar, but by the time they recorded their classic album *If I Should Fall from Grace with God* in 1988 it was clear that there was brilliance behind the mania.

By now, Shane MacGowan had proved to be a thoughtful songwriter, despite his (no doubt genuine) alcoholic stage image, and the band had acquired new musicians, including folk veterans Philip Chevron and multi-instrumentalist Terry Woods – who, remarkably, had played in the very first Steeleye Span line-up. They also had a celebrity producer, Steve Lillywhite (of U2 and Peter Gabriel fame), who managed to retain the Pogues' energy in a set that matched traditional songs against Chevron's thoughtful reflection on Irish migration, "Thousands Are Sailing" and MacGowan's angry and political "Birmingham Six". And then, of course, there was that bitter-sweet Christmas classic "Fairytale Of New York", in which the folk punks were now backed by sweeping strings, with MacGowan singing alongside Kirsty MacColl, daughter of folk hero Ewan MacColl.

A few weeks after the album's release, in March 1988, The Pogues made a triumphant return to London with six sold-out shows at The Town and Country (now the Forum) in Kentish Town, and an extra show at Brixton Academy. Their range was remarkable, from Irish dance tunes treated with punk energy through to "Fairytale" and Ewan MacColl's classic, "Dirty Old Town". Their guests included American country star Steve Earle, and Joe Strummer, who revived that Clash classic, "London Calling", with them. After seeing the show I wrote "get a ticket to see them if you can – preferably twice".

Other fine shows would follow, of course, but so would the problems, thanks to MacGowan's drinking and increasingly erratic behaviour. He left The Pogues in 1991 and Joe Strummer took over on lead vocals for a while before the band broke up five years later. Meanwhile, MacGowan had founded a new band, The Popes, where he continued to act out his now predictably chaotic lifestyle on stage. I remember waiting for hours for the band to turn up for a St Patrick's Day show in London, where MacGowan eventually staggered on stage clutching a pint for what seemed to be an unrehearsed set. He and The Pogues were eventually re-united in

2001 for occasional tours that continued until 2014, a year after
Philip Chevron had died. They should be remembered for those
glory years in the eighties. When they were at their best, The Pogues
were unique.

THE OYSTERBAND

Down in Kent, another band was trying to give English traditional
music a post-punk makeover in this difficult decade, as they edged
from folk into rock. Oysterband were, they say, "determined that
traditional music should not be just a branch of the heritage industry".

They weren't exactly newcomers. Back in the seventies, violinist
Ian Telfer was studying for a PhD at Canterbury University ("which
I wasn't very good at") when he had met guitarist Alan Prosser
(who was "pretending to study chemical physics") and they both
became members of a local acoustic band, Fiddler's Dram. To the
astonishment of all concerned, they notched up a huge hit with "Day
Trip To Bangor", a sing-along, knees-up song, which sold half a
million singles and landed them an appearance on *Top of the Pops*.

Looking back, Telfer says he is not embarrassed by the experience.
"Some people think it was terribly unfashionable nonsense, but
personally I was happy to have sold 502,000 singles... that gave me
and Alan enough money to go on trying to be musicians."

They had a second group, The Oyster Ceilidh Band (so called
because they played at a successful folk club in Whitstable, a town
famous for its oysters), in which they were joined by John Jones, a
teacher and melodeon player. They played at folk dances and
recorded their own albums, but their fortunes dramatically improved
after they had changed their name and were invited to record for a
new indie label, Cooking Vinyl.

"They thought we were the noisiest thing they had to hand," said
Telfer. "Initially we were 'anything but Fairport'... we were a bit
rougher and wilder in performance... though years later we found
ourselves on tour with them and realised that was an absurd position
to have taken. We got on like a house on fire."

The Oysters' first album for the label, *Step Outside*, began with a
traditional song, a treatment of the Cornish song "Hal-an-Tow" that
had been recorded by that legendary a cappella vocal harmony folk

group The Watersons back in the mid-sixties. The Oysters' upbeat stomping treatment began with crashing electric guitar chords.

It was a song that typified their early approach, as a rousing, good-time band who became popular on the festival and concert circuit, mixing self-written material with reminders of their folk roots, often with a Celtic edge. The British music scene may have been tough for folk-rockers in the eighties, but they survived. They never played pubs ("it's hideously difficult to get out of that unless you are Dave Edmunds", said Telfer), but they did play extensively outside the UK. Their brand of English folk-rock was performed across "thirteen countries in Asia", in the USA, but mostly in Europe – where they acquired a "frighteningly young" and enthusiastic audience, and opened for The Pogues on a German tour. And then came one of the more unexpected and successful collaborations in the story of English folk-rock.

June Tabor is one of Britain's finest interpreters of popular song, a singer with a remarkable musical range, and the ability to mix emotion, passion and drama in her widely varied material. But she was certainly no punk, and seemed an unlikely folk-rocker, though she says she "never was very ordinary".

She had started singing as a schoolgirl in the sixties, after hearing a record by Anne Briggs and deciding "this is what I want to do... and locking myself in the bathroom to practise". She studied French and Latin at Oxford, where she became president of the Heritage folk club, and it was here that she first met Maddy Prior, who was singing at the club along with Tim Hart, in the days before Steeleye Span. Maddy and June went on to work together as an occasional duo, Silly Sisters, whose debut album in 1976 featured experiments in Bulgarian-influenced harmonies and backing from the folk scene's leading acoustic musicians including Martin Carthy and Nic Jones – who would also play on her first solo albums.

She said she "didn't want to depend on singing for money", and for eleven years she worked as a librarian in London, emerging from the books to record albums or John Peel sessions for the BBC. In the difficult eighties she ran a restaurant in Cumbria, while occasionally recording with that fine guitarist, Martin Simpson, but when the restaurant folded she "went for music full time – some people do come to things late in life". She recorded a jazz album of work by

Ellington and Mingus, backed by pianist Huw Warren. And then came the Oysters.

They met up during the Sidmouth Folk Festival in 1987, in the musicians' social pub, The Dove. Ian Anderson, the editor of what was then *Folk Roots* magazine, remembers: "June and some friends were somewhat hilariously the worse for pints and had just burned an effigy of a music journalist in the ash tray. The Oysters were obviously impressed. The rest, as they say, is history."

"We didn't know she was like that," said Telfer, and asked to be introduced, and by the end of the evening June and the Oysters had decided to work together. "They said they wanted to do something different and have a woman singing with the band," June remembers. "Something along the lines of 10,000 Maniacs. They said they wanted someone who could 'float their voice over what the band does and throw themselves about a bit on stage'. I said I'm up for throwing the voice but not sure about the rest."

The idea survived, and both sides met up in Ian Telfer's basement kitchen to decide on songs. "I said straight away 'they have got to have good words'," said June. "That's the way I chose a song and they were up for that. We looked at all sorts of things, some traditional, some contemporary... and in the end the choice was very strong from the lyric point of view." So as a famously intense musical story-teller, how hard was it for her to sing with a band bashing away behind her? "It's a matter of learning. But the songs were strong enough to carry, the words were really strong, and what we tried to do was emphasise the content. But it just happened to be a rather loud backing!"

For those who thought that June only sang folk songs, the *Freedom and Rain* album (1990) was a revelation. It began with "Mississippi Summer", a song by American Labour activist Si Khan that she had heard in the USA, as well as songs by Richard Thompson, John Tams, Shane MacGowan and Billy Bragg. The traditional material included "Dives And Lazarus", "which includes the line 'hell is dark, hell is cold, hell is full of mice'... I love that!" said June. "I found that really strong, moving and powerful. It was certainly not dampened by a rock backing."

The experiment had worked, breathing new life into guitar folk-rock, and enhancing the reputation of both parties. It was followed by a tour that included a wild night in the Spanish town of Oviedo. The band went on late, around 2 a.m., at an outdoor festival where, said June "considerable amounts of alcohol had been consumed. The Oysters finished with the Clash favourite 'I Fought The Law' and the audience invaded the stage. I had to part them to get to the microphone."

When the tour was over, June returned to her solo acoustic career singing all kinds of music, arguing "what I prefer to do is take songs from different backgrounds and link them in some way. It's always down to the words." She recorded concept albums about roses, and mixed traditional songs with contemporary work by anyone from Tracy Chapman to her massive admirer Elvis Costello – who composed songs for her, including "All This Useless Beauty". "If you can't appreciate June Tabor, you should just stop listening to music," said Costello.

And for their part, the Oysters continued touring and recording, but now (like the Fairports) concentrating more on new songs than traditional material and moving away from "the clichés of the 'Celtic' style" with albums like *Meet You There*. They also held a series of their own festivals, The Big Sessions, which, says Ian, "didn't last ferociously long... we had Steve Earle on once at Leicester. And a Steve Earle audience – entirely male and aged around 50 – came in and hollered for him and then left." But the Oysters' shows also helped to provide a platform for the next generation of folk musicians. *The Big Session Volume 1* album (2004), recorded in a small hall in west London, set out to "attempt to bring to a larger stage the spirit of an after-hours music session", and included not just June Tabor but also the younger experimental artists, Eliza Carthy and Jim Moray.

Then, twenty-one years on from *Freedom and Rain*, "everything was turned upside down yet again", as Ian put it. June and the Oysters had not lost touch, and had occasionally performed together, and now decided to make a reunion album. *Ragged Kingdom*, released in 2011, was an extraordinary success, winning a whole batch of BBC Folk Awards (Best Album, Best Group, Best Trad Track and Folk Singer of the Year for June). It was followed by a two-year tour and an appearance on BBC TV's *Later... With Jools Holland*.

This was an album of greater maturity, emotional depth and variety. The contemporary songs included a powerful duet between June Tabor and John Jones on "Dark End Of The Street", a pained acoustic version of Joy Division's "Love Will Tear Us Apart" (which June had sung on the *Big Session* album) and a gutsy re-working of PJ Harvey's "That Was My Veil". But there were more traditional tracks on this album, because, said June, "we looked at a huge range of stuff but those were the ones that worked for all of us." They included a stomping treatment of "Bonnie Bunch Of Roses" that didn't detract from June's no-nonsense story-telling, along with delicate vocal harmony work on "(When I Was No But) Sweet Sixteen", and fine melodeon and fiddle work on "Fountains Flowing".

Ragged Kingdom was such a success that June and the Oysters got together to tour again – a mere eight years later, in 2019. There would be no new album this time, but they did release a ten-track "tour memento", which was on sale at the concerts. Playing in London they mixed old Oysterband songs like "Put Out The Lights" with new traditional material that also appeared on the "memento" album. "I'll Show You Wonders" was a jaunty folk-rock treatment of the murder ballad "Twa Sisters", while "False True Love" was treated to a more acoustic backing, with acoustic guitar, cello and violin.

June described it as "one of those songs of what might have been... it's traditional but so apposite. Which is one of the things I always come back to, time after time... that traditional music understands the human heart and human nature like nothing else... because it is absolutely timeless."

She is now in her early seventies but still in intense, powerful voice. She and the Oysters had enjoyed a curious, truncated history, but between them had created one of the great folk-rock bands.

BILLY BRAGG

The Oysters/Tabor tour in the autumn of 2019 coincided with a British tour from Billy Bragg, another surviving hero of the eighties punk-folk-rock scene, though Bragg is far harder to categorise. An ardent punk and Clash fan, he would go on to be embraced by the English folk scene before also being hailed in the USA as a great exponent of Americana. And he achieved all this while developing his role as a thoughtful left-wing activist and commentator on British and global politics – as well as the author of a book on skiffle.

Billy Bragg has enjoyed an unlikely and unique career. Born in Barking, east London, he started out working as a clerk and messenger, played in a pub band, Riff Raff, and briefly became an army recruit (he bought himself out after ninety days). And then, in the early eighties, he emerged in the punk era as an electric guitar-playing soloist and singer-songwriter with a pronounced East End accent.

But he was a punk fan with eclectic musical tastes – and that included folk.

As a teenager, back in the seventies, he was, he said, "really into Simon and Garfunkel and Bob Dylan… and recognised that some of the people Dylan talked about, Bert Lloyd and Ewan MacColl, had appeared on Topic Records compilations." His family didn't have a record player, so he went down to Barking Public Library, which included a record section, "and recorded a lot of them at home". Then he started listening to Shirley and Dolly Collins, "who really connected with me more than anything else that was going on", and to The Watersons. He also played Steeleye Span albums, "which made me a bit weird at school… there was nobody else into that shit. So I kind of had a layman's knowledge of traditional English music, that was derailed by punk."

The young punk soloist was a success. His solo album *Life's a Riot with Spy Vs Spy* (1983) reached the Top 30 and included a series of highly original songs, including "The Busy Girl Buys Beauty", a reflection on the consumer society, as well as the upbeat "A New England", which would become a hit single for Ewan's daughter, Kirsty MacColl. His second album, *Brewing Up with Billy Bragg* (1984), included an attack on the right-wing tabloid press, "It Says Here", and broke into the Top 20.

In the same year he toured the USA for the first time, where he became increasingly fascinated by the American radical folk tradition. "It really opened my mind to the labour songs," he said. "The British tradition was not as vibrant as the American tradition, because theirs was more twentieth century and ours more nineteenth century." In Britain, he had been connected to The Clash, but "because of the way I appeared they connected me to Woody Guthrie. I had read that Dylan was influenced by Woody, but hadn't been able to buy a Woody Guthrie record until then..."

The American tour rekindled his interest in American folk, but he wouldn't reconnect with his English folk roots until he became actively involved in one of the most bitter industrial disputes in recent British history, the miners' strike of 1984–5. Conservative government plans to close collieries led to a strike led by the National Union of Mineworkers, and violent clashes between miners and the police. Billy Bragg supported the miners with benefit shows around the colliery towns and it transformed his attitudes to folk. "Initially you would not see my folk influences because I'm hiding them until the miners' strike," he said, as he explained the importance to his career of a miner and traditional singer called Jock Purdon.

He was the support act for Billy at a benefit show in the north-east where Purdon "sang a cappella with his hand over his ear... and all his songs were more radical than mine. I thought to myself, 'I'm going to be in trouble here, this old geezer is going to slaughter me'." When Billy expressed his concerns in the dressing room, the miner reassured him by saying, "listen son, it doesn't matter what you sing. By standing in solidarity with the miners you are part of the tradition now, whatever you do."

On stage, Purdon mixed his own work with far older songs like "The Trimdon Grange Explosion", which deals with a nineteenth-century mine disaster. "Explosion" had been recorded by Martin Carthy, along with other songs he had heard sung by The Watersons. Bragg said, "it was that experience, and re-connecting with The Watersons, that gave me the confidence to let my folk side come to the fore."

The result was "Between The Wars" (1985), his most successful, and most folk-influenced song of his career up to that point. It sounded more like some sturdy and long-established union anthem than a pop song, and included lines like "I kept the faith and I kept voting, not for the iron fist but for the helping hand". And yet it reached number 15 in the singles charts, and earned Billy an appearance on *Top of the Pops*. It was released on an EP that also included "The World Turned Upside Down", a song by folk singer Leon Rosselson about the Diggers, a radical group who set up an agricultural commune in Surrey during the seventeenth century. And then there was "Which Side Are You On?", originally a miners' song from Kentucky, written by the wife of a union organiser, which had earlier been recorded by Pete Seeger.

"And with that EP I came out in, shall we say, 'folk style', not to upset the purists," said Billy. "I have always felt I am of the tradition but not part of it." So was this solo work folk-rock? Well, it was certainly folk-influenced, and "Upside Down" in particular involved some decidedly punk-influenced crashing guitar chords.

The folk scene was delighted. Ian Anderson put Billy on the front cover of his magazine, and he even accepted an appearance to play electric guitar at the Trowbridge Folk Festival. While there he heard the Blowzabella band playing his song "Between The Wars" "with a hurdy gurdy! I don't know if they expected me to be outraged but I was totally chuffed. I thought 'great, this is like welcome home, you are part of this'."

There were limits, of course. He certainly wouldn't play acoustic guitar in folk clubs. He explained "I play electric guitar so I don't have to play fucking folk clubs! I didn't want to be there – I wanted to be off with The Clash. If I had played acoustic guitar they would have said fuck off and play in the folk clubs – that's how it was then!"

Billy was still firmly a part of the post-punk scene, and when he toured with Red Wedge in their campaign to win youth support for the Labour Party before the 1987 elections, it was in the company of Paul Weller, Jerry Dammers and The Smiths' guitar hero Johnny Marr. But at the same time Bragg was making friends on the folk scene, meeting Leon Rosselson and his heroes The Watersons, including Martin Carthy, Norma Waterson and their then-teenage daughter, Eliza Carthy.

Billy remembers, "the first time I met Martin I told him 'I saw Johnny Marr the other day and he told me that his guitar playing is "just Martin Carthy, speeded up".' And Martin said 'that's lovely... who's Johnny Marr?' Eliza was like... deeply embarrassed!"

On his third album, *Talking with the Taxman About Poetry* (1986), Billy was joined on some tracks by other musicians, including Johnny Marr on guitar. Several of the songs, from Levi Stubb's "Tears" to the Clash-like "Help Save The Youth Of America", showed his continued interest in America, and the most powerful political anthem in the set, "There Is Power In The Union", was written back in 1913 by American labour activist Joe Hill.

His fascination with the history of the American radical folk scene included, inevitably, a growing interest in the work of that extraordinary singer and songwriter Woody Guthrie, who travelled through the Dust Bowl in the thirties, singing about unions and strikes, and whose work was a major influence on the young Bob Dylan. Bragg's 1991 single "You Woke Up My Neighbourhood" (on which he was joined by Peter Buck and Michael Stipe from R.E.M.) took its title from a drawing by Woody that he had seen in the Smithsonian Institute.

Within a few years, the names of Woody and Billy would be interlinked. He had been performing alongside Woody's son, Arlo, and Woody's old colleague Pete Seeger, at a Guthrie tribute show in New York ("at a time when I only knew one Guthrie song"), and here he met Woody's daughter, Nora. When she later discovered a large collection of her late father's lyrics that had never been recorded, she asked Billy if he could provide melodies for them. "Because, like me, Woody was not the kind of songwriter who writes music," Billy told me at the time. "The music for his songs was in his head and it was lost when he died."

The *Mermaid Avenue* project (named after the Coney Island street where Woody once lived) was a collaboration with the American band Wilco, whose front man Jeff Tweedy was also involved in writing some of the melodies for a set that veered from rolling country rock to folk balladry and occasional echoes of Dylan's *Basement Tapes*. It proved to be a massive success, earned a Grammy nomination, and led to two further *Mermaid Avenue* releases, with some tracks involving the band and others where Billy sang solo. In the USA the fusion would be termed Americana, while in the UK, this was folk-rock.

Joining Billy on some of the tracks, including the charming "California Stars", was a young violinist, Eliza Carthy, who was about to shake up the English folk-rock scene.

SOURCES

Author Interviews

(All 2019)
Billy Bragg
June Tabor
Ian Telfer

Written Sources

Billy Bragg, *Roots, Radicals and Rockers* (Faber & Faber, 2017).

Andrew Collins, *Billy Bragg: Still Suitable for Miners* (Virgin Books, 2007).

Robin Denselow, "Review: The Pogues At Brixton Academy", *Guardian*, December 22, 2004.

Robin Denselow, "Review: The Popes At London Forum", *Guardian*, March 19, 1999.

Robin Denselow, "Review: The Pogues At Town And Country", *Guardian*, March 16, 1988.

Robin Denselow, "Songwriters Of The World Unite (Bragg and Guthrie)", *Guardian*, May 14, 1998.

SEVEN

THE NEW FOLK-ROCK

ELIZA CARTHY

"My daddy wouldn't let me listen to folk-rock when I was little," said Eliza Carthy, and gave a characteristic cackle. "Not because he thought it was naughty – he thought I should listen to traditional singers. He said 'don't listen to us, listen to those who went before us', so I haven't heard Steeleye or Fairport – I just haven't got round to it." There was another cackle. "He was being modest. The only thing of Steeleye I have heard is when you go round the supermarkets at Christmas and 'Gaudete' is playing…"

Martin Carthy, her folk-guitar-hero dad and one-time member of Steeleye, explained what he had been trying to achieve. "I'm disappointed by a lot of the new crop (of folk singers)… they listened to us, my lot – I don't understand why they don't go back one step further, when all that stuff is available. It's really intriguing because all those old women and old blokes do odd stuff when they are singing, they make odd choices, and it's part of the pleasure, the deal…"

As the daughter of Martin Carthy and Norma Waterson, Eliza comes from a family regarded as folk royalty, who have played a unique role in the British folk scene. On the one hand they are distinguished traditionalists, fascinated by the roots and history of the music, while on the other hand they have been happy to experiment, to bring the songs to new audiences. And Eliza would do more than anyone else of her generation in matching acoustic work against new forms of folk-rock experimentation, bringing a new dynamic to the music while also emerging as an original singer-songwriter.

As she explained to me back in the nineties: "I like the stories and I like the poetry, and the words have a real power over me. As for the tunes, they are so brilliantly odd, they are like nothing else you'll hear. I want to do this because it's different, and being different is good."

Billy Bragg, who helped Eliza when she was starting out, describes her as "fabulously new... I played with her in the nineties at Glastonbury before she played on *Mermaid Avenue*... and before she went on stage she put mud in her hair! I think Eliza is key for that new generation, because... they are a rum bunch, the folk audience, if you want to do something different and new. But because of her pedigree you can't really argue with her!"

Eliza has always had eclectic taste. When she was young she had listened to "a weird combination of Queen, Mozart, George Formby and The Wombles, Mike Batt", as well as traditional music. Her dad's folk-rock but may not have been allowed, but she was able to join her parents' celebrated family band — "I had the chance to belt along with The Watersons all the time."

There was, she says, "a natural feeling to the music flowing through all the time. And I didn't just have a Brit-centric view of folk. Friends were coming to the house from everywhere, from Louisiana, India or France... and when world music hit big I was interested in that. We went to the Vancouver Folk Festival when I was 13 and I saw *gnawa* musicians and African choirs. And then I would come back and listen to Fred Jordan [that great singing Shropshire farm worker]. And I adored Billy Bragg because he reminded me of Dick Gaughan [the political Scottish singer-songwriter]. We used to go to the Inverness Festival, and Dick would get up on stage with just an electric guitar, and I thought it was the coolest thing I had ever seen..."

All of this would be reflected in her freewheeling approach to music, both as a singer and as an instrumentalist. She had started playing violin after listening to Dave Swarbrick (who had played with her dad as a duo) and Chris Wood, whom Martin was mentoring. "And I was thinking 'this is interesting — you can play violin and sing at the same time!'"

She began recording while still a teenager, first with fellow fiddler Nancy Kerr, and then in 1994 joining her mum and dad in a new family band, Waterson:Carthy. It was the start of a musical career that would always include regular work with her parents, alongside all her many other projects. Her first solo album, *Heat Light & Sound* (1996), was a fresh, confident set that showcased her already excellent fiddle work, her singing (a fine treatment of "10,000 Miles") and even her song-writing. And with sturdy electric bass guitar playing from Barnaby Stradling it showed more than a nod towards folk-rock.

Stradling reappeared the following year playing on the cheerfully upbeat album that Eliza recorded with The Kings of Calicutt, and went on to play a key role in Eliza's most ambitious project to date, in which she set out to update the folk-rock style her dad had helped to pioneer.

By now she had moved to Scotland, excited by the vibrant music scene that included bands like Shooglenifty and The Peatbog Faeries, and was "hanging out with circus performers and playing loads of different things with various street theatre companies... and I wanted to express that". She also wanted to "subvert the idea of what was a traditional album and what wasn't a traditional album". The result, *Red Rice*, was a remarkable double set.

Red was a boldly experimental album that updated the original aims of folk-rock by reflecting the late nineties music scene, with traditional songs now given a contemporary drum and bass backing, or matched against almost jazzy riffs or programming (making music through use of electronic devices and computers). She was backed by a band that included drummer Sam Thomas, electric guitarist Olly Knight and piano-accordion work from Martin Green, later a founder member of that remarkable experimental folk trio Lau. But the key player was Barnaby Stradling on electric bass, percussion and Moog, who had spent years playing with "grungy, punky bands before joining Eliza".

They developed an unusual way of constructing new settings for the songs, with Eliza "singing a traditional song, free-form, and then Barnaby will just work out some weird circular rhythm that goes underneath it. Then I have to shift a little bit, he shifts a little bit, and it comes together." That was how they constructed some of the best songs on the album, like "Greenwood Laddie", while others were more experimental, like the track "Red Rice", which features Eliza on fiddle and programming from the Halifax duo, Shack and Paul. As Eliza explained to me at the time, "they do raves and parties and a bit of DJ-ing and we all got drunk together and went into the studio to do a bit of singing and playing. They looped my fiddle playing after I'd gone and a couple of weeks later they sent me their versions of the songs."

The second album in the set, *Rice*, was completely different – a straightforward and classy set of folk songs backed by an acoustic band that included melodeon and acoustic guitar. Inevitably, it was the experimental *Red* that gained the most attention, and led to Eliza's invitation to a whole batch of summer festivals, including Glastonbury – where she joined a line-up that included Dylan, Pulp and Tricky. She was just 22, sported red hair and studs in her lip and nose, and was seen as the experimental leading lady of the new folk scene. Her only rival was that exquisite, but less experimental, singer Kate Rusby.

Looking back at *Red* and *Rice* over two decades later, Eliza explained the difference between them like this: "People think of *Rice* as the traditional album and *Red* as the experimental album – but that's not the way I saw it. I saw people like Kate Rusby making pretty-sounding acoustic music on expensive instruments... so my 'modern' album showing I can do this, was *Rice*. *Red* was what I think of as the traditional way of doing things – expressing the music you love with the people you love... and I was hanging around with drum and bass DJs and people that grew up in reggae bands... *Red* for me was going into the family business, because that's what my dad did! People were going 'you're such a rebel', and I was going 'I'm doing exactly the same thing as my dad. Exactly the same!'" The famous cackle returned. "It was me seeing if I could do pretty on *Rice*... but actually what I wanted to do was make squealing noises with my friends in Edinburgh – so that's what I did on *Red*!" So was this Eliza's equivalent of sixties folk-rock? "Yes, but with a new set of tools! Folk hip hop, hip hop clog dancing, all that..."

Red Rice (released first as a double album, then as two separate albums) was a triumph. It was nominated for a Mercury Award (for Best Album from the UK) and led to Eliza signing with a major record label, Warner Brothers USA. And now she changed direction yet again, to the dismay of many of her folk followers. Back in 1998 she had told me, "it was never my aim to shake up the folk scene. I just do what I do and never let that get boring."

So she did just that, and instead of the new experimental folk-rock album that many expected, she recorded *Angels and Cigarettes*, a classy but inevitably more tame-sounding folk-influenced pop album of her own songs. She said she was "trying to write English pop music, like

Kirsty MacColl – I wanted to write something that didn't have its basis in the blues... I wanted to write informed pop music from the background I have in studying traditional music... and I'm still doing it. It's never been an either/or thing for me... I like doing everything." So when she toured across the USA promoting *Angels and Cigarettes* she "opened every set with an unaccompanied ballad".

Angels and Cigarettes was less of a commercial success than *Red Rice*, and Eliza followed up with a return to traditional music, to the delight of her folk fans. Though when someone said "welcome back" to her at an Oysterband Big Session Festival show she responded angrily. "You are saying this to me at an Oysterband festival? This is my return to traditional music? I had made two Waterson:Carthy albums in that period that nobody bought..."

But her next traditional album, *Anglicana*, was an undisputed success, a clever blend of delicate acoustic songs, including a duet with her dad and a solo piano piece, matched against a thoughtful return to folk-rock. Her backing musicians included the fine duo of John Spiers on melodeon and Jon Boden on fiddle, and Stradling was back on bass, but for Eliza the key player on the folk-rock songs was the Scottish drummer, Donald Hay. Her father had stopped her from listening to folk-rock when she was young because he wanted her to appreciate the twists, turns, decorations and subtleties in the work of traditional singers, so now she set out to follow their approach. Many of the songs were taken from Topic Records' *Voice of the People* albums, and Eliza set out to follow the style of the great veterans, rather than let a regular drum beat dictate her approach.

Donald Hay had an eclectic background, "playing in an incredibly loud Scottish folk hip hop group called Mystery Juice, as well as Shooglenifty and loads more", and he laughed when she told him this was a folk-rock album "because the Scots hate the term folk-rock". But she insisted "I don't want any suggestion of the seventies on this album – this is not *Liege and Lief*! I want the drums to serve the music and not the other way round. I have heard so many songs that have guitar and drums going 'boom-ching-boom-ching' and the poor song has to somehow still be music over the top. So what we are going to do is stretch, wait, breathe... and then in the bits when we are not stretching and breathing... you can bash the crap out of those! I'd

245

rather we had those fantastic moments when we are hanging in the air, and then – bang! You come down again."

So with "Worcester City" and "Pretty Ploughboy" she maintained the "ebb and flow of traditional music", but now with a folk-rock backing. Her dad's lessons had been understood.

Once again, Eliza was nominated for a Mercury Award, but once again she didn't win (this time it went to Dizzee Rascal for *Boy in da Corner*). But *Anglicana* didn't go unrecognised. Back in 2000 the BBC had marked the arrival of the latest folk revival by launching the now annual Radio 2 Folk Awards. The first winner had been Kate Rusby, with Eliza's mum Norma winning in 2001 and her dad Martin winning in 2002. In 2003 the Folk Singer of the Year was Eliza, while *Anglicana* won Album of the Year... and Spiers and Boden picked up the Horizon award.

So now, predictably enough, Eliza changed direction yet again and started a new and excellent acoustic band, The Ratcatchers, that included Spiers and Boden, and with them she recorded the *Rough Music* album. When that band broke up, she went back to song-writing and working with her parents, before returning to new forms of folk-rock. And as for Spiers and Boden, they went off to form the most commercial band that the English folk scene had produced since the glory days of Steeleye Span.

JIM MORAY

2003 was an interesting year for the English folk scene. Not just because of Eliza and *Anglicana*, but also because of another new folk-rocker who happened to be a fan of Dizzee Rascal and made one of the more startling London debuts of the year.

Jim Moray walked on stage at the ICA clutching an electric guitar and looking like an indie rock musician in his leather jacket, jeans and red sneakers. On the table in front of him was a laptop, and behind him a drummer, double-bass player and video screen.

He was there to promote his new album *Sweet England*, and his opening song was "Early One Morning", a choice so corny that no one would ever dare sing it in a folk club. But then it had never been played quite like this before, with Moray's cool vocals backed by a wash of sound, dub effects and electro percussion. Like Richard

Thompson back in the sixties he set out to "get traditional music – which I like – and rock music I like, and try to put them together". The one difference being that the rock music had changed. Eliza Carthy had brought drum and bass into the mix with *Red*, while Moray's influences were "Radiohead... I'm still the biggest Radiohead fan, and things like Massive Attack, Portishead... so the slightly hip-hoppy edge to *Sweet England* is entirely down to that... and the bowing guitars with drumsticks and droney things is down to Radiohead, and Sonic Youth a little bit. And then there were bits of electronic music... it was trying to make folk-rock with the rock being nineties Britpoppy stuff..."

Jim Moray had a folk background – his parents had met while running a university folk club, and took him to the Sidmouth Folk Festival every year – but he says "most of my folk education was through records – which is why my thinking is based on records being the core activity". He studied classical composition at Birmingham Conservatoire "because there were no folk courses in the UK at that point... and by the fourth year I had bent it into being a song-writing thing, and doing things with traditional music".

He was now performing, playing in a power pop band before moving towards folk and solo work. In 2001 he was a finalist for the BBC Young Folk Musician Award (Maddy Prior was a judge) and he went on play Glastonbury, opening for Billy Bragg, and join Eliza Carthy and Spiers and Boden on The Oysterband's Big Sessions tour.

Then came *Sweet England*, which he says was "recorded in a student bedroom... with a lot of the drums sampled off vinyl because you couldn't play drums in the house". It was a clever, original album that proved that – at this stage, at least – he was even more successful as a recording artist than a live performer. Moray played most of the instruments himself – guitars, keyboards, drums, bass and programming – and also produced the album, with help on one track from Simon Emmerson of the Afro Celt Sound System, who also assisted in the mixing. At the 2004 Folk Awards, *Sweet England* won Best Album, and Moray also won the Horizon Award, with Emmerson making the presentation.

Moray said, "It was the right place and the right time for a young male English folk singer – because the people that had been breaking through to mainstream consciousness were Eliza Carthy and Kate Rusby."

The follow-up, three years later, was simply titled *Jim Moray* and was less of a success. Moray said it was done to "please the major labels, and the A&R people". He had hoped that *Sweet England* would be "re-mixed and re-released on a major label – but that fell through at a very late stage". But he had "signed a publishing deal for a lot of money... so I moved to Bristol, rented a studio for two years, and went crazy!" There were some good sections on the new work but perhaps inevitably it sounded over-produced and lacked the freshness and excitement of his debut set. He says now, "I can barely listen to it... it was hugely over-reaching... though it's some people's favourite record. It was on the soundtrack to *Dr Who* and on an advert!"

Moray said he had "gained momentum with *Sweet England*, but now lost it all... I was licking my wounds". So he went back to recording in a bedroom with two microphones and a computer, and produced another inventive album that proved that traditional songs could be revitalised by contemporary technology. *Low Culture* (2008) was a far calmer affair than his earlier work, but impressively varied. The opening "Leaving Australia" reflected the growing popularity of world music with its delicate use of African *kora* and *mbira* thumb piano, while a stomping treatment of the XTC song "All You Pretty Girls" was treated as a brass-backed sing-along shanty. And bravest of all was the clash of traditional balladry and hip hop on his version of that bleak folk song "Lucy Wan", which now included the Ghanaian rapper Bubbz.

Moray said that he "wanted to do 'Lucy Wan' in a grime-ish way because that's what the song seemed to say to me. It felt like a gang-violence, inner-city thing." But was his aim to bring a new audience into folk? "It was in my head... I thought that a lot of people find traditional music alienating, so I was trying to make a record for people who are not from that background to understand it a bit..."

SOURCES

Author Interviews

(All 2019)
Billy Bragg
Eliza Carthy
Martin Carthy
Simon Emmerson
Jim Moray

Written Sources

Eliza Carthy, "Letter to the *Guardian*", January 26, 2010.

Robin Denselow, "Festivals Are Finished? Try Telling That To Eliza Carthy", *Guardian*, June 22, 1998.

Robin Denselow, "Review: Jim Moray At The ICA, London", *Guardian*, November 7, 2003.

Colin Irwin, "Rap, Grime And The Hurdy-gurdy", *Guardian*, July 16, 2008.

Sophie Parkes, *Wayward Daughter: An Official Biography of Eliza Carthy* (Soundcheck Books, 2012).

EIGHT

GLOBAL FOLK

EDWARD II

The new folk scene was becoming more experimental thanks to Eliza Carthy and Jim Moray, but there had been little attempt to find common ground between English folk and the music of Britain's increasingly multi-cultural society. This was despite the fact that musical taste was broadening with the growing popularity of world music in the eighties and nineties and the success of the world music festival WOMAD.

The one brave exception was the Manchester band whose changing line-ups were known as Edward the Second and the Red Hot Polkas, then Edward II, and finally e2K. Matching Caribbean influences against traditional hornpipes, polkas and ballads, they started out in the early eighties as something of a fun band, mixing English dance styles with a lilting reggae beat, and then added in vocals and brass. They may not have shaken up the folk scene in the way that The Specials helped transform English pop, but they showed how reggae bass lines could be matched against melodeon, accordion and brass, and became a successful live band, touring the world and giving over 200 shows a year, including performances at Fairport's Cropredy Festival.

Many of Edward II's songs are self-written, but they continued to use traditional material. Their 1998 album *This Way Up* re-worked the dance tune "Speed The Plough" (now titled "Plough The Speed") and included an original reggae treatment of "Early One Morning" (before Jim Moray got his hands on it). There would be triumphant reunions further down the line, but the band split in 2003 after opening the door for new fusion styles.

THE IMAGINED VILLAGE

Now came a far more ambitious, high-profile project attempting to match English traditional music against not just the Caribbean but the African and Asian sounds of modern-day, multi-cultural Britain. With The Imagined Village, Simon Emmerson set out to bring the folk and world scenes together.

He had the perfect eclectic musical background. He was a punk rocker but also a folk fan and a massive admirer of Martin Carthy, and had joined his first band Scritti Politti after meeting the band's leader Green Gartside in the audience at a Carthy performance at Cecil Sharp House, near where Emmerson was then squatting. He went on to co-found the more jazz/soul influenced Working Week, and as a producer worked with the Senegalese world music star Baaba Maal. In 1995 he was co-founder of that still massively successful fusion band Afro Celt Sound System, who do exactly what their name promises, with their classy, cheerfully adventurous blend of Celtic and global styles.

The folk-global project started after Emmerson had been nudged towards the idea by a remarkable array of different musicians. He said that Baaba Maal had advised him it was "important for me to explore my own roots as a musician", while Joe Strummer had said much the same thing to him, soon before his death. "I bumped into him at Glastonbury, sitting around a fire as you do. And he asked me why I am doing so much with Celtic music? Why not do an album based on English roots music and folk music?" It seems he might have been involved in the project, had he lived.

Then there was journalist Ian Anderson, who "had been saying for a while that he felt there was a blind spot among English musicians who were embracing global culture but had ignorance of their own cultural roots".

Emmerson decided to put that right, and recruited a remarkable line-up to join him. For a start there was Billy Bragg, who lived near him in Dorset and had now switched from Woody Guthrie and Americana back to a reflection on his multi-cultural homeland with his 2002 album England, *Half English*. Recorded with his new band, The Blokes, which included Ben Mandelson, Lu Edmonds (of Mekons and PiL fame) and Ian McLagan (Small Faces) it had shown

Billy edging towards global sounds – the title track was set to a bhangra beat.

Billy was keen to be involved. He said that "the *Mermaid Avenue* sessions taught me a lot about the joys of collaboration, about writing and playing songs with other people". So as he and Emmerson walked their dogs on the beach, they discussed possible songs and what Billy describes as "ideas of belonging rather than national identity... I thought [the project] was a really good way of creating that head space around Englishness which is hard thing to get at from the left."

Martin Carthy, whom Emmerson describes as "a lovely, open-minded wise old Nordic god head", was also "really keen and open to it". And his involvement attracted yet more musicians, including the sitar player Sheema Mukherjee, "who had always wanted to play with Martin Carthy" according to Emmerson, and former punk hero Paul Weller, "a huge Martin Carthy fan". Eliza Carthy was also involved, of course, along with a cast that included everyone from traditional singers The Young Coppers to the writer, dub poet, and later professor, Benjamin Zephaniah.

This may have been the experimental folk event of the decade, but it would take time for The Imagined Village to succeed. Their debut concert was a high-profile event, held in a large tent which provided welcome relief from the mud at the 2007 WOMAD Festival, out in the Wiltshire countryside. It was a patchily entertaining affair that felt like a work in progress – as did the subsequent album, simply titled *The Imagined Village*, which was a little unwisely promoted as 'arguably the most ambitious reinvention of the English folk tradition since Fairport Convention's *Liege and Lief.*'

It began with what sounded like a radio documentary feature, in which John Copper discussed the history of his celebrated family of Sussex singers, and the way in which "'ouses, 'ouses, 'ouses" had been built across the Downs, against a wash of beats and effects. The best tracks were Billy Bragg's version of "Hard Times Of Old England", from the repertoire of The Copper Family, which was now updated with new lyrics about rural poverty and holiday cottages, and on which he was joined by The Young Coppers, Eliza Carthy and Simon Emmerson. Then there was a sturdy re-working of that traditional Steeleye favourite "Cold Haily Rainy Night", with vocals from Chis Wood, Eliza and Martin Carthy, with added sitar backing. Even more adventurous was Zephaniah's re-telling of "Tam Lyn", with dub effects and brooding backing from Emmerson and members of Transglobal Underground.

Looking back now, Eliza says she found that first album "a smorgasbord, with some great bits in it... it was less of a band, more of a project", while for Martin it was "a cut-and-paste job – and I got slightly fed up that the whole thing seemed to be based on my repertoire".

But The Imagined Village kept going, went on tour, and evolved into an effective, adventurous and increasingly successful band. In 2008, dhol drummer Johnny Kalsi led them through a stomping performance of "Cold Haily Rainy Night" on BBC TV's *Later... With Jools Holland* (the song would win Best Traditional Track at the Folk Awards later that year), and they played at major summer festivals, from Glastonbury to Cambridge.

Their second album, *Empire and Love* (2010), was a massive improvement on the debut, with a powerful opening track, in which Martin Carthy re-worked "My Son John". Originally a song about wounded soldiers from the Napoleonic wars, it was now updated for the era of conflicts in the Afghanistan and Iraq era, with Martin Carthy backed by sitar and Asian-influenced percussion. "I was very happy with that," he said, "but I had been wary of doing it. I wanted to keep a lot of the original five verses and add a few things on and tweak a word here and there... and it was lovely to discuss rhythm with [drummer] Andy Gangadeen and Johnny Kalsi." Elsewhere, Martin added an equally brave and totally unexpected slow treatment of Slade's "'Cum On Feel The Noize", while "Scarborough Fair" – one of the best-known songs in his repertoire – now had a sitar backing.

It raised a few eyebrows at the time, but Emmerson compared it to the experiments in the early days of the folk scene, back in the sixties, when guitarist Davy Graham mixed English and global influences in his solo work and collaborations with Shirley Collins. "So I see ourselves in that context – there was a huge amount of experimentation that went on in the sixties and seventies. Davy Graham was doing very similar things. And then of course you have The Incredible String Band..."

The Imagined Village had become an intriguing fusion band – but also took on political and cultural significance at a time when the far right, led by the Chairman of the British National Party, Nick Griffin, had been trying to claim English folk music as their own – to the fury of many musicians. Griffin said he was a fan of Eliza Carthy (as well as Kate Rusby), and in a letter to the *Guardian* Eliza hit back by pointing out that "at the moment I'm touring with The Imagined Village, an English folk band that includes British Asians alongside guests such as Billy Bragg and Benjamin Zephaniah... Bollocks to Nick Griffin."

For Eliza "every album was a step up... and by the time we got to *Bending The Dark* we were really getting a handle on something". Released in 2012, this was the band's third album, and marked yet another change of direction. It started with a brooding, chugging reggae work-out that segued into an a cappella traditional song, "The Captain's Apprentice", sung by Jackie Oates (Jim Moray's sister), who had now joined the band. Then there was a subtle arrangement of the bleak traditional story of the "New Yorker Trader", now featuring beats and fiddle, and Eliza Carthy's "Sick Old Man", a state-of-the-nation re-working of "Raggle Taggle Gypsies". Best of all was the lengthy title track, written by Sheema, and remarkable for its complex, ever-changing mix of moods and rhythm patterns, and for a furious percussion battle between Kalsi and Gangadeen.

It was a confident, original set but this would be the last Imagined Village album – at least until now. After a final tour, the band called it a day, partly because Simon Emmerson wanted to concentrate on the upcoming 20th anniversary of his other multi-cultural band, the Afro Celts. As their success continued, the chances of a Village reunion seemed increasingly unlikely. Though Eliza, for one, is certainly keen that the Village should get together again.

"I know she is," said Simon. "I get a slightly drunken text from her about twice a year! And I do want to do another album, and I've got some ideas... I thought it would be nice to do an album of English soul music..."

SOURCES

Author Interviews

(All 2019)
Ian Anderson
Billy Bragg
Eliza Carthy
Martin Carthy
Simon Emmerson

Written Sources

Robin Denselow, "Review: The Imagined Village At WOMAD", *Guardian*, September 6, 2007.
Robin Denselow, "Review: The Imagined Village: Empire and Love", *Guardian*, January 7, 2010.

NINE

FOLK BIG BANDS

BELLOWHEAD

In 2006, Jon Boden was a man with a problem. He was simply too busy. After all, he was a member of the increasingly successful acoustic duo Spiers and Boden, both he and John Spiers were also members of Eliza Carthy's excellent band, The Ratcatchers, and he had recorded his first solo album, *Pained Lady*. And on top of that, he and Spiers were working with a folk big band they had started. It was called Bellowhead and had just released its debut album, *Burlesque*.

"My daughter had been born the previous year," said Jon, "and I had to cut back. I'd been thinking Spiers and Boden is important, and it's bread and butter... and The Ratcatchers is important... it was a great band... lots of fiddles, and the unaccompanied singing was particularly enjoyable. So I thought if I drop anything I'll drop Bellowhead... But then *Burlesque* came out, and it was clear this was going places. So I thought, this is my chance to be lead singer with a cool band, so I'm going to stick with that. But it was really hard to leave The Ratcatchers..."

Bellowhead did indeed go places. It became the most commercially successful British folk band of the new century, concentrating almost exclusively on re-working traditional songs, and becoming "more folk-rocky as it went along". Along with Eliza Carthy, Boden now became one of the most passionate, high-profile advocates for English folk music – but he had come to the music through a very different route.

Jon Boden's mum had liked Steeleye, but he grew up as a rock fan, "listening to Eurythmics, Dire Straits and Paul Simon. Then I got into Zeppelin, and came to Sandy Denny after hearing her on *Zeppelin IV* [where she famously joined them on "The Battle Of Evermore"] and that led me down the rabbit warren." He was a "later convert to folk music, discovering it at university", and while studying medieval history at Durham he listened to "Kate Rusby – because you could put her albums on when your friends came round and not be embarrassed by it". He was also a fan of Eliza, but preferred *Rice* to *Red*. When it came to sixties styles, he "never played Steeleye for a good decade – I was in the acoustic mindset", but did listen to that great singer Peter Bellamy, and to The Watersons.

Music and theatre became his great passions. He played fiddle at pub sessions and studied at the London College of Music for a Masters in Composition for Musical Theatre, "not realising that people don't really earn a living writing music for theatre". He wrote the music for a production of John Webster's *The White Devil* in Oxford, and while in the city he "had a night off, went to a session, and met John Spiers".

Spiers was a melodeon player who had a master's in genetics from Cambridge, but did come from a folk family – his dad was a Morris dancer. After that initial meeting at the Elm Tree pub, Spiers and Boden started working together, helping to shake up the acoustic folk scene with their energy, enthusiasm and originality. Boden developed a vocal style that echoed Tom Waits as well as Peter Bellamy. He was always keen to add a dash of drama to the show, noting that "even a tiny thing, like John playing a solo and I walk on unannounced can be a theatrically powerful moment".

They released their first album in 2001, and for the next thirteen years they kept working as a duo, despite their other projects, from Eliza's Ratcatchers to the extraordinary Bellowhead, a band that would go on to sell over a quarter of a million albums, headline at festivals, and win a whole batch of awards.

The idea came from discussions between the duo as they drove between gigs. John Spiers had been listening to the French Canadian band La Bottine Souriante, and was excited by the way in which they mixed a horn section with accordion and fiddle. He was also a big disco fan, said Jon, "and he was very knowledgeable about it. He was a seventies disco DJ at college, and while we were stuck in a traffic jam we were playing loads of stuff and talking about disco string sections... not something I had thought about! So then we started talking about... maybe we could do something with English music, with a fiddle section that would turn into a disco string section... and have a Brass Monkey-style brass section that turned into disco brass. Wouldn't that be cool!" Boden may not have been listening to Steeleye, but he had been listening to Martin Carthy and John Kirkpatrick's later project, Brass Monkey – who also happened to have been an inspiration for La Bottine Souriante.

Spiers and Boden decided that a big band would be good for the English folk scene "because it was a pity there were no big headline bands for festivals. Even Eliza wasn't really a festival headliner, and Kate Rusby was more a concert artist... you couldn't jump up and down to her as you could to Irish and Scottish bands." And The Oysterband? "At that stage I was completely unaware of them – but they were more non-trad..."

The duo did nothing about the idea until Jon was contacted by the organiser of the Oxford Folk Festival, who asked him if he could think of a good band to headline their Saturday-night show. It so happened that he did. "I said 'I know a band who can headline. It doesn't exist yet but I'll put it together for you!' He said yes, agreed to pay £1,000 – John and I would not get paid – and I thought it would be a random gig and that would be the end of it."

So it was that the (then) ten-piece Bellowhead made their debut performance at Oxford Town Hall in April 2004. "And we got away with it – just," said Jon. "John has got a recording and it's such a mush of echo and reverb that you can't hear all the mistakes. But the energy was there, the audience was great and everyone loved it. And even if it sounded pretty atrocious at the first gig, the visuals probably saw us through – there was always something going on, all the time."

This might have been a "random" gig, but Boden had put thought and effort into it. He had written out all the parts and "spent days printing out the massive scores... if you have ten people on stage all playing at the same time you have to orchestrate it or it will be a complete racket. They got a chance to play it through before we went on stage."

To stop it all becoming a "complete unfocused mess" he had also laid down a couple of rules. "I stated from the beginning that we'd do only traditional English songs and tunes – and we could then do anything we liked with them. Anyone could arrange or bring in material. And the other stipulation I made was that I was the singer... no particular reason why me and not anybody else – but it was my idea!"

In 2004 Bellowhead released an EP, *E.P.Onymous*, which included a big-band treatment of the stomping "Rochdale Coconut Dance", which had appeared on the debut Spiers and Boden album, and two years later they followed up with *Burlesque*. It landed them a performance on *Later... With Jools Holland* and sold 20,000 albums, "which in folk terms at that point was massive". By now the band was an eleven-piece, with tuba player Gideon Juckes joining a line-up that included such varied musicians as fiddle and oboe player Paul Sartin, guitar and mandolin exponent Benji Kirkpatrick (the son of John Kirkpatrick), trumpeter Andy Mellon, who had studied at the Royal Academy of Music, and percussionist Pete Flood, who would become increasingly important to the band as an arranger. On *Burlesque*, Flood set the lyrics of the traditional song "Across The Line" to a melody by the Brazilian star Milton Nascimento.

Bellowhead were classy players, fine harmony singers and great entertainers. As Boden put it, "we had this huge palette of visual and musical things we could use theatrically... and I became more theatrical than I imagined I would be." But there was one problem. "The big limiting factor with Bellowhead is that we were a party band – which was also a great strength. But when we did something serious, it's not that it didn't work, but I got the sense that the audience were always waiting for 'when are we going to start jumping up and down again?'"

For over a decade they dominated the English folk scene, after surviving a scare when their self-produced second album, *Matachin*, failed to sell, leaving Boden to worry that "that's the end of that little jaunt". Then their record label brought in producer John Leckie, celebrated for producing everyone from Radiohead to Baaba Maal, and Bellowhead returned in triumph. Their 2010 album *Hedonism*, which kicked off with one of their best-loved songs, the furious treatment of "New York Girls", sold a remarkable 60,000 albums.

They had created a distinctively English form of popular music that really was popular – and eventually edged towards old-style folk-rock, with the introduction of electric guitar alongside the strings and brass. Like much of the new folk scene (with the exception of Jim Moray), Boden had started out opposed to electric guitars, but he had become aware that attitudes were changing. As the folk revival developed, spawning sub-divisions from nu-folk to psych-folk, and the term "folk" now being applied to artists as varied as the highly commercial Mumford & Sons and the alt-folk band The Owl Service, Boden took note.

"These nu-folk people came out of nowhere and we went 'who the fuck are these guys?' They are dressed like it's the seventies and playing drums like Dave Mattacks... and initially it was like having the rug pulled from under us because we had spent a decade bringing in French Canadian and French influences and re-inventing the music in terms of how you play English music on the fiddle and the squeezebox... It's not so much that they were successful... if you went to an Owl Service gig not many people were there... but it gradually changed our resistance to seventies folk-rock. I had always thought that what we were doing with Bellowhead was a bit like what Steeleye were doing, but we were using a different palette of instruments..."

Bellowhead used electric guitar for the first time on a second John Leckie production, *Broadside* (2012), another boisterous set that included a typically gutsy treatment of the Carthy/Swarbrick favourite "Byker Hill" and would bring the band their first Top 20 album success. "I thought, yes, I'm lead singer with a rock band – it's brilliant!" said Boden. "I think we were folk-rock before but the electric guitar is pretty key. When nu-folk came in, and the seventies aesthetic, it started making me remember the Steeleye stuff... and what I loved about Steeleye was the electric guitar, particularly on the earlier records before they brought the drums in."

Bellowhead's final studio album, *Revival*, even included a treatment of that seventies folk-rock classic, Richard Thompson's "I Want To See The Bright Lights Tonight". And Boden, who had once rejected the instrument, now decided "there is something about the aesthetic of the electric guitar that really works with English folk song... the dirty sound. For me it's the natural instrument to play English folk songs on."

Bellowhead were a phenomenon best experienced live, playing anywhere from outdoor festivals to the Royal Opera House. My personal favourite show was a New Year event in 2010–11 at London's Southbank where they were joined on stage by a sword-swallower, and their performance paused at midnight so the band and the audience could go outside to enjoy the fireworks exploding around the Festival Hall. They then returned to the stage and welcomed in 2011 with a set that included anything from Abba to The Carpenters.

Despite his pop-star status with Bellowhead, Boden says he was still "evangelical" about promoting English traditional songs to new audiences and getting more people to start singing them, "so while Eliza Carthy is more evangelical about it as an art form, I'm more evangelical about it as a social activity. I wanted Bellowhead to be a gateway drug into getting people singing in pubs!" Many Bellowhead shows ended with an invitation for the audience to join the band for a session in a nearby hostelry, where Boden would play his fiddle, and "ask them to sing a song", hoping to "make people aware that there is music there that you own, but you don't know you own it. It's like not knowing about a public footpath."

Between June 24, 2010, and June 24, 2011, the workaholic Boden had followed up the idea of promoting social singing by releasing "a folk song a day" of traditional songs that he didn't perform on stage but which would be "fun to sing in pubs".

Bellowhead broke up in May 2016 after a lengthy farewell tour that was recorded for a live double album and DVD. Jon Boden had decided to leave because, he said, he had done everything he wanted to do as an arranger for Bellowhead and wanted to get back to more song-writing. In his years with Bellowhead he had somehow found time to continue the duo Spiers and Boden, write for the theatre (including work for the Royal Shakespeare Company), record a second solo album, *Songs from the Floodplain* (2009) and start new a band, The Remnant Kings, to perform his new songs on tour. Looking back now, he said that "Bellowhead was such a massive thing, I'm sure it will be the greatest commercial and quite possibly artistic achievement of my life... but it completely overshadowed everything else that I did."

Jon Boden said that he had hoped that Bellowhead would continue without him "and it was a strange situation – it ended with me lobbying for them to carry on. I was really sad that they stopped – I was looking forward to seeing a Bellowhead gig!"

THE WAYWARD BAND

Bellowhead was no more, but the idea of a folk big band was too good for others to ignore and Eliza Carthy was the obvious person to take up the challenge. After all, she had joined Jon Boden and John Spiers in their discussions about big bands, the importance of La Bottine Souriante and her dad's band, Brass Monkey, back in the days when they were all working in The Ratcatchers together, and Bellowhead was first being planned.

Nine years later, in 2013, Eliza would be on stage with her own big band – in the company of that folk-rock maverick Jim Moray. She was celebrating twenty-one years as a professional musician with the release of *Wayward Daughter*, a double album of traditional and self-written songs recorded throughout her career, and she decided to celebrate with a brave and unique tour. She assembled a Bellowhead-style band including brass and a string section to help her perform the songs, with Moray playing guitar and keyboards, and Sam Sweeney from Bellowhead playing fiddle. The result was a new departure for them both. In London, the show opened with a set from Moray, who included a string-backed treatment of "Sweet England", while Eliza's songs included big-band treatments of anything from a composition by her aunt Lal Waterson to a whalers' song she had recorded with Waterson:Carthy and the Latin-edged "Grey Gallito", which she had originally recorded with that exuberant, Scottish-based fusion band, Salsa Celtica.

The tour led to a live album, but then this extraordinary line-up disbanded, as Jim Moray continued his solo career and moved off to a new folk-rock project. The Wayward Band returned without him, making an appearance at the Cambridge Folk Festival in 2016 – just weeks after the demise of Bellowhead – and releasing their studio album *Big Machine* the following year.

Inevitably, comparisons would be made, especially as both bands included violin work from Sam Sweeney. But Eliza insisted that this was certainly not Bellowhead part 2. "God no! Has it been described like that?" But she agreed "Bellowhead had to finish for us to be able to do it – you can't have two big bands..."

The Wayward Band were indeed very different, even if many of their songs were traditional. *Big Machine* included a furious, edgy treatment of "Devil In The Woman", a story of domestic abuse driven on by brass and electric guitar, and the gently emotional fiddle-backed lament, "I Wish That The Wars Were Over". And then there was an angry burst of folk hip hop, with MC Dizraeli joining Eliza Carthy on her reflection on the refugee crisis, "You Know Me". She described it as "the perfect album for me – such a crystallisation of so many ideas and plans and agendas".

This was not a party band but a more serious affair, though they had the energy to enthuse a festival crowd, as they did with a memorable performance at WOMAD in July 2017. It seemed that after constantly changing direction throughout her career, Eliza had found a perfect big band. By matching her violin and vocal work against brass, strings and melodeon, as well as guitar and percussion, she could cover her many styles and interests, from traditional material to her own increasingly inventive song-writing.

Then, sadly, it all went wrong, as Eliza Carthy and the band faced major financial problems. "We were badly ripped off by a private investor – or he was supposed to be a private investor but he turned out to be a bit of a Walter Mitty character," said Eliza. "We budgeted everything, started making the record, but the money never came."

So in order to pay the band the money they were owed, she recorded a new album DIY album, *Restitute*, and gave them the proceeds. It was a largely solo affair, much of it recorded at home in her bedroom, but with help from other musicians, including her father and Jon Boden.

As for The Wayward Band, she said, "they are not dead – just sleeping". And it was Boden who now once again picked up the folk big-band concept.

THE REMNANT KINGS

Jon Boden had left Bellowhead to follow a solo career and concentrate on song-writing and writing for the theatre, and it seemed at first that he really would do something dramatically different. His third solo album, *Afterglow* (2017), was a follow-up to his solo set *Songs from the Floodplain*, in that it was another post-apocalyptic concept set, though much of it sounded more prog rock than folk, "with extra added guitar and more overdubs". And while on *Floodplain* he had played everything himself, from guitars and drums to concertina and bagpipes, he was now joined in the studio by his band, The Remnant Kings.

In 2019 he released another album with the band, *Rose in June*, and now at last he was back to arranging and recording traditional songs. "It was very comfortable," he said. "Like riding a bike." The album included a charming Ewan MacColl song, "Sweet Thames Flow Softly", new versions of songs from *Floodplain* and even a re-worked Bellowhead folk favourite, "Rigs Of The Time". On tour, Boden was backed by different-sized versions of his band for different shows, and for his performance at London's Union Chapel in November 2019 he fronted an eleven-piece band. Electric guitars were matched against strings and brass, and comparisons with both Bellowhead and The Wayward Band were inevitable, especially as the line-up included both Paul Sartin (ex-Bellowhead) and Sam Sweeney (ex-Bellowhead and Wayward Band) who was now playing drums as well as fiddle.

The show was, of course, highly theatrical, with Boden explaining the story of *Afterglow*, six fiddles providing the backing for "Rigs Of The Time", and five squeezeboxes providing an unlikely new treatment for Kate Bush's "Hounds Of Love". He was clearly delighted by the standing ovation. The folk-rock big band lives on.

SOURCES

Author Interview

Jon Boden (2019)

Written Sources

Alex Gallacher, "Jon Boden: A Folk Song A Day", *Folk Radio*, May 31, 2010.

Robin Denselow, "Review: Eliza Carthy & The Wayward Band: Big Machine", *Guardian*, February 2, 2017.

Nathaniel Handy, "Eliza Carthy: Wayward and Free", *Songlines*, April 3, 2018.

Will Hodgkinson, "Folk Has A New Sex Appeal", *Guardian*, September 19, 2008.

Colin Irwin, sleeve-notes for Spiers and Boden: *The Works* (2011).

Colin Irwin, "Wayward Ho!", *fRoots*, April 2017.

TEN

THE RETURN OF THE
ELECTRIC GUITAR

FALSE LIGHTS

For Jim Moray and Billy Bragg, the folk scene has one great advantage – if you are good enough, you can just keep going. "I wanted to do something where I could go on getting better rather than hit my peak when I was 25," said Moray. "And I feel I have been getting better at it." For his part, Billy argues "folk audiences actively encourage you to grow old! They are OK if you have grey hair and a grey beard – they are totally cool with that!" Both have survived lengthy careers in style, and done so while playing electric guitar, which was rejected by many of the young musicians who founded the new folk revival back in the 1990s, but is now back in fashion.

After touring and recording with Eliza Carthy's prototype big band, Jim Moray set out on a very different venture: a new, no-nonsense folk-rock band, False Lights, that he formed with singer-songwriter Sam Carter. The duo met up at the folk industry showcase English Folk Expo in 2014, began discussing their musical tastes and shared love of Radiohead, and came to the conclusion that what the scene needed was a new guitar band. Carter's agent learned of their discussion, and sold the idea to the Folk East Festival in Suffolk, who were looking for a headliner.

"I was told that the band had a gig," said Jim, "and I said, 'what band?'" The duo were given money to rehearse, added bass, drums, violin and melodeon to the line-up, and were ready to debut at Folk East that summer. For Moray says it was an ideal continuation of his early experiments back in the "Sweet England" days. "It's probably what I should have done from the word go, surrounding myself with really good people and not taking the weight entirely on my own shoulders. It's what the 'Sweet England' era should have been... but I'm relatively shy and not good at making friends."

The band's debut album *Salvor* (2015) was an entertaining mixture of energy, experiment and emotion. It began with the Child ballad "The Wife Of Usher's Well", with this traditional tale of the supernatural now starting with Sam Carter singing over a suitably startling and otherworldly loop of sampled and treated voices, before bass and then guitars move in. Elsewhere, they included a stomping treatment of "Skewball", an American nineteenth-century shape-note[1] hymn, "The Indian's Petition", and – best of all – an exuberant final track on which Rani Arbo's setting of Tennyson's poem about the acceptance of death, "Crossing The Bar", was re-worked with organ, drums, bass, violin and Latin-edged percussion.

This was guitar-based folk-rock with a new twist. Moray, who always regarded recording, rather than live performance, as his "core activity", was False Lights' producer, and his technique was always experimental. As he explained it, "Sam records a vocal, and the next time he hears it it's completely different. So he put the words of 'The Wife Of Usher's Well' to a shape-note tune... I think he was envisaging someone like Neil Young – and I sent it back to him with the cut-up samples and drum beat on the off-beat. That's how we work best."

The duo continued their folk-rock experiments on *Harmonograph* (2018) which featured bass work from Barnaby Stradling, that veteran of Eliza Carthy's folk experiments. Again, the songs were mostly traditional, including an exquisite re-worked shape-note hymn "Far And Distant Land", along with the gutsy ballad "Murder In The Red Barn", and a treatment of "Drink Old England Dry" that sounded like a Bellowhead festival favourite. "I still like the term folk-rock," said Jim Moray, "but I think of it in different terms to other people I suppose."

---

[1] As defined by the Library of Congress: "Nineteenth century American song books that used notes in different shapes to aid singers came to be known as 'shape-note hymnals' and the style of singing from these 'shape-note singing'. Christian hymnals using this system were among the most enduring uses of this notation."

Alongside the work with False Lights, he continued his solo career, with the aim – as ever – of taking traditional songs and making them sound fresh. He had been dismayed by many of the nu-folk bands "who were writing new songs and trying to make them sound as if they were from the sixties, while I was taking old songs and trying to make them sound as if they were from now. I was thinking I have nothing in common with those people... because I am constantly playing to audiences who are expecting something different."

So he continued to experiment. His 2016 album *Upcetera* (which he regarded as being his best to date) included two of his own songs, along with narrative folk ballads transformed by string and brass arrangements and by his electric guitar work. He followed its release by joining the big-band movement, and touring with a thirteen-piece band, aiming to be "the polar opposite to Bellowhead. Bellowhead was about having a good time but *Upcetera* was deadly serious."

A lifelong fan of June Tabor, he said that his aim was to follow her approach to traditional songs and story-telling "because the thing about June is that you believe that she believes it. I have always wanted to do that and maybe haven't had the vocal ability to pull it off... it's been a long journey to learn how to do it... but I have always wanted it to be serious."

For his 2019 solo album *The Outlander* he had changed direction again, to a more minimal approach, singing traditional English songs backed by a band that included Sam Sweeney on violin, but with Moray playing electric guitar. When he started out, the folk clubs rejected him because of his noisy experimental approach. Now he had become a still-experimental part of the established folk scene, regularly playing in the clubs. In the autumn of 2019 he gave a solo show at that folk-scene Mecca, Cecil Sharp House in London – and played electric guitar throughout.

OLIVIA CHANEY AND OFFA REX

The return to fashion of the electric guitar led to a re-working of the music of the bands that had started the folk-rock movement, back in the sixties and seventies. Jim Moray may have disliked the revivalist style of some of the nu-folk scene, but he very much approved of

Offa Rex, a band who featured "a once-in-a-generation singer... and managed to make a retro folk album that is actually good".

Offa Rex were an adventurous and most unlikely band. For a start they were American, and better known as The Decemberists, a Grammy-nominated indie guitar band from Oregon on the American West Coast. They changed their name to Offa Rex when they set out to revive classic English folk-rock from the seventies in the company of an English female singer, Olivia Chaney. She is a singer-songwriter with a remarkable voice who is rightly admired in the folk scene – at Richard Thompson's 70th birthday bash she was chosen to sing Sandy Denny's classic "Who Knows Where The Time Goes" – and yet she had no history as a folk-rocker and wasn't even sure she was a folk singer. As she put it "I love singing folk songs but certainly don't regard myself as just a folk musician because I've got my love of classical music as well... and good pop music."

For a new folk heroine, she had an unconventional career. Classically trained in "piano and operatic stuff" she went to Chetham's School of Music and then the Royal Academy, before becoming a "crazy jobbing musician", collaborating with film-makers, choreographers and composers and "steeped in the contemporary classical scene". She had also developed a love of folk music. Her father, an artist, was "passionate about music", and she grew up listening to Sandy Denny and Joni Mitchell, along with Mozart and Michael Jackson. Later she heard Shirley and Dolly Collins and "could not believe my ears... this untrained, English voice with those ancient songs and her sister playing a sort of Handelian organ".

Now she began to develop a style of her own. "I never try to imitate," she said, "but because I had been trained as a singer I was thinking about how to find my own singing voice, departing from just having an operatic technique." She started "getting into folky stuff", and gigging around pubs with a friend, singing English and American traditional songs. Then came a stint singing and performing in Shakespeare plays at the Globe in London, followed by a "weird hiatus". She joined those chill-out ambient pop favourites Zero 7, who invited her on a world tour as their singer.

By now, the folk world had begun to take note. The ever-attentive Ian Anderson, editor of what was now called *fRoots*, included her on a compilation set, *Looking for a New England*, which was given away

269

free with the November/December 2009 issue, and also included songs from Jim Moray, Jon Boden and one great veteran, Shirley Collins. It was followed by showcase appearances in the USA, in which Chaney was joined by Moray, The Unthanks and that great Scottish band Trembling Bells.

Then came a series of residencies at Aldeburgh in Suffolk, on projects where she was able to combine her folk and classical interests – and on one occasion found both Shirley Collins and Ray Davies watching from the front row. She was joined by Concerto Caledonia and singers including Alasdair Roberts and Jim Moray for an early music/folk fusion project which was recorded as the rather curiously titled album, *Revenge of the Folksingers*, which also provided a reminder that Chaney was becoming a powerful songwriter. A later project involved re-interpretations of the music of Purcell, one of Chaney's favourite composers. "For me, folk music is the root of all music," she said. "That's why I have a love of composers like Henry Purcell and John Dowland – they were much more connected to traditional music."

Eventually, after much anticipation on the folk scene, she was signed to a major album, Nonesuch, and released her debut album. *The Longest River* (2015) was a gently intriguing, subtle set on which she played guitar as well as piano and harmonium, with some tracks performed solo and others on which she was backed by strings and synth. It began with the traditional "False Bride", included songs by Purcell as well as Alasdair Roberts, but was dominated by her own song-writing.

It was an impressive set that demonstrated the range of her exquisite, haunting voice – but was most certainly not folk-rock. And neither was her contribution to the *Folk Songs* compilation, on which she was backed by the Kronos Quartet on an album that celebrated the 50th anniversary of her record label, Nonesuch, and which also featured her celebrated American label-colleagues Sam Amidon, Rhiannon Giddens and Natalie Merchant. Olivia sang two songs on the album, one of them in French.

But the leader of an American rock band had other ideas about what she should be doing. Olivia was on tour in America and sitting in a Brooklyn hotel when she read a Tweet from Colin Meloy of The Decemberists that read "I'd lose my shirt if Olivia Chaney sang

'Willie O'Winsbury'." She said she knew exactly what it meant. Meloy is a fan of English folk from the sixties and seventies, and "Willie O'Winsbury" is a traditional song famously performed by that legendary English singer Anne Briggs. Back in the sixties Briggs had recorded an EP, *The Hazards of Love*, which would later inspire the title song to a Decemberists album. "I was double honoured," said Olivia, "because I was a massive fan of Anne Briggs and Willie O'Winsbury is one of my favourite songs of all time... and because of that, I'd never dared do it."

That Tweet led to Olivia working alongside The Decemberists as their support act, and then touring the States and recording with them as they got together as a new folk-rock band, Offa Rex. She said she was hesitant at first "because I didn't want it to be just a derivative thing that wasn't going to do anything new. I wanted to have enough creative freedom for it to feel interesting and a bit fresh."

The Offa Rex album *The Queen of Hearts* (2017) was an exercise in nostalgia that worked because it did indeed sound fresh, with the band's no-nonsense, respectful playing matched against strong vocals from Olivia and Melroy, with production work from Tucker Martine (of R.E.M. fame). It of course included "Willie O'Winsbury" (but not the Anne Briggs version, though that is still Olivia's favourite), along with a treatment of "Flash Company" inspired not by folk-rockers but by the gypsy singer Phoebe Smith. Then there are Morris dance tunes from the Ashley Hutchings/Albion repertoire, along with the Steeleye Span favourites "Blackleg Miner" and "Sheepcrook And Black Dog", yet another new version of Ewan MacColl's "The First Time Ever I Saw Your Face" and Lal Waterson's "To Make You Stay" (sung by Meloy and included after Olivia had rung the family to ask permission).

The sleeve-notes, written by Olivia and Meloy, were another great homage to English folk-rock and traditional music in the seventies, with references to Steeleye, the Fairports, Martin Carthy, June Tabor and Anne Briggs. If American indie rock fans weren't already aware of them before, they certainly were now. "I wanted them to go back to the originals, as well as listening to our versions," said Olivia.

The following year, Olivia released her second solo album, *Shelter*. It included her own songs, an Everly Brothers cover and more Henry

Purcell, but there were no folk songs, apart from a brief snatch of "Molly Malone". But those wanting to hear Olivia Chaney sing more traditional material didn't have long to wait.

To celebrate their 80th birthday, that great British folk label Topic Records released *Vision & Revision* (2019), a double album on which contemporary artists were invited to re-interpret songs from Topic's vast back catalogue. Olivia was asked to sing "Nancy Of Yarmouth" with Eliza Carthy, who sent her the original recording by the Suffolk singer Fred Ling, so she could learn the song. The duo recorded in Eliza's bedroom, and according to Eliza, Olivia corrected her singing, saying "that's not quite how they do that bit…" Eliza found that Olivia "had every single variation off pat, exactly as the old guys did it. I said 'I'm supposed to be the expert here and you just kicked my arse!' I was absolutely delighted!"

Later that year Olivia Chaney was nominated in the Folk Singer of the Year category at the Folk Awards. But she still insisted "I'm never going to shy away from folk being an influence. But when I keep getting included in the folk world it can sometimes seem a bit awkward, because I'm like… 'I'm not a proper folk singer like all of you'."

Eliza Carthy says she "adores" her work.

THE RAILS

While Offa Rex set out to revive classic seventies folk-rock, the children of the original folk-rockers were creating their own new folk fusions. Eliza Carthy had been involved in re-working traditional styles alongside anything from hip hop to big-band styles, working with almost every new major English folk artist to have emerged this century. She even played on the first album by The Rails, a folk-rock electric guitar band co-founded by Richard and Linda Thompson's daughter, Kami.

Kami and Eliza may both come from celebrated folk families, but they have very different musical histories. Eliza was brought up listening to her parents singing together, while Kami was born at the time of her parents' break-up, and had "barely seen them in the same room" when she was growing up. She didn't listen to folk music during her school years in the eighties and nineties, because, she says, it was "not on the agenda with any of my peers or anyone I would talk to – ergo it was deeply uncool". But she did listen to her dad playing when she visited him in California, "and got into my mum's music later, when I was 19 or 20 and she started singing again, and then [I] delved into what she had done".

When she started out as a musician she "wasn't folkie at all... the only folk music I knew and loved was Fairport Convention, and Sandy Denny. I have always felt connected to her, in a strange sort of way." There was no traditional material on Kami's first solo album, which included a George Harrison song, but all that changed, strangely enough, when she met her partner, a rock guitarist. James Walbourne is lead guitarist with Chrissie Hynde's band The Pretenders, has worked with The Pogues and Ray Davies, and is also a folk-rock fan. He and Kami first met when he played on Linda Thompson's album *Versatile Heart*. So when they later decided to form a band of their own, the main influence on their writing and playing was "seventies folk-rock records by the Fairports. That's the sound we wanted to aim up to."

The debut album by The Rails, *Fair Warning* (2014), included two traditional songs and a series of self-written pieces with decidedly English and London-oriented lyrics, all treated with energy and using electric guitars. Eliza joined them on fiddle for two tracks, including "Send Her To Holloway". The album was *Mojo* magazine's Folk Album of the Year and won them the Horizon prize at the Folk Awards.

Their second album, *Other People*, was less successful – "we weren't getting on professionally, we were in a bad place", said Kami – but it did include one great London song, "The Cally". And then they came crashing back to form with the 2019 set *Cancel the Sun*, in which they were both "completely involved". It was more rock than folk-rock, included the angry and funny "Save The Planet (Kill Yourself)" and was launched in a small London venue where Kami's parents were in the audience. On stage, Walbourne prowled the stage bashing out guitar chords, while Kami sounded uncannily like the young Linda.

Her brother Teddy Thompson, another fine singer-songwriter, may have moved to New York, but Kami and James live in Camden

Town, London. Asked how she would like to describe The Rails, she said "'English' is the term I like best."

BACK TO BILLY BRAGG

The return to fashion of electric guitars meant that the folk scene had caught up with Billy Bragg, who had been playing solo electric guitar throughout his career (though he admitted he had "started being more reasonable about things and playing acoustic a bit" in the nineties). Now in his sixties, he argues that "folk audiences are very open-minded, and not everything has to be new. They actively encourage you to grow old! They are OK if you have grey hair and a grey beard – they are totally cool with that!"

Not that he was a predictable folkie, of course. He continued to switch styles, sounding distinctively English while continuing to explore his love of American folk. After appearing alongside the Carthys on the Imagined Village project he recorded an album with his band The Blokes that included solo versions of the same songs. Then he recorded a solo album in the USA with production help from singer-songwriter Joe Henry, and joined Henry to record *Shine a Light: Field Recordings from the Great Americana Railroad*. They did so while travelling by train from Chicago to Los Angeles, with sessions held on platforms, in waiting rooms or in local hotels.

It was an original and entertaining idea that tied in well with Billy Bragg's book on skiffle. As Henry explained during the duo's London show, "our patron saint was Leadbelly", the inspiration for so many skiffle songs. But the times were changing, and Bragg quickly moved from Americana and nostalgia to angry political comment, noting "it may seem strange to be singing railroad songs with what's been going on. But I didn't see Brexit or Trump coming." He broke off from the railroad ballads to include a new song of his own, "The Sleep Of Reason", that warned of complacency and the destruction of truth leading to "monsters".

It appeared on an EP of new political songs, *Walls Not Bridges*, released later that year, which also included "Full English Brexit", a brave and thoughtful piece in which Bragg, a passionate Remainer, wrote from the viewpoint of an elderly Leave voter complaining "nobody's listening to me".

274

In late 2019, just before the General Election, Billy Bragg toured the UK with a solo show, in which he appeared for three nights at the same sizable venue, with a different set list every night, covering songs from throughout his career, all mixed, of course, with a hefty dose of political comment. In London the concerts were packed out every night – an impressive achievement for a solo artist – as Bragg mixed the old punk-era hits with recent songs, as well as reminders of his folk influences, from "Thatcherites", his re-working of the traditional "Ye Jacobites By Name", to the Joe Hill anthem "There Is Power In A Union".

He's still a solo folk-rocker with an electric guitar.

SOURCES

Author Interviews

(All 2019)
Billy Bragg
Olivia Chaney
Jim Moray
Kami Thompson

Albums

Concert Caledonia: *Revenge of the Folksingers* (BBC Music, 2011).

Written Sources

Tim Chipping, "A Voice In A Million", *fRoots*, June 2013.
Robin Denselow, "Review: Billy Bragg And Joe Henry At Union Chapel", *Guardian*, January 17, 2017.
Elizabeth Kinder, "21st Century Folk-Rock", *fRoots*, spring 2018.

ELEVEN

AND NEXT...

When the folk-rock movement started, back in the late sixties and seventies, the English folk scene was a place for experiments of all kinds. From the thrilling unaccompanied vocal work of the early Watersons and The Young Tradition, through to the extraordinary fusion experiments of Shirley Collins working either alongside blues/ jazz/world music maverick Davy Graham on guitar or her sister Dolly on flute organ. Then there were the guitar heroes Bert Jansch and John Renbourn, singer-songwriters like Roy Harper or the wild folk-global-theatrical experiments of The Incredible String Band.

And today? The folk scene has kept expanding, with the best veterans still playing, and new singers emerging. In the process, paths keep crossing, and new formats for tackling traditional songs evolve. The early folk heroes may be getting older but many are still in impressive form. Shirley Collins has made a glorious comeback after years in which she was unable to sing. Steeleye Span celebrated their 50th birthday with a line-up that Jim Moray considers "one of their best" – and a celebratory concert that featured past and current members of the band, including John Kirkpatrick and his son Benji, showing how the music has evolved. And Carole Pegg, of Mr Fox fame, went on to become a music academic specialising in Inner Asia, and fused traditional English influences with Tuvan styles in her work with Radik Tülüsh, the celebrated throat-singer from the group Huun-Huur-Tu.

Fairport Convention remained as active as ever, with the Cropredy Festival still the high point of their year. The 2021 programme (which promised a very similar line-up to the 2020 festival, cancelled because of the Covid-19 pandemic) included the return of Richard Thompson and other veteran folk-rockers. Home Service had acquired a new look in 2015 when John Tams left and John Kirkpatrick was invited to take over. Now Tams decided to return and would be appearing alongside Kirkpatrick.

The bill also promised another comeback band, folk-reggae pioneers Edward II, who had re-formed in 2015 to promote their best album to date, *Manchester's Improving Daily*, a tribute to the broadside ballad traditions of their city.

Then there are those re-working traditional material in other ways, such as that excellent guitarist Martin Simpson, and singer-songwriters from Chris Wood and Seth Lakeman through to Steve Knightley of Show of Hands. There are new unaccompanied harmony singers like The Young'uns, and the art-folk of The Unthanks, with the haunting singing of sisters Rachel and Becky Unthank backed by anything from piano and strings to jazz-influenced brass.

The list is extensive, with new performers still emerging who might not associate themselves with folk-rock but are following the same philosophy of setting out to re-work traditional songs in new ways and create a new English popular music.

SAM LEE

Sam Lee is one such maverick. He insists "I never wanted to just be a musician", and devotes much of his time to eco-campaigning, conservation work and encouraging others to enjoy his love of the countryside and fight for its survival. But he is also a singer, arranger and song-collector who set out to take folk in new directions and create music for people who had never heard traditional songs before. Inevitably, he has critics in the folk world, and claims, "I'm not welcome in a lot of folk places... I'm persona non grata because I have a very different view on it and can sometimes be a bit hot-headed." He argues that the music "needs to be heard by as many people as possible. It needs to be re-introduced and played in different ways, and abused and taken apart. The worst thing you can do to a folk song is not challenge it. For me, the line that has been my compass is Mahler's quote 'tradition is tending the flame and not worshipping the ashes'."

Lee is very much the folk outsider. He's from Kentish Town, north London, has very rarely played in folk clubs, doesn't come from a folk background, and only discovered music – and nature – when he attended Forest School Camps, where city schoolchildren learn about wildlife and sing around the campfire. He was a huge fan of Michael

Jackson, but once he discovered folk he realised, "I was as free as anybody else to sing these songs... and went into a pure diet of just folk music." It was an "obsession" that would lead him to song-collecting, especially from the Traveller community and the great Scottish traditional singer Stanley Robertson. Having collected them, he set out to "highlight the beauty of these songs in an unusual and different setting".

So in his first album, *Ground of Its Own* (2012), he matched his direct, almost crooned singing style against backing that included jew's harp, trumpets, fiddle, banjo and the drone-like effects of an Indian shruti box. It was short-listed for a Mercury Prize. Next came *The Fade in Time* (2015) which included backing from cello, ukulele and willow flute and was most remarkable for a charming a cappella version of the traditional "Lovely Molly", on which he was backed by the massed voices of the Roundhouse Choir. They performed it at the 2016 Folk Awards, where it was awarded Best Traditional Track.

In 2020 he changed direction yet again. He had always avoided using guitars in his music, questioning whether the instrument could bring anything new to the folk scene, but now he teamed up with a producer and celebrated rock guitarist Bernard Butler (of Suede and McAlmont and Butler fame) to record *Old Wow*, which features Butler's electric guitar work. Sam explained that "if it's played beautifully and sensitively you wouldn't necessarily know that it was electric guitar".

The songs on the album were, he said, "nature-based – it's about heart, hearth and earth – our relationship to the earth and nature". It included folk songs and re-written folk songs, many of them dealing with conservation and the natural world. It includes "Balnafanen", a Scottish "love song to nature" which included snatches of the better-known "Wild Mountain Thyme", along with the Copper Family song, "Spencer The Rover", "for me an ancient medicine song in which nature is the healer". And then there's a "not re-written enormously" treatment of "Turtle Dove", a traditional song about the once-common bird that now faces extinction in the UK. For Lee "the song speaks so clearly about impending loss, and the verses 'the hills shall fly, the billows will burn, the rocks melt into the sun' – it almost speaks of climate catastrophe... how could they sing that, unknowing of what was to come?"

By now, Sam Lee was as well known for his conservation work as for his music. He organised pilgrimages to the remaining haunts of the turtle dove, and held Singing With Nightingales events, at which small audiences were invited out into the woods to learn about the local bird life, eat around a camp fire and then follow Sam out into the darkness, where he would sing and play shruti box as the birds noisily sang back. Some in the folk scene disapproved, but this was a powerful and emotional way of introducing outsiders to this beautiful and endangered bird and "getting people into nature".

He's an unusual singer who agrees he is "a workaholic and very entrepreneurial". His other ventures include singing with the Yiddish Twist Orchestra, creating new venues for musicians through the Nest Collective and Campfire Club movement, and helping the RSPB campaign to highlight the problem of endangered birds through *Let Nature Sing* – a single of bird songs that became a Top 20 best-seller.

And then there's his work with Extinction Rebellion (XR), the protest movement that demands urgent political action on climate change and the environment. In April 2019 the movement burst into action with a two-week "rebellion" that brought parts of London to a standstill. Before it started "when none of us had any idea how enormous it would be", some of XR's leaders came down to the woods to listen to the nightingales. And when the first phase of protests ended, Sam helped organise a celebratory gathering in London's Berkeley Square. Police stood by and "watched me climb a tree and put a banner up", without complaining, and he later led the crowd through an emotional sing-along of his re-written version of "A Nightingale Sang In Berkeley Square" – with the sounds of nightingales singing added in.

It may not have originally been a folk song, but it sounded like one now, as it echoed across London's West End. The man who once hated guitars would hate to be called a folk-rocker... but he has the same experimental spirit.

STICK IN THE WHEEL

And then there's Stick in the Wheel, a London duo with their roots firmly in east London, who have a fascination for both unaccompanied traditional singing and electronica. As singer Nicola Kearey explains, "at the one end you have the hard-core super-trad, which is folk sing-around, no mikes, very raw and unadorned, and then right at the other end you have the super-experimental stuff which we also do because it's part of our culture. The bit in the middle, which is most of the commercial scene, we don't really have anything to do with and we are not interested. It might seem a paradox but it's completely natural for us to inhabit those two extremes."

They too have an unlikely folk history. Instrumentalist and producer Ian Carter says he "grew up with folk music... my favourite records were Bert Jansch and a Young Tradition sampler. I was impressed by the older generation – people like Martin Carthy and John Kirkpatrick." He was, it seems, particularly impressed by Carthy's solo album from 1976, *Crown of Horn* (on which his acoustic guitar is backed by Moog synthesiser on some tracks). "Holy shit!" he said. "That album is amazing."

When he started playing and producing it was on the dubstep/grime/hip hop scene, where he was involved in electronica experiments with Various Production, but also played the guitar and dobro. When he and Kearey started singing folk songs together they listened to the old singers, turning to the internet, where they "did a lot of YouTube research on the folk scene to see what it was – and it didn't seem we were doing anything radically different".

But the clips they loved were not the slick concert events, but intimate DIY performances. So for Ian "my favourite recording of Martin Carthy doing 'Georgie' is him singing in his back garden. And The Watersons... we didn't listen to their records but we used to watch clips of them, when they are singing in some big old pub and doing 'Hal-an-Tow' and everyone is smoking fags. It's as good as being there, and almost better than listening to records."

The other highly individual way in which they learned about folk was through their memories of the *Bagpuss* children's TV series, which was broadcast in the seventies and featured an impressive musical background that involved many traditional songs. "None of us knew we were listening to folk music when we were watching *Bagpuss* as kids," said Nicola. "But hearing that music as a kid... it plants itself in your brain."

As an East Ender she was also "motivated by what was happening around me – the gentrification of east London, and the places I had an attachment to being knocked down or changed... and the medium of folk music, discovering that tradition, is how I dealt with it".

All of which was reflected on their first album, *From Here* (2015), an acoustic album with attitude. Nicola sang in a harsh, no-nonsense East End accent and brought a new contemporary edge to old traditional songs like "The Blacksmith", which now became an angry story of betrayal, or Ewan MacColl's "Champion At Keeping Them Rolling", which now sounded like a contemporary truckers' ballad. New songs included "Me N Becky", a contemporary story of London riots, looting, jail and remorse.

Having established their credentials as the most exciting new band on the folk scene, Stick in the Wheel then demonstrated their love of live, DIY music (and their respect for other singers) by releasing *From Here: English Folk Field Recordings*. A collection of "immediate and intimate" live tracks, recorded in kitchens, gardens or back rooms, it included new performances from, among others, Martin and Eliza Carthy, John Kirkpatrick and Sam Lee. A second set would include June Tabor, Nancy Kerr and her mum Sandra Kerr (who was responsible for writing and singing many of the *Bagpuss* folk songs).

Now the band began to branch out. On *Follow Them True* (2018) they matched Nicola Kearey's no-nonsense treatment of traditional songs and new material with increasingly complex backing from Ian Carter, making use of his production skills and background in experimental electronica. The album began with the furious stomping "Over Again", matching electro-percussion and guitar riffs. Elsewhere, there was a new setting for the traditional "Weaving Song", which had appeared on the *Bagpuss* TV shows that the duo had listened to growing up. At the end of 2019 they released a "mixtape", *Against the Loathsome Beyond*, which included re-mixes of work from Cambridge guitarist C Joynes along with spoken passages matched against electronic soundscapes, and an edgy, clattering and gutsy treatment of "Down In Yon Forest".

Kearey and Carter concluded 2019 by curating the English Folk Dance and Song Society's *Perspectives on Tradition* project. Three very different musicians – bass player Olugbenga Adelekan, DJ and turntablist Jon1st and musician/producer Nabihah Iqbal – were all invited to investigate the hallowed library at Cecil Sharp House, although none of them had a background in English folk. They didn't want the project to end with a concert or album, but rather to introduce the musicians to the archives and see what happened.

Stick in the Wheel insist they are not a folk-rock band (Kearey finds the term "a bit middle-of-the-road") but in their bold fusion of the ancient and the modern they are following what is now a folk tradition. Richard Thompson wanted to create a new English music by mixing the pop styles of the sixties with traditional songs. So too did the musicians who followed, mixing in the musical influences of later generations while keeping the old folk songs alive. As Martin Carthy said, "You can't hurt this stuff by messing with it."

The English folk-rock pioneers can't claim to have started everything, of course: they had been influenced by Dylan and The Byrds in America, who had begun re-working folk songs with a rock backing. Fairport Convention, and those who followed, had wanted to create an English equivalent. But when the Fairports met to rehearse the songs from their *Liege and Lief* album in a London pub back in September 1969, with the extraordinary gang of young musicians that included Richard Thompson and Sandy Denny joined by the somewhat older distinguished folk fiddler Dave Swarbrick, they helped to launch a musical revolution. As Swarbrick told me that day, "I'm still a folk fiddler, and maybe this is the folk revival."

The revival led to the creation of great new music across Britain and beyond. Eliza Carthy says that Scottish musicians hate the term folk-rock, but there has been an adventurous Celtic folk-fusion scene running alongside the English projects. The nearest Scottish equivalent to the Fairports is Battlefield Band, formed in the Glasgow suburb of Battlefield back in 1969 and still going. They are not rockers, for sure, but they are certainly adventurous, with a line-up that has included electric keyboards along with fiddles, bagpipes, bouzouki and cittern (the medieval mandolin), and a repertoire that has ranged from traditional dance tunes to the inspired, often angry and political songs of founding member Alan Reid. Later came Capercaillie, who started out in Argyll as an acoustic band but went on to appear at festivals and concert halls around the world and to sell over a million albums after adding in electric guitars, synths or drum machines in the late eighties. Led by keyboard player and accordionist Donald Shaw and his wife, the fine, versatile singer Karen Matheson, they mixed contemporary songs with traditional material, along with a dash of jazz and global influences, and introduced new audiences to

Gaelic songs that ranged from laments and love ballads to the waulking songs originally sung by weavers.

Then there was the extraordinary Martyn Bennett, who learned to play pipes and fiddle after being introduced to many of Scotland's great traditional singers by his folklorist mother. He was also a fan of contemporary music and the rave scene, and set out to create something completely new. He bought a sampler and keyboards, and began recording his own albums, mixing traditional styles with programmed beats, showing how respect for tradition could be matched against furious experimentation. And he succeeded, even if he shocked some of the more musically conservative folk fans when he appeared at the 2000 Cambridge Folk festival. Bennett was a great innovator, but died of cancer at the tragically young age of 33, after releasing his best-received album *Grit* (2003), which fused beats and pipes with samples of traditional singers.

He has remained a major influence in Scotland, helping to lead the way for everyone from the bagpipes-and-beats festival favourites Peatbog Faeries through to The Burns Unit, Shooglenifty and the twelve-piece Treacherous Orchestra. He even encouraged a new Celtic-Latin fusion scene. In 1995 he was at a meeting in an Edinburgh bar, along with trumpeter Toby Shippey and Scottish-based Venezuelan singer Lino Rocha, where they discussed their mutual love of Tito Puente, and similarities between Salsa and Scottish styles ("the energy and passion", according to Rocha). The result was Salsa Celtica, a band that mixed the two styles, toured the bars of Edinburgh and the Highlands, travelled to Cuba to study Latin licks, and even won over Latin dance fans in New York. Their 2006 album *El Camino* included Eliza Carthy, then living in the Scottish borders.

It's an approach that was reflected in a whole batch of other Scottish fusion experiments. Breabach matched their pipes and fiddles against Indigenous Australian and Māori styles, while that fine singer-songwriter James Yorkston, a key figure in the influential indie-folk label The Fence Collective, went on to explore Asian styles in the Yorkston/Thorne/Khan trio. Joined by double bass player Jon Thorne and Suhail Yusuf Khan, an exponent of the bowed, stringed instrument the *sarangi,* used in Hindustani folk and classical music, they re-worked anything from traditional material to songs by Lal

Waterson and Robert Burns – whose "Westlin Winds" was given an Asian makeover on their exquisite 2020 album *Navarasa: Nine Emotions*.

And then, of course, there's the magnificent (and two-thirds Scottish) trio Lau, who established their reputation thanks to the exquisite, thrilling and often hypnotic interplay between guitarist and singer Kris Drever, fiddler Aidan O'Rourke and accordion exponent Martin Green. They are special because of the emotional intensity and changes of mood in their playing, and their ability to improvise. In 2012 with *Race the Loser*, Green began to add electronica to the intriguing Lau mix.

That same adventurous approach was reflected across the British Isles. The Welsh language folk scene included everyone from eighties prog-rockers Pererin to Georgia Ruth, who matched harp against *sarangi* and synths, or 9Bach, who fused traditional songs with dub effects or Indigenous Australian styles. And that superb Welsh harpist Catrin Finch provided surely the finest folk-classical-global fusions of them all by collaborating with the Colombian band Cimarrón and the West African kora virtuoso Seckou Keita.

In Ireland there was much the same free-wheeling approach, with the country's best-known folk band The Chieftains leading the way by playing with musicians from China, Spain, Mexico or the USA – while still remaining true to their traditional roots. And here – as in Ireland – amplified styles flourished in the eighties, just as the English folk-rockers faltered, with Christy Moore, Ireland's finest interpreter of songs of all kinds, very much at the heart of it all. He had spent much of the early seventies playing in that glorious acoustic band, Planxty, but in 1981, he and Dónal Lunny decided to move on, mixing new and traditional songs in a contemporary rock setting. Moving Hearts was a seven-piece that matched electric guitar and bouzouki against synths, bass, drums, uilleann pipes and saxophone. They recorded two albums, including angry political songs, before Christy decided to leave for what would become a triumphant solo career, while Lunny went on to record an instrumental set that now included traditional songs re-worked for pipes, electric bass and synth.

The eighties were a great time for Celtic folk-rock, and the ever-changing Waterboys deserve an honorary mention. Were they Irish? Well no, not exactly, for the band was founded in Edinburgh by a Scot, Mike Scott, who started out playing rock anthems, before moving to Ireland, where he invited traditional musicians to join him, and in 1988 released the massively successful *Fisherman's Blues*, followed two years later by *Room to Roam*. Among those traditional musicians was the young and brilliant Irish accordionist, fiddler and whistle player Sharon Shannon, who remembers that "there were no rules as to the type of music played... We could move very easily from a punk song to an old-timey American waltz, to Irish jigs and reels and on to New Orleans-type blues."

She quit when the band moved the emphasis from folk back to rock, and in 1991 released her first solo album of traditional music – a massive commercial success. Since then she has continued as a soloist, leading her own Big Band and proving how Irish traditional styles could be fused with just about everything. Her 2008 album, *The Galway Girl*, started with her Celtic-Alt Country collaboration with Steve Earle on his song "The Galway Girl", a massive hit in Ireland, and included demonstrations of her work alongside Jackson Browne or Kirsty MacColl, whose gloriously slinky Libertango demonstrated Shannon's skills as an accordion tango player. Her 2017 album, *Sacred Earth*, even brought African influences into the mix.

Elsewhere, the Irish experimental folk scene ranges from the exuberant Damien Dempsey, who has mixed stories of Dublin life with rap and reggae, through to the fusion work of The Gloaming, in which those distinguished traditional musicians fiddler Martin Hayes and guitarist Dennis Cahill are joined by a cast that includes singer Iarla Ó Lionáird and the inventive, gently dominant American pianist and producer Thomas "Doveman" Bartlett, who transforms the music with his decidedly un-traditional musical interventions. And then there's Lankum, with their intense, edgy blend of harmony vocals and drone and ambient effects bringing new life to even the best-known Irish songs, like "The Wild Rover".

Richard Thompson described the early folk-rock experiments as "revolutionary... people in other countries saw what we did, and thought 'we should do this with our culture'. Bands in Spain, Netherlands, Sweden – even Los Lobos in the States – thought 'we should be looking at our own tradition', so it changed things." American blues musicians would of course point out that they were there first, re-working the blues on electric guitars since the late thirties and forties, but if the Fairports' achievements included getting those Mexican-American heroes Los Lobos to revitalize their musical traditions, that's no mean achievement.

And elsewhere? In Africa, musicians like the Congolese virtuoso Franco had been playing electric guitar, and mixing local and foreign styles, long before the British folk experiments. But the popularity of folk rock in the seventies surely helped British audiences to develop a broader, more adventurous musical taste. And that made them more receptive to the musicians from Africa, and elsewhere around the planet, who would win an international following with the rise of so-called world music – especially as many of the new bands followed the folk-rock format of matching local instruments and traditional styles against guitar, bass and drums. And the story still continues, with experimental folk-rock-electronica scenes flourishing anywhere from Turkey to South Korea.

The Electric Muse has gone global.

SOURCES

Author Interviews

Billy Bragg (2019)
John Kirkpatrick (2019)
Sam Lee (2019)
Sharon Shannon (2017)
Stick in the Wheel (Nicola and Ian) (2019)

TWELVE

THE YEAR THE MUSIC PAUSED

The planet has had a depressing, frightening year in 2020, as the Covid-19 pandemic wrecked lives, hopes and jobs. The arts were, of course, seriously affected, and the performing arts suffered particularly badly. Lockdown and social distancing meant that festivals, tours and even small-scale concerts were cancelled in a way that had never happened before – not even in wartime.

The folk scene was among the sectors that suffered. In England, this meant the cancellation of not just Fairport's 2020 Cropredy Festival (the entire line-up was re-booked for August 2021, by when the situation will hopefully have improved), but other major folk festivals, from Cambridge to Sidmouth. Describing his feelings in the weeks after the cancelled Cropredy Festival, Fairport's Simon Nicol described the situation as "calamity/catastrophe/nightmare/frustration. I have the odd blue period when all seems utterly 'over' and I'm defeated. In point of fact, you catch me there at the moment. And I am putting it down to simple grieving – grieving for a Cropredy that couldn't happen; yet something in me changed when that weekend went past. While it was still a date on the calendar that was in the future, it was a vivid 'almost-memory', something readily conjured to mind. A field and a weekend packed with reunions, encounters, chatter, laughter and unexpected as well as anticipated climactic moments of music to listen to and to perform. Now it's ashes in the mouth – and the weather has turned cold and grey to echo the feelings within..."

The joys of live shows before an audience were suddenly and unexpectedly gone. But lockdown didn't mean that music was no longer being created. It just meant that performances had to take on new forms, made possible by the internet, such as artists live streaming from home. But further innovation was possible, and one of the bravest and most remarkable musical events of the lockdown period came from Sam Lee. On April 22 he celebrated Earth Day by hosting a three-hour late-night concert streamed from a wood "somewhere in Sussex", surrounded by nightingales, which sang throughout the broadcast. The event featured both live and pre-recorded music, along with poetry, readings and talks from an impressive cast, including the Poet Laureate Simon Armitage, the broadcaster and wildlife campaigner Chris Packham and even the Pet Shop Boys, who "sent in" a lush, gently sturdy instrumental, "Night Sings (Popa's Theme)". Proof that experimentation could still take place during lockdown came from artists who played live while listening and reacting to the birdsong. Bernard Butler's guitar improvisation was moody and atmospheric, while Jocelyn Pook and singer Melanie Pappenheim contributed two delightfully quirky tracks, both of which had lengthy pauses filled with nightingale songs. As for Sam Lee, he started and ended this notable event with two live folk songs from the woods – both about nightingales.

Lockdown affected the folk scene in other ways. Many musicians earn most of their income through performing, and the halting of live music brought them severe financial problems, as well as to stage crews and venues. It was little surprise then that many of the live streamed events were fundraisers. Among those taking part was Richard Thompson, who sang from his home in New Jersey, USA, in aid of the Royal Albert Hall in London, where he had held his memorable 70th birthday concert the previous year.

Richard was also among the artists who took part in the increasingly ambitious podcast and online Folk On Foot events, organised by the broadcaster Matthew Bannister. He started the project in 2018, with the aim of "walking with leading artists in the landscape that has inspired their music – which is performed on location". High production values, combined with the choice of musicians, made this an excellent series, but Folk On Foot took on new importance with lockdown. A series of "festivals" set out to raise money for musicians who were suffering financial hardship (and for those who were taking part) and did so with enormous success.

The third festival, Together Again, streamed on August bank holiday Monday, featured leading folk artists playing live in small (socially distanced) groups from different locations around the country – and they were obviously delighted at the opportunity. The star cast included Kris Drever from Lau, playing with Phil Cunningham and John McCusker; Sam Lee accompanied by a small band; and Peggy Seeger with her sons, Neill and Calum MacColl, providing a timely reworking of her song "When Will the Good Times Roll". Then there was Eliza Carthy with guitarist David Delarre; Rioghnach Connolly (Folk Singer of the Year at the 2019 Folk Awards) performing with Stuart McCallum, her colleague in The Breath; Steve Knightley and Phil Beer, aka Show of Hands; and the welcome reunion of John Spiers and Jon Boden. Almost all the music was acoustic – though actor-singer Johnny Flynn had an electric bass in his four-piece band – but Folk On Foot was a bravely original way of lifting the gloom brought by Covid.

There was further innovation in the albums released during lockdown, which included impressive new sets from two great veterans. In the States 79-year-old Bob Dylan returned to classic form with *Rough and Rowdy Ways*, while in England there was the magnificent *Heart's Ease*, from the (slightly older) Shirley Collins. The follow-up to *Lodestar* – the 2016 record that marked her comeback after thirty-eight years – was a glorious reminder that Shirley was still in a class of her own, both as a singer with a distinctive style, and as an innovator. In her early career she had matched traditional songs against the blues/jazz/world music styles of guitarist Davy Graham, and sung with folk-rockers The Albion Band, but now she moved in a new direction. On the album's final track, "Crowlink", named after a cliff on the South Downs overlooking the English Channel "where I love to be", she sang against a moody, atmospheric fusion of hurdy-gurdy, electronica and field recordings of waves and sea birds, provided by Matthew Shaw. Now in her mid-eighties, she was still happy to explore new folk fusions. "I'm happy to experiment if it all sounds right," she said, "not just for the sake of doing it."

From the younger generation of British folk-rock-electronica innovators, there was intriguing new music from the London duo Stick in the Wheel. Their third album, *Hold Fast*, was an exhilarating, intense fusion of ancient texts (and slang) with contemporary sounds, which ranged from the pounding psych-folk of "Gold So Red" to a startling new treatment of Rudyard Kipling's anti-war poem "Soldier, Soldier", with Nicola Kearey's no-nonsense vocals set against crashing electric guitar chords from Ian Carter. Then there was the spooky electronica of "Nine Herbs Charm" and a rousing, epic anthem "Forward", while on "Budg & Snudg", the story of a seventeenth-century house burglar, they matched exuberant post-punk ferocity against a Morris tune on melodeon provided by that veteran of earlier folk-rock experiments, John Kirkpatrick.

Peter Knight, Kirkpatrick's one-time colleague in Steeleye Span, offered calmer, elegant new styles on *Natural Invention*, the debut studio album from his Gigspanner Big Band, in which he was joined by a celebrity cast, from the award-winning multi-instrumentalist duo Phillip Henry and Hannah Martin to John Spiers. It was a virtuoso record, mixing new settings for traditional songs from England and Ireland with bluegrass, with Roger Flack's electric guitar matched against the violins, dobro, squeezeboxes, bass and percussion to provide a reminder of Peter Knight's folk-rock roots.

Elsewhere, lockdown releases ranged from nostalgia to protest – the latter provided by an angry single from Show of Hands. They originally released "The Bristol Slaver" on their 1997 album, *Dark Fields*, but decided to revamp it as their contribution to a summer that had seen a rise in the Black Lives Matter movement and the toppling of the statue of slave trader Edward Colston, which was pushed into Bristol Harbour. The new version of the song, produced by Matt Clifford, best known for playing keyboards with The Rolling Stones, was furious, stomping and timely.

Then (of course) there were the Thompsons. For followers of classic British folk-rock, one of the releases of 2020 was Richard and Linda Thompson's *Hard Luck Stories*, an eight-CD box set of 113 songs, which featured all six studio albums released in the years they worked together (1972 to 1982) along with thirty-one previously unreleased tracks. One such song was "Amazon Queen", written and recorded by Richard at the start of his solo career, and there were also intense and haunting reminders of Linda's vocal work. There were previously unheard versions of songs from the duo's best-loved album *I Want to See the Bright Lights Tonight*, such as an exquisite, pained version of "The End Of The Rainbow" in which Linda takes the lead, along with unreleased tracks from live performances, including reminders of the duo's now legendary farewell tour of the USA in 1982. Folk-rock's greatest couple may have been in the process of splitting up that year, but they were in extraordinary form.

For those wanting to hear more of Richard, he also featured on a track released by Fairport Convention to raise money for Help Musicians UK. The 2020 Cropredy Festival may have been cancelled, but twenty of the artists who would have taken part, including the Fairports and Ralph McTell, recorded a new version of Richard's song "Meet On The Ledge", with which the Fairports traditionally conclude their Cropredy set. Written by Richard when he was still a teenager, it's a rousing anthem with lyrics about death and hope that made it popular at funerals. It ends with the optimistic line "if you really mean it, it all comes around again", which seemed particularly apposite for the lockdown months. Traditional songs have survived because they have lasting power and relevance, and – in the right hands – can be fused successfully with a remarkable variety of styles.

The summer of 2020 was a miserable period, and the situation had become even worse by the winter, when lockdown returned. But there was musical activity amidst the gloom, with Bellowhead reforming to cheer followers stuck at home and deprived of live music with a one-off concert stream to mark the 10th anniversary of their *Hedonism* album. There was new music from Edward II, while (to the delight of Eliza Carthy) Imagined Village started planning their long-awaited return, once the Covid crisis allowed – and even recorded a new version of the Sandy Denny song 'The Quiet Joys of Brotherhood'.

For my part, I was helped through lockdown by listening to anything from new music by Cosmo Sheldrake, mixing folktronica instrumentals with bird song, through to the stark, 'post-apocalyptic' work of Lunatraktors, and the folk-scat-jazz singing of Lizabett Russo. Along, of course, with the established favourites, ranging from the instrumental brilliance of Spiro, with their complex fusion of traditional melodies and the repeated phrases and patterns of systems music, through to Richard and Linda Thompson and the ever-remarkable Shirley Collins. But live music was desperately missed. Let's hope it has returned by the time you read this.

SOURCES

Author Interviews

Shirley Collins (2020)
Simon Nicol (2020)

Farewell, Farewell

Many great folk musicians have died since the first edition of *The Electric Muse* appeared in the seventies – from Ewan MacColl, a key figure in the original folk revival, through to Fairport Convention members Sandy Denny, Judy Dyble and Dave Swarbrick, Tim Hart from Steeleye Span, Scottish folk-fusion exponent Martyn Bennett and those masters of folk-blues, Davy Graham, Bert Jansch and John Renbourn.

Then there were three of the original authors of this book.

Dave Laing, who died in 2019, was the driving force behind the project, a thoughtful editor and music academic who was one of Britain's leading writers on popular music. Dave was also a trustee of the folk music charity Square Roots Productions, which celebrates the links between American and British folk music and promotes fledgling and legacy musicians. It is through the support of this charity that this book has been re-published.

Karl Dallas, who died in 2016, was a journalist, singer-songwriter and political activist who played a crucial role in the emerging folk scene of the fifties and sixties.

And Robert Shelton, who died in 1995, will be remembered as the first major critic to boost the career of the young Bob Dylan – and for helping a whole batch of other great performers.

It's to their memory that this latest edition of *The Electric Muse* is dedicated.

Robin Denselow
London, January 2021

INDEX